Poetry
New Zealand
Yearbook
2018

Edited by Jack Ross

MASSEY UNIVERSITY PRESS

Contents

ESSAYS

Editorial

A live tradition

To have gathered from the air a live tradition
or from a fine old eye the unconquered flame
This is not vanity.
— Ezra Pound, 'Canto LXXXI'

Just as our previous issue focused on younger poets, this one has as its overarching principle 'the tradition' — however you want to define that term. In pursuit of this aim, I've chosen to feature the poetry of Alistair Paterson.

Alistair was the managing editor of *Poetry New Zealand* for 20 years, from 1994 to 2014, and before that he edited *Mate / Climate* between 1974 and 1981. He is, however, principally a writer. Alistair had a poem in the very first issue of *New Zealand Poetry Yearbook*, in 1951, and since then he has published nine books of poetry and three of prose, as well as editing numerous other books and journals.

He represents, then, a very important thing: perseverance in the writing life. Alongside this, though, his tireless work showcasing the talents of others shows a generosity of spirit which is also an essential part of the sense of poetic community I wish to celebrate here.

Another aspect of Alistair's career is perhaps less well known: a pronounced taste for experimentation and theory. As a result, Alistair's poetry has never stood still. The free-flowing, associative poems he is writing today seem to me to represent a considerable technical advance on the more formal long poems of his middle years. Whether or not other readers agree with this diagnosis, the one constant factor in his writing is undoubtedly change.

For an author to be creating interesting new work after 70-odd years of writing is not a phenomenon for which there are many parallels.

Thomas Hardy published a book of poems in his eighty-eighth year; John Masefield in his eighty-ninth; Allen Curnow in his ninetieth. Alistair Paterson's poetry now spans a similar period, but neither Hardy nor Masefield could be said to have kept up with new developments in poetics to the extent that Paterson has. Only Curnow provides a real precedent.

There's a strong focus on mortality in many of the 21 new poems included here. How could there not be? What's perhaps even more noticeable is the delight and curiosity about nature, travel, time and the sea that most of them display. Paterson's energy seems inexhaustible. His wide acquaintanceship with so many of our poets, old and new, makes him in many ways the perfect embodiment of the ideal of a local tradition.

The Pound quote I began with speaks specifically of a live tradition. That's the real point, I think. Of course it can be interesting and valuable to celebrate the past, but it's what the past has gifted to the present that really matters. Good poems don't die, but grow in the memory, inspire us to speak out about our own times, our own problems, our own causes for celebration or despair.

The same can be true of essays and reviews, more strongly in evidence than ever in this issue. As well as a long interview, I've been fortunate enough to be able to include Owen Bullock's essay on Alistair Paterson's long poem *The Toledo Room* (1978), and thus to provide maximum coverage of his work to date.

Alongside this, you'll find a passionate defence of confessional poetry against its many, many detractors by poetry student Jeanita Cush-Hunter; an eloquent centenary tribute to T. E. Hulme, the (so-called) 'father of imagism' — and certainly founder of a certain notion of the Modernist poetic tradition — by poet and classicist Ted Jenner; and an amusing account of a family poetic tradition by Reade Moore.

More controversially, perhaps, Robert McLean has written a reply to Janet Charman's essay 'A Piece of Why', included in the previous edition of *Poetry New Zealand*, in which he takes issue with Charman's avowedly psychoanalytic reading of Allen Curnow's choices as an anthologist.

Celebration and inclusiveness are one thing, but it must be emphasised that the right to *dis*agree is also part of a 'live tradition'. Both Charman and McLean argue passionately in support of their positions, but on the issues, never *ad hominem*. Both, it seems to me, deserve a hearing. Perhaps it's my evangelical upbringing, but I've never felt that there was much to be feared from robust debate.

The review section here, too — larger than ever — is not short of strong opinions, cogently expressed. In her generous and thought-provoking review of our previous issue, *Poetry New Zealand Yearbook 2017*, poet and literary critic Paula Green announced as her own guiding principle that: 'A good poetry review opens a book for the reader as opposed to snapping it shut through the critic's prejudices.'

I would certainly agree with that — in principle, at any rate. A book should always be given the benefit of the doubt, if at all possible. Unfortunately one cannot always leave it at that. In the essay 'Confessions of a Book Reviewer', George Orwell put the issue very neatly: 'If one says . . . that *King Lear* is a good play and *The Four Just Men* is a good thriller, what meaning is there in the word "good"?'

If we like and admire *all* books, then it's much the same as liking and admiring none. Differentiation is the point of criticism, after all, and sometimes one bad review can teach us more than catalogues of praise.

To conclude with another quotation from Pound's *Pisan Cantos*:[1]

The wind is part of the process
The rain is part of the process

Of course there is another important point to make about book reviews. The masthead of the *Poetry New Zealand* website has always read 'International Journal of Poetry and Poetics'. There have certainly been questions in the past about just how many international publications can be mixed with the local product without obscuring the central *raison d'être* of the magazine.

This issue, for instance, includes reviews of 33 books. Twenty-three of these come from New Zealand publishers. Of the remainder, five come from Australia, one from Hong Kong, one from Spain, one from the UK, one from New York, and one from Hawai'i. However, seven of these 10 constitute single-author collections by New Zealand writers. The other three are anthologies. Of these the first, *5 6 7 8* is an Australian-published sampler of work by four poets, two of whom are transplanted New Zealanders; the second, *A TransPacific Poetics*, has a New Zealand-based co-editor, includes substantial local content and was in fact launched here in July 2017; only the third, *Zero Distance*, might seem an anomalous inclusion. When I explain that its editor, Yiang Lujing, is studying at Victoria University of Wellington, and has contributed translations to earlier editions of *Poetry New Zealand Yearbook*, the status of his work as a deliberate attempt to introduce contemporary Chinese writing to a Pacific audience may seem clearer. It is, of course, fortunate that we were able to find a reviewer, poet and critic Hamish Dewe, who is bilingual in Chinese and English.

It might be objected that few of these books are likely to be found on the shelves of local bookshops, but this is an uncomfortable reality for much poetry publishing in New Zealand now. In any case, in the age of online ordering, international books are often easier to obtain than those issued by some of our less tech-savvy local publishers.

The second round of the *Poetry New Zealand* Poetry Prize has been as much of a delight to judge as the first one. I've ended up making the following choices:

First prize ($500):	Fardowsa Mohamed, for 'Us' (page 126 in this issue)
Second prize ($300):	Semira Davis, for 'Hiding' (page 89)
Third prize ($200):	Henry Ludbrook, for 'The Bar Girl' (page 117)

Fardowsa Mohamed's poem is, quite simply, magnificent. Its breadth of theme, its honesty and its directness speak of a region of experience I long to know more about.

It's always a good sign when a poem scares the life out of you.

Semira Davis's poem is clipped and condensed, but there's a sea of pain submerged under its surface. And yet, among other things, one would have to admit that it's also very funny.

Henry Ludbrook's 'The Bar Girl' is lush and romantic — or should that be pervy and voyeuristic? — all at the same time. It expresses perfectly a very real feeling, and that's probably why I found it irresistible.

There are 87 poets in this issue (besides Alistair Paterson, our featured poet). There are also six essayists and 13 reviewers: 98 authors in all.

If variety is the spice of life, then I think you'll find it here. I'm particularly happy to be able to present new work by some of the luminaries of our antipodean poetic tradition: Jennifer Compton, David Eggleton, Sue Fitchett, Ted Jenner, Bob Orr, Albert Wendt, Mark Young and many, many others.

However, the preponderance of poems is by younger writers — some still in their teens — which is as it should be. More than 300 submissions were received for this issue, making the selection particularly difficult. So please don't be discouraged if you sent in work and had it rejected. Perseverance, and receptiveness to change: those are the two principles embodied in Alistair Paterson's long literary career — keeping at it, despite all disappointments and discouragements; above all, always being ready to try something new.

Dr Jack Ross
September 2017

---

1   Ezra Pound, 'Canto LXXIV', in *The Cantos of Ezra Pound* (New York: New Directions, [1970] 1996), 455.

Featured
Poet

Alistair Paterson ONZM

Alistair Paterson is a poet, critic, fiction writer and editor, with considerable achievements in each of these fields. Born in Nelson in 1929, he has managed to combine a busy literary career with his professional life. He worked as an instructor officer in the Royal New Zealand Navy from 1954 to 1974 (retiring as lieutenant commander) and in public service education (New Zealand Police 1974–78; Department of Education 1979–89). A list of his many books and prizes is included below, but it is perhaps as a tireless champion of excellence in New Zealand poetry, both as an editor and as a practitioner, that he has left his most enduring mark. Many poets will remember with gratitude the voice of this long-term editor of *Poetry New Zealand* on the phone, questioning their word choices, inspiring us to do better, and providing mini master classes year after year. *Passant: A Journey to Elsewhere*, a memoir of his early years, came out from British publisher Austin Macauley in late 2017.

SELECT BIBLIOGRAPHY

Poetry
- *Caves in the Hills.* Christchurch: Pegasus Press, 1965.
- *Birds Flying.* Christchurch: Pegasus Press, 1973.
- *Cities & Strangers.* Dunedin: Caveman Press, 1976.
- *The Toledo Room: A Poem for Voices.* Dunedin: Pilgrims South Press, 1978.
- *Qu'appelle.* Dunedin: Pilgrims South Press, 1982.
- *Odysseus Rex.* Drawings by Nigel Brown. Auckland: Auckland University Press, 1986.
- *Incantations for Warriors.* Drawings by Roy Dalgarno. Auckland: Earl of Seacliff Art Workshop, 1987.

- *Summer on the Côte d'Azur*. Wellington: HeadworX, 2003.
- *Africa: // Kabbo, Mantis and the Porcupine's Daughter*. Auckland: Puriri Press, 2008.

Prose
- *The New Poetry: Considerations Towards Open Form*. Dunedin: Pilgrims South Press, 1981.
- *How to Be a Millionaire by Next Wednesday: A Novel*. Auckland: David Ling, 1994.
- *Passant: A Journey to Elsewhere*. London: Austin Macauley, 2017.

Edited
- *Mate* (editor, issues 22–27: 1974–78).
- *Climate* (editor, issues 28–32: 1978–81).
- *15 Contemporary New Zealand Poets*. Dunedin: Pilgrims South Press, 1980.
- *Garrett on Education: A Selection of Papers by Denny Garrett*. Wellington: Tutor Publications, 1984.
- 'Seven New Zealand Poets'. *New Directions* 46, ed. James Laughlin (New York, 1983): 78–97.
- *Short Stories from New Zealand*. Petone: Highgate/Price Milburn, 1988.
- *Poetry New Zealand* (managing editor, issues 8–48: 1994–2014).

Prizes
- 1982 — John Cowie Reid Memorial Award for longer poems (joint winner).
- 1993 — BNZ Katherine Mansfield Award for short stories.
- 2007 — Officer of the New Zealand Order of Merit.

Online
- Aotearoa New Zealand Poetry Sound Archive
  http://aonzpsa.blogspot.co.nz/2007/11/paterson-alistair.html
- The Depot: Cultural Icons
  http://culturalicons.co.nz/episode/alistair-paterson

- HeadworX author's page
  http://headworx.co.nz/author/patersona
- NZ Book Council author's page
  http://www.bookcouncil.org.nz/writer/paterson-alistair/
- The Poetry Archive (UK)
  https://www.poetryarchive.org/poet/alistair-paterson
- Wikipedia page
  https://en.wikipedia.org/wiki/Alistair_Paterson

A poem for Thomas Merton & Ernest Hemingway

I can't remember its name
      — the capital of Belgium —
but I ought to remember it
because people live there

& even though they speak
      another language they're
still people & it's important
we remember they are.

But people are everywhere
      & poet Thomas Merton
who became famous, lived in
Kentucky & became a monk

(which seems a strange place
      for anyone to become
anything — least of all a monk
& a Trappist) wrote a poem

about Ernest Hemingway
      when no one was writing
poems about him & certainly
no one at all in Belgium. But

people have to live somewhere
      & Kentucky & Belgium
are both as good as any when
you need some place to live.

I don't think I want to live
      in either of those places
but I like Merton & Hemingway
& this is a poem for them.

How to write fiction

James Wood has written a book
(strangely) on how to write fiction —
      with exemplars: Amis, Austen,
Camus, Dickens, De Quincey,
Hawthorne, Lawrence, Lessing
        & the rest of them.

The girl in the library sits & waits
for what comes to her from the book
      she's reading, from life —
from fiction, what's to be written,
what she'll write in her essay
        on the page in front of her.

And the way James Wood puts it
suggests it's a beginning,
      (the assignment she's writing)
is imaginary like everything else
that's of course & in its own way
        as always, fiction . . .

But of the best kind, a masquerade
as James Wood describes it,
      written with plainly 'the best
of intentions', to help transcribe
what's happening in the present
        & might lead her to the future.

And that's what it is — fiction —
her pausing, stopping to make notes
      thinking of weekends spent
at the beach or travelling
to somewhere she's never been —
        will never visit . . .

James Wood tells her how
it's done, what she should be doing
        & she knows if she stops
working, reading, taking notes
doesn't finish his book, nothing
        will get written at all.

Journey to elsewhere

I wish I could have met you
                Greville Texidor
when you came to Auckland
all those years ago,
   to a city still in part a frontier town
to a country ignorant of itself
a farming country
                a soldier country . . .

A 'deep red silence' was there
   a pervading unease, a foreboding
on the hills & the beaches exactly
   the way you described them . . .

But what difference does it make
   when all days become one day
all nights one night
           when what's happened
is still happening & yet all of it
     is long since over: Barcelona
Holloway, Paparoa —
   what you worked for, hoped for . . .

      Tanks exchanging fire at Alamein

You walked to the top of the pass
from where the village could be seen
dreamed night after night
       you could walk down to it . . .

But there was nowhere to go
except back to where you came from
          to return to where
the farm boys, road workers
                         miners, railway clerks
anyone who could carry a gun
had been sent to endure
          what was happening where

  sand tumbles, the sky falls . . .

You counted on getting there
                    that there wasn't much risk
no more than in anything else
          you'd done or might yet do . . .

Yes, I wish I could have met you
at the hardware store in Takapuna
              on the North Shore
looking out over empty farmland
towards Rangitoto & the sea
                    writing about it, about Spain
what you did there wishing
you could have done more

  in Aragon, Huesco, Almudeva . . .

But what difference does it make
                    when what's happened
is still happening & yet all of it
                    is long since over

Raison d'être

(for Dumont d'Urville)

It's raining
          on Condé-sur-Noireau
(where you came from)
        the streets of Copenhagen
Lambton Quay in Wellington
        on everything, everywhere

sur les oiseaux dans l'herbe —
               les choses petites

on the people in the paintings
   in the dark — the almost dark —
figures, silhouettes
   as William Hodges saw them
in 1773 amidst the ferns, the trees
            there in Dusky Bay

And the words — the words
        are still there on the pages
where you put them
       in Watering Cove as well
& with *les oiseaux sur la plage*
           on D'Urville Island

the rain in the streets, on hilltops
that falls in time & place,
          on the places you visited
Auckland's Toi o Tamaki
   French Pass, Cape Stephens

seascapes with figures
     Cook's Strait, Blind Bay
& the birds, *les oiseaux exotiques*
as in the landscape:
  Adele Island, Torrent Bay

Rangitoto ki te Tonga
     Te Aumiti — Current Basin —
the resting place
       of Te Kawau-a-Touru
et toujours, toujours, toujours
    le bateau sur la mer

Rick's place — maybe . . .

You're in Tauranga
   to take the waters, salty, hot
at the base of 'The Mount'
     famous, of course for

what happens there — famous
   for being famous . . .

But at the end of the wall
     (the great wall of China)
clearly visible on a good day
      you can see

the 'heavenly mountains'.

And the elements of language:
you put them together
   bits of them (verbs) listed
by those who know such things
      'strong' or 'weak' . . .

The ice has melted, hasn't
   been seen around here much
since the last glacier finally
      slid into the sea

& now the volcanoes (except
for White Island, still active)
   others merely resting . . .

Sports gear can be bought
   around the corner at *Bronco's*
all of it perfect for swimming
      surfing, fishing.

'We've hats here' the girl tells us
　　'for the out-of-towners —
they make them look' (smiles)
　　　'kind of perky'.

Nobody wants to talk about it

The mountains have hit pay dirt,
they play golden trumpets in the National Orchestra
the music steers them into the world of oblivion
where everything comes from, everything finishes
— the world of *nada*, no place, of nothing.

The beginning of it all is in France, in America
where the mountains may not be the tallest
but if you choose a good day, offer easy climbing
providing you're properly equipped, wear crampons
& have clothing suitable for high altitudes.

Whiteouts are plentiful, & tend to obscure the sound
of the music the orchestra's making, the shrill
whine of the violins and the deeper tones
of cellos, double basses, the book of avalanches
from Mt Erebus or invisibly further inland,

I wouldn't want to go there because mountains
are difficult to climb & you can make mistakes,
die on their slopes, in the dry valleys where
geologists have found the desiccated bodies of seals
& penguins that have become lost there.

People who play in the National Orchestra know
about such things because they've travelled overseas,
have performed in Europe, been praised
for performances no one back home has noticed
& the local papers haven't reported because

they prefer articles about rugby players
& celebrities. But the mountains won't stop —
they keep pushing up into the clouds, distorting
the landscape & throwing things around
whenever they want to & no one expects it.

Stopping by a cornfield late in the afternoon

Along the edge of the river
near the trees — elms, oaks planted
in the nineteenth century we
        stop — leave our bicycles,
go into the field across the road
where the corn's sweet cobs locked
    in the green sheaths that protect

them from wind & rain, have
ripened & are ready for picking —
        which we do because my father
says he's been given permission,
    & we're allowed to take them.

We choose what seem the best,
put them into the bag we have with us,
        carry them home & set them
to cook, when they're ready
    take them out, put them on plates.

I remember
that summer we stopped by
    the river — not because the corn was
so sweet but because I don't think
        my father told us the truth.

Te Kooti's War

This is where it finished
at Te Porere —
         not a long walk from
the main highway . . .
National Park
         to Turangi

The ghosts are there waiting
for what was to happen —
         McDonnell, Major Kepa.
It's a steep climb
through the brush
         up to the gun pits.

The weather's bad
the outer defences
         too cold for comfort
& the skiers
leaving their buses
         looking for shelter

talk about chalets
the ski lift on Ruapehu
         the weather in Aspen.
The dead were buried
near where they fell
         in the action.

Therapy

You're going to a therapist because you need help
    need someone to talk to about things.

He asks you to sit, so you sit on a couch next to a
    table with a glass of water on it.

You're there because you have problems, need to see
    a therapist, because you're a mess

and everything you've done and have been doing is a
    mess, continues to be a mess.

Somewhere outside where you can't see it a dog is
    barking because it knows you're there

wants to draw attention to itself, to warn you of awful
    things happening, that therapy won't help

which it knows because it's a dog, has a therapist who
    has tied it up, left it there as a warning.

It remembers the tree outside the house where you
    lived — where people once lived —

but you don't want to talk to your therapist about that
    don't want to remember any of it, don't

want the dog to let anyone know about it because it's
    too important to discuss, to talk about

the dark that's the order of it all — begins to move
    when you don't expect it, least expect it

and eventually covers everything, takes control of
    your life, everybody's life, of all there is.

The Talisman

That was it I suppose
     the *Talisman* — a scow
sometimes at the wharf
     moving in & out of port
Wellington, Greymouth
       Nelson . . .

always on the water
      with its green paint
off white sails
in a way that seemed suitable
for summer, out of
     place in winter . . .

And my grandfather
     there on the veranda
sipping his tea & smoking
     his pipe, watching the sky
the sun moving over
     the wavering sea . . .

That word of course
     that name, *Talisman*
one to remember
  lifted perhaps from the novel
written by Walter Scott
     on the third crusade . . .

My grandfather sits
     in his sea grass chair
exactly the way he likes to,
     the little town behind him
invisible,
      no longer there . . .

The Tannery

We broke into it —
the one-time tanning factory
(tannery) where no one had worked
     for perhaps forty years

Nor visited it for months or more

The dust covered machinery
vats forgotten, unforgiving
where for so long they'd been silent
     doing nothing

We thought we were
Tom Sawyer (Houlker really) there
with Huck Finn & another
     whose name I've forgotten

We shouldn't have been there

where the past
lifted from the benches, floorboards,
in an odour of death & decay
     intractable, alien

as of the vanquished
suggesting that something
someone angry, violent, inconsolable
     had been there before us

broken the windows, the doors

torn open the cupboards
in order to tell us something, hold us
there motionless, frozen
     silent & afraid . . .

The way things are

In the morning — the dawn chorus —
      well, what's left of it, invisible birds
inhabiting an invisible world
      & your voice saying nothing as if

like my uncle you were coming home
      in the dark of night or was it
in the morning early, when he thought he
      saw a hat on a fence post

& reached out to grab it — a top hat he said
      or thought it was but it wasn't
as he discovered when he touched it because
      it turned out to be an owl that took off

simply, immediately vanished into the dark
      the way he said his car almost did
when he was coming home from a delivery
      & his brakes failed on Gentle Annie

the usual thing which of course (& it goes
      without saying) is what you'd expect —
the windows didn't 'open to the south'
      & the door stayed locked.

Sometimes it's like that — clouds race round
      as they always do when nothing's
happening, isn't going to happen
      & morning nudges the window

'in russet mantle clad' the way it does when
      no one wants it to & it hasn't
the slightest intention of giving up on anything
      or leaving things alone for a while.

Thus when the voice in my head starts talking
          because it knows I'm awake
& even if I'm not listening & don't want to,
          my uncle hears what I'm saying —

& talks to me which is what he seems always
          to have been doing — making up stories
that might or might not be true, which I believe
          because they sound so convincing.

It's out there, everything's out there & doing
          what maybe it's always been doing:
the wind in the hedgerow or whatever it is
          crossing the motorway or tackling

the Harbour & the bridge, Auckland, the Shore
          the Norfolk pine — the one at the foot
of North Head in the street in Devonport where
          you used to live & we'd visit you

tells me as it does even if I don't want it to
          that there's always something to worry
about & even if you try to say it's otherwise
          that's the way things usually are.

The valley of the kings

'In the corridor leading to the pyramid
[the red pyramid] Hassein
     found a secondary tomb
from the Late Period with bones from
     a young man of small stature . . .'

Hollows in the mountains show where
limpets hold hard to rock-rimmed pools
     near Piha & Anawhata

as Miroslav Verner described them in
The Pyramids, Grove Press NY, p186
     & in Takaka, the long walk
home from the District High School
     past the dairy factory.

I could hear them — the bells —
  ringing out over half a century ago.

Books take you there & to other places
where you've never been
     & indeed, you'll never be going —
to the Temple of Apollo
     Iona, the Book of Kells . . .

If it's written in a book it must be true
even if there's nothing there
     anyone can believe . . .

where the bells rang out half a century
& two years ago as they might have
     almost certainly rung
for Nefertiti, King Tut, Akhenaten

& the poets — yes, those poets

near the hills where there are no pyramids
    the caves, their shattered hollows —
where they step out of the canvas
  & take the track that leads nowhere
not even as far as
        the District High School . . .

Navigator

The cement surface of the courtyard
is covered by a thin layer of quiet
      there is another person in the room
he walks in to being the rehearsal —
some things can never be counted
          are too numerous for one location

there are places in the great pyramid
channels open to the North Star & Orion
      you get there by compass, by dead
reckoning, direction & drift, the tides
take you to where there are two elephants
      tigers, other animals, to the zoo

no two places are alike, they're different
even twins if you look at them carefully —
      the sea opens a channel towards
other locations, valleys, the Swiss Alps
geometry tells you how to find things
      mark out boundaries after rain

in Egypt there's always a need for water
ferries sail from Piraeus or Corfu
      pearls are his eyes, full fathom five
in the depths of the northern winter it's best
to take precautions, wear a thick coat
      in summer umbrellas give shelter

sheets need trimming when the sails are set
travelling overland is another matter
      it's uncertain when you'll get there
'where' is always the place you're going to
get it onto paper where you can see it —
            you can do it with a sextant

Reading Alan Brunton

At first reading Alan Brunton
seems something like a puzzle.
You're adrift somewhere at sea
in a race across the Pacific
going any place, elsewhere
into Asia, Kathmandu
the Wild Mountains, Pueblo
      Duchess County

He says you have to be cautious
walking between stones
because the mountains are always
there & the stones are hungry
ready to eat you
You need a dog & at sea
a weapon against the waves
      that are equally hungry

Reading Alan Brunton is
something of a puzzle, a pathway
pulled up on a lonely beach
where the tide coming in lifts it
& drops it in New Mexico
on Broadway, New York.
Least expected, they're all least
      expected, ready to talk

because they wear masks, everyone
wears a mask, the kite maker
& the kite maker's daughter
lying in the sun on the beach because
in Copacabana they wear a mask
& the god is Kotakawana,

is androgynous, lives in Titicaca
    & the only conversation

you'll have is with yourself because
it's difficult to hear what's said
in the mountains where usually
the winds are strong, the air thin.
In summer there's Starnbergersee.
You can take coffee at the Hofgarten
as Eliot (T. S.) did with Marie
    the arch-duke's cousin.

And then there's the price
because nothing's free.
But you know it because shelter
& food cost money as do trains
buses, & even if you're walking
shoes wear out, dogs follow you,
winter's coming on
    your time's running out . . .

The Moon and Sixpence

The moon is full of memories
      sits in the fork of a tree
is taken down & put in a bag
            with six oranges

It isn't forgotten . . .
      Nightfall brings a torrent
floods the plain with yellow light
      the moon, sixpence
   Gauguin, Vincent van Gogh

There are so many people
      we haven't met: Anya Sinclair
The Garden of Forking Paths
McLeod, *The Painter in the Painting*

Moana a Toi, Tauranga,
      music in the Atrium, things
you've never seen before
         discover the moon in
  the lonely reaches of the sky . . .

The moon is full of memories
         sits in the fork of a tree
is taken down & put in a bag
            with six oranges

It's not forgotten, nor that
      nightfall brings a torrent
floods the plain with yellow light:
'The Moon, Sixpence' — the movie —
  Gauguin, Vincent van Gogh

There are so many of them
we've never heard of: Anya Sinclair
        The Garden of Forking Paths
McLeod, *The Painter in the Painting*

Moana a Toi, Tauranga, the Atrium,
the Long Gallery
            the Vault, Cube, Gallery One
things you've never seen before
                you need to see

How to get to the bus stop,
            the airport — how to discover
the forest's edge, people, places —
        the lonely reaches of the sky

Survival

The city's in disarray because those
appointed to manage it aren't able
            to manage everything

I wish I could understand them . . .

be like Magellan or Columbus
travel the world to parts unknown
            rediscover the Dodo

We carry them with us — the dead . . .

while officials & their supporters
who know how to care for themselves
            seem certain of survival

I wish it were possible to remember . . .

the way to the Galapagos, Mauritius
travel on a ship like the *Beagle*, make
        discoveries, invent a theory

one that might offer a prescription

for how things work or don't,
the theory of evolution & how finches
            differ from island to island

Perhaps it's a matter of where you live . . .

which suburb you can afford, or whether
you can pay for a flight from Auckland
            to Paris, Arles, Le Pay

I want to go to cities I've never seen

take the pilgrimage, Camino de Santiago
visit the Musée d'Orsay, go to places
            I've never been . . .

The Forest of Tane

They've always been here (well, almost)
& those others — the cedars of Lebanon
               treasured of Gilgamesh

those that went down to the edge of the sea,
& moved over the water — *Tokomaru*
               Takitimu, Te Arawa, Tainui . . .

Maatua that landed at Te Manuka-tu-tahi
while the trees of the forest waited through
               the days, months & years

They lean into themselves, lean over
each other, rocks, gullies, rivers, mountains
               rimu, totara, pohutukawa

They (the trees) have become planks, become
bridges, have become ships cresting
               the Pacific, the Atlantic

breathing the air, riding out the storms
the *Niña, Pinta & Santa Maria*, all of them —
               Endeavour, Golden Hind

circling an endless passage of days, shaping
the outermost edges of the world,
               the forest of Tane

that came from Te Kore, from the great void
from Ranginui & Papatuanuku & formed
               the wind & the sky . . .

The fiddler of Dooney

Well W B, it's a great poem
   & I wouldn't want to be without it —
      as you put it so succinctly
          — so memorably —
'the merry love the fiddle
     the merry love to dance.'

But sometimes there's that other thing
you wrote about — that evil chance
     lurking in the forest
in black water, close to the mountain
where people who've never danced
       stare into the dark.

Summer's last flicker has gone
     the sedge has long left the lake
& the lady 'mystic, wonderful'
       'clothed in white samite'
lifts her arm from the water,
    reaches for the king's sword

while here in Drumcliffe churchyard
       not far from the ancient cross
I turn towards Ben Bulben
hoping to hear the fiddler —
       hoping to hear him play
but the clouds come down
    bringing with them a scatter of rain.

Looking at the message carved
       on your headstone
the message you left for horsemen
riding out to the hunt or for home
    I listen for the sound of the fiddle
hear the sigh of the wind —
      nothing more . . .

Eine kleine Nachtmusik
(a serenade)

Driving towards town thinking
of my grandfather — the other —
from Edinburgh, dead at forty
& of everybody else because
　　　everybody dies

A little music from the radio
Mozart's *Eine kleine Nachtmusik*
Serenade No. 13 for strings
in G major —
　　　for a chamber ensemble:

Two violins, viola & cello
optional double bass (but usually
performed by a string orchestra)
everybody dies — Mozart died
　　　& the ensemble as well.

Edinburgh's on the other side
of the world — & Vienna —
but they remembered, sent a cross
(Caledonian) to mark the grave
　　　the place he's buried.

Maybe my grandfather heard it —
maybe he heard the *Nachtmusik*
at a concert in Wellington before
he was taken to Porirua,
　　　locked up & died there . . .

A traveller's guide to Venice

Of course they've decided it —
    the way things ought to be:
privileges, perks, parliamentary travel,
mermaids singing opera
        Italy, America, Spain.

This morning's newspaper says it —
    whatever newspapers say
Richardson's Pamela might have said
if anyone has asked her: we'll
        all be a long time dead.

Protesters seek freedom in Libya
are hit by the Army & Air Force,
        pigeons strut on the windowsills
of the Beehive trying to see whatever's
    happening inside.

Somewhere beyond Jupiter or Saturn
outside London, New York, Paris
        ten million light years away
there are planets dying & dead, stars
        going supernova.

If you can manage a few days off
    take the ferry to Devonport
sit on the beach at Takapuna watching
rain come in from the Tasman
        cruise ships going out to sea . . .

It's not exactly like being in Venice
Paris, Valencia, Rome
        wherever you might want to go
but you have to be somewhere
        or you're nowhere at all . . .

Always becoming: A life in poetry
Alistair Paterson with Jen Webb

Alistair Paterson has been a central figure in New Zealand poetry for many decades, as poet, editor and mentor. In late 2014, as part of a research project which involved conversations with senior poets about how creativity emerges, how it circulates, and what people do with this capacity, Professor of Creative Writing at the University of Canberra Jen Webb and Alistair met in Alistair's Auckland home to talk about poetry and his own practice. He began by saying: 'I don't think of myself so much as a poet. I think of myself as still trying to become a poet — or not so much *become* a poet, but to *write poetry*. If you want to *become* a poet, give it up; you'll never be any good.'

Why is it that you don't identify yourself as a poet?
Because then you're identifying yourself, instead of what you do or what you're trying to do.

So the idea is, if I say 'I'm a poet', that freezes it?
It freezes the whole thing, because it says you've got somewhere, you've achieved something. In fact poetry is a lifelong learning process; and if you say *I'm a poet*, or if you say *I've found my voice* . . .

Then you're actually dead in the water.
You're dead in the water. You're finished. That's why I don't like to see, in some creative writing courses, the teachers talking about *finding your voice*. My personal view is: don't try to find your voice, you're wasting your time, because then it's about *you* and it's not about the verse, it's not about the work. If you're trying to write poetry, to create poetry, that's an entirely different thing from finding out something about yourself. And anyway, if you're trying to write poetry, you will discover yourself anyway. You don't have to make an effort to do that.

I suppose, too, that saying 'I'm a poet' suggests that you're actually a finished being, when really we change constantly as we go through our lives; we don't become a thing, but we're always becoming who we are.
Yes. We're always becoming, we're never there. Because there is only the present and there's only the now, and there's only the person in the present and now. You're always becoming, in the present. The future? Well it's not here, it doesn't exist. By the time we get to it, it's *now*.

I think this is quite important. While I try to write poetry, I also try to learn about writing poetry: I read poetics and other people's poetry all the time. And in the process of editing magazines, over the past 30 years, one of the great benefits I've found is seeing the poetry that comes in — hundreds and thousands of poems come in to you in 30 years. You learn so much from other people.

So how do you identify yourself then? Do you say 'I'm an editor', or 'I'm a teacher'?
I'm a human being. And I try to do things. One of the things about poetry or editing — or anything else — is that we are what we do. And in being what we do, we discover, or do something about, our identity. It's not necessarily an identity we're fully conscious of: it's to some extent subconscious, and inside ourselves. So when I say *we are what we do*, I think that's important.

One of the questions you sent me in advance of this meeting was about when I first came into contact with poetry, or learnt something about it. It was quite early, when I was starting school. My grandmother used to teach me spelling, and I became enamoured of words and language. So by the time I was in Standard One, I was reading everything I could get my hands on.

Then, at the age of seven, I became ill: I had pain in my gut. The local doctor said 'rumbling appendix', or 'it might go away'; but I kept going to see him for two years. Then I started crawling up the wall — literally trying to crawl up the wall to escape the pain. I was just one week off my ninth birthday, and I was put into hospital, and had surgery, and there I remained for two years: in the same room, in the same bed.

I was in a children's ward in a hospital in a New Zealand provincial town, with no radio, no television, no toys, and nothing to do except read. I discovered, when I came out of the operation and slowly came back to myself, that my reading knowledge seemed to have been blotted out. I was given books and started sounding out the words and learning to read all over again. I spent two years in hospital reading books, day after day after day after day. Although I didn't always understand what I was reading, it gave me an absolute enthusiasm for language, particularly written language: the sound of it, the feel of it, the range of it, and the arrangement of it.

I didn't know it at that time, but I actually have what is called synaesthesia, where a word doesn't just have sound or meaning, but also has colour and feeling and rhythm.[1] That's important from the point of view of poetry, because if you're trying to write poetry and you don't have some sense of those aspects of language, then much of the writing is dead on the page.

So I think that's how I became obsessed with language and with reading. Most of it was prose, but when I went back to school I started to discover poetry because there was a teacher there, Mrs Riley, who ran what was called 'verse speaking'. I used to reel out of that classroom, drunk with words, absolutely intoxicated with words.

When I was getting towards the end of my school years, I was trying to write poetry, and my music teacher said to me, 'I hear, Alistair, you're writing poetry'. I said, 'I'm trying to write poetry'. 'Just give it up', he said, 'it's unhealthy'. But I didn't stop writing poetry, even though at that stage, back in Nelson where I come from, people looked upon poetry writing as effeminate, as not a proper thing to do.

Subsequently I went to Teachers' College at Canterbury University and discovered Allen Curnow's *A Book of New Zealand Verse*.[2] I was absolutely entranced by it, and so relieved that there were actually men who wrote poetry in New Zealand: it wasn't just something that came from brilliant minds overseas; you could have it here. That gave me some encouragement.

Later on I transferred from Canterbury to Victoria, because Alistair

Campbell, James K. Baxter, Louis Johnson were there, and I thought I should get to know some poets. I became a kind of junior member of the Wellington Group at that stage.[3] This helped me, in that Louis Johnson particularly, and Campbell and Baxter, gave me the feeling that poetry could be a profession. It did not have to be something that you did just to occupy your time. I recognised in those people a true professionalism, and I've been doing it ever since: I don't know that I've reached that stage, but I have worked in that direction.

So far you are telling me about reading prose, and writing poetry. What was the impact, for you, of reading poetry?
I read poetry every day, and all the time. I read it every day, from wherever I can get it.

I am a re-reader as well as a reader. Because when I'm reading it's not just the story or the characters; it's the language, the language itself, that makes books enjoyable. And you can get that from anything, from trashy pop magazine writing to enormously heavy, complex and boring academic writing. Within that range there's a tremendous range of writers, many of whom aren't fully aware of what they're doing. Perhaps we never are fully aware of what we're doing? Certainly not as poets . . .

Were you mentored, as a young poet?
I was never mentored myself.

Really? So Baxter and Johnson and people like that were models, for you, of how a poet might work, rather than people who'd look at your work and give you feedback?
Yes. I took years to learn some little tricks in poetry, and I taught myself. For instance, the use of the word *of*: '*the moon of kindness*', or '*the moon of* something else'; I just threw away the word *of* and I tell people not to use these kind of constructs, because they are poeticisms. And I learned about excessive adjectival disease, which is absolutely frightful. And then of course in doing all this I found myself mentoring others, but I think the real reason for this was because I was teaching, and I hated it.

Then I saw an advertisement for instructor officers and trainers in the navy, so I joined the navy, and became an instructor officer, and finished up after 20 years as a lieutenant commander. During that period I was training people in boat sailing, navigation, elementary electronics, mechanics, and so on. As a result, it was almost inevitable that I would fall into mentoring poets, because I just could not abide something that wasn't quite as good as it could be. The habit persisted and I became a mentor.

I've done an awful lot of mentoring, because when people would send work in, I would find little things in it I didn't like, or I thought were rather rough, and I found it irresistible to give a few words of advice, and that's how I developed into a poet or a would-be poet who mentors others. I worked on *Poetry New Zealand* for 21 years, and the labour was great! Try getting a thousand submissions a year, and writing an answer to every one of them.

You mean you never just rejected a submission, you always wrote them a response? That's a huge commitment.
I never just rejected anything; but I rarely just accepted anything either. That was the educator part of me, unable to resist the temptation to get the poetry to be what I considered to be the best we could publish.

Can you tell me a little about how you started to develop as a writer?
I got interested in the question of longer poems because, back in the 1970s, nobody seemed to be writing long poems. A single one-off poem seemed to be the limit of what you could do with a poem. Also around about then, in the mid-1970s after I left the navy, I was living in Wellington and I had a close association with actors, and with Jennifer Compton: she's a poet and a playwright who now lives near Sydney, near where Grace Perry used to live.[4] Before she moved from Wellington to Australia, she introduced me to people in the theatre world, and I found myself trying to write a poem, which turned into that longish poem 'The Toledo Room'.[5] That was my first long poem, and I did it in theatrical form under the influence of these people in the theatre. It has

been performed on radio as a play, and it was performed at Downstage Theatre in Wellington — with music by Jonathan Besser — as a kind of Shakespearean mime, which went quite well.[6]

I was very pleased with that. I thought it was a great success to have a first long poem done like that. Looking back now I see it's got weaknesses, it could have been done differently, but that's the way one feels about everything. You're never happy with it in the end.

Then I got into reviewing, for all sorts of magazines, and I started writing the odd essay, which led me deeper into poetics, into your favourite Foucault, and semiotics, and so on. I'm very interested in avant-garde writing — not that I'm an extreme avant-garde writer myself, but I'm very interested in it because it's from avant-garde writing we can learn so much about the art of poetry writing. Lisa Samuels is an interesting avant-garde poet who uses semiotic techniques. I've published some of her in *Poetry New Zealand*, and she's featured and has an interview in the recent issue, *Poetry New Zealand* 49.[7] It's about opening up the boundaries, and reimaging how language might be used.

There's a characteristic about it that concerns me deeply when people are writing what they think is avant-garde semiotics — the academic world is such that it actually causes people to write in a manner which is reminiscent of the French philosopher-linguists, which is almost incomprehensible at times — and actually they're rambling through the ideas of how to do it. I'd rather hear what they're doing, and what it means: what is poetry; how does it work; what does it do to people; what is reality? These are the questions that come to my mind. But you don't often find that among people writing about semiotic practice.

And when they do use the word 'reality', they're not necessarily writing about the kind of reality that interests me. Maybe I'm being too negative about this . . . when you know that death is only a short distance off, the question of reality is very, very important.

Poetry can't remain just an abstract language game. It has to be lived.
Yes. So I want to know more about the nature of reality: what is it all

about? That's why Max Tegmark's book on mathematics interests me.[8] He talks about three realities: external, internal and consensual reality. But in fact I think he missed the most important: *apparent* reality, which covers the whole three. And that takes us to the question of the nature of poetry: what is the nature of science in relationship to the arts? And what is reality in relationship to them and human beings?

It's like Descartes' *cogito ergo sum*; I think, therefore I am. But it's the other way around.

That's what Heidegger said: it's *sum ergo cogito*; I am, therefore I think.[9] Or, I am *because* I think. I am *because* I write poetry. I am *because* I build a bridge. And when you consider those aspects, you have to take it a step further and ask about aesthetic qualities. What are aesthetic qualities? The nature of reality, and the aesthetics related to it, is extremely important.

I am interested in these sorts of questions, and especially — for poets — what connects us back to the world; what is it that makes things real for you, and that finally matters.
What is the world? Max's view of the internal, external and consensus reality is right into it. But I say apparent reality covers the lot, because no matter what we say about anything, it's how it appears to us. Human beings evolved not to deal with a real world out there. They evolved to deal with the apparent world as it affects them, because otherwise they wouldn't survive.

So perhaps we can talk about finding ways into what might be a world, or our points of connection with that apparent or possible world. Certainly maths gives us a language to explore this.
And we do that in poetry all the time: poetry explores the apparent world. But in exploring the apparent world, it is doing stuff to us, and when a poem is written, it's not a fixed object in any way. As you and I both know, it changes — for the writer — from time to time, and like Auden said, the writer doesn't know what he's saying until it's said, and

even then probably doesn't know what he's saying. And when a reader reads it, the reader doesn't read the poem the author wrote: readers read the poem they read, and that is something inside themselves. That's why I say that a poem is largely just a set of marks on a piece of paper. That is, the poem is the sign; but the signifiers exist in the person who reads it, not anywhere else.

Given that condition of openness, what effects do you want to have on your readers? Do you hope to have an effect, or do you just leave it entirely in their eyes and in their hands?
Well, you write a poem for all sorts of reasons. One of the reasons is that it's something you can't help doing, because you love language so much. But when the reader gets it, you expect them to use the poem in a slightly similar way: to use the poem as a means of self-construction.

Are you saying that the business of reading poetry is part of the business of being? That as you read, you take it in like food and it nurtures and feeds and 'grows' you?
Yes. Yes. And if you take it seriously enough, if you read hard enough, it restructures you. But it's not the poem that the author wrote: it's the poem that the reader constructs on what the author wrote.

But for the poet: what you've got to be able to do is to detect what the poem is doing, on a subconscious level, and when it brings something up to the surface, be able to comprehend it in terms of yourself and what you're doing. The conscious mind is a mind that deals with apparent reality, and some of the apparent reality is what floats out of your subconscious. I can take the irrational that comes from my subconscious mind and I can embody that, as much as I am able, into a poem. That 'irrational' aspect gives the poem a variety and depth it might not have otherwise. And when a reader reads it, if the reader finds some of this irrational material that doesn't apparently relate to the poem, hopefully it will relate to the reader's subconscious and the reader will use this irrationality to help construct his or her self's subconscious, and ultimately the whole person. Does that help?

So it's about paying attention, then, it seems to me.
It's paying attention to everything that's there. And of course this apparently irrational element, that doesn't actually match the poem, can be put in such a way that it helps to create the aesthetic construct that is the poem. The unifying factor in a poem is the aesthetics of it. That's why we should be suspicious of narrative in a poem. If the poem is essentially narrative, don't write a poem, go and write a novel.

So you're not a keen reader of verse novels?
Not really. Although I recently actually edited a verse novel of 120 pages for someone. I could understand what he was doing. But I didn't think that his emphasis was as much on the aesthetic as on the narrative. That's why, when I'm trying to mentor people, I'm trying to help them steer towards this concept of the aesthetic as the primary element in the structure of a poem. Because the structure of the poem is not just the language: it's what it does to the reader, what it does to you when you write it.

You write very long, book-length poems, but you are resistant to narrative. What is the attraction for you of the really large space, if not narrative?
The attraction about a large space is that when you're working on this piece of writing, the elements in your subconscious keep stirring up and rising out of it. And these things keep coming. Why cut the poem short when there's all this stuff surging out? You only stop when it doesn't happen any more. Do you write long poems?

I don't. Actually, I write really quite short poems.
I'll give you a prediction. You'll be writing long poems.

Well, I've actually started easing into it, sneakily, by putting together several short poems that are on the same issue. And then when I put those together there'd be eight or so, and then I'd have to rework all of them so that it becomes a thing in itself and not cobbled-together bits.

And that's how you start writing long poems! Because these pieces are coming out in a way that relate to each other aesthetically, and you can't help it. They don't have to be continuous. They don't have to be rational. They don't have to be narrative. But there has to be a flow of musical language, a flow of language that integrates with itself, and overall a kind of aesthetic development that takes place when you're doing it and you can't fully recognise or understand. You feel it's there.

I'm interested in your earlier question of what writing does to one as a writer. You've been writing and editing for many, many years now: what makes it matter still, to you? Why do you keep doing it?
I don't really fully understand why I do it; and I'm sure most others would say the same about their writing. But once you become enraptured of language and you start doing something with it yourself, it becomes so much a part of your process as a human being that you can't stop it. And if you don't do that, you might just as well finish off now because you'll go nowhere, you'll just become somebody who turns out the same ideas, who does the same things, and you're no longer a person but a kind of tool in society. So I keep doing it because of those things, and because I would really like to write a really good poem. I can never be Shakespeare, but I would like to do it really well.

Let's roll with that one. Where do you find those words, in an attempt to do it really well? Because W. H. Auden has an essay on writing poetry, where he says: 'When we genuinely speak, we do not have the words ready to do our bidding; we have to find them, and we do not know exactly what we are going to say until we have said it, and we say and hear something new that has never been said or heard before.'[10] Does that make sense to you?
Yes. You can't possibly know what you're going to write until you've written it. You can't, because it comes along as a phrase into your mind or your head, and the phrase starts off a process that may or may not become a poem, but you hope it does. And it's not what you *need* to say, because you're not actually saying anything, but you're creating

an aesthetic. The language comes by familiarity with language, as much as possible. Vast reading, vast thinking about what you read. Vast experience of language, even a little foreign language learning: I've been doing a course in Māori lately, and writing one or two poems with a few Māori bits in them. It's that wide range that fills your subconscious up with things, and those things are part of you. They are part of the stuff that creates you, makes you. And when you draw on that making — well you don't actually draw on it, the poem forces your writing — then the words come up. But they have to fit together in an aesthetic kind of manner.

And then of course you ask, *how do you know when a poem's finished?* As far as I'm concerned, one never knows when it's fully finished; it's just that you've exhausted your capacity to deal with it any longer.

So you don't finish it, you abandon it, as somebody said.[11]
Well, in a sense you abandon it; but in another sense you never abandon it because it's always somewhere in your mind and you wish you'd done it better, or you redevelop it elsewhere. Those sorts of questions seem very important to me. It's not just about where you get the words from; it's also about where you get the ideas. I get them from moving about, because travel affects you. Well, everything affects you. Everything.

This is a piece on Shakespeare I wrote when I was at Stratford-upon-Avon earlier in the year:

> Stratford-upon-Avon. Visiting actually and wishing the Bard were here could see it. *The morn on yon high eastern hill.* That it were possible to meet him on the bridge that Clapton built over the Avon. Anywhere at all he might have been with Burbage, Marlowe. Where what was written was written because it had to be written and what was done was surely done here or in London at an ale house close by the Thames where they talked about how to deal with the Lord Chamberlain. The river's still here and not far off, Marlborough's Palace built to celebrate victory, success in warfare, richly rewarded. The first Duke, a good subject for a play at the

Globe. All those skirmishes and battles and the many others that followed after. Nelson at Trafalgar, the Bellerophon at the Glorious First. The Battle of the Nile. Guns and pikes, the nameless dead. But it's Antony who's remembered. Cleopatra. The barge she sat in burnished like a throne, and the plays. The plays that captured the poor and powerless, villains and outlaws. The frailties and follies of knights and kings.

In doing this, I'm hoping that it becomes an aesthetic experience both for the reader and the poet, because it's an aesthetic experience that gives shape to the self, the unconscious, the way one thinks and feels.

Do you find you write quickly, as you come to do this sort of work? Or for the first draft anyway.
No. I'm slow, I think. It's slow. I find it extremely difficult. You have to open yourself up to the unconscious, and you have to be in that mental state where things are reasonably in balance in your life. If you're not in that reasonably balanced sort of state, where you can get access to your subconscious, it won't come. If other things are overwhelming you, you can't do it. You're really drawing on everything you experience and know, in order to construct something more of yourself and, hopefully, give it to other people who might be able to use it to construct themselves as well. That's a kind of expansion of the reader response theory but that's what I feel is right.

So in practical terms, then, when you've done the first draft and you think, okay, I think there is something there, I'm going to keep going with this: does the process feel different to you, when you move from the initial drafting into starting editing?
At first when you look at the poem — the thing you've written and you feel that you have to go on working at — you look at it as an editor might: identifying the rough patches. But then, when it comes to actually working on those, you have to go back into a poetry writing mode in order to get the thing out.

So editing is still a form of poetry making? It's not a different state of mind?

No. It's still a form of poetry making; it's the same state of mind. But there is this process of working into it from the editorial perspective to get started on it. Finally, well, there might be a line or two you can hardly do anything with; and it might take several weeks before a solution comes, or it may never come; in which case maybe discard it, not deal with; but then on the other hand, one's always tempted to publish the stuff, damn it [*laughter*].

How do you know, then, when you think, okay, I will publish it? Either you believe it's pretty much as perfect as it can be, or you think, I'll never be able to resolve those two lines, but everything else is really good so I'm going to publish it. How do you identify that point?

Well, if it's got two bad lines in it, you know they're bad, then don't publish it.

But if those two lines weren't there, how would you know when to say to yourself, 'those 312 lines are good, this is ready to go'?

You don't say it. You feel it. And sometimes you find that when you're trying to write something else you can draw on that thing that didn't work, and use parts of it. If the concept was good and what was coming up into you felt good, but it didn't seem to work because of that one fault in it, or two faults . . . It's your physical being that tells you it's ready to go.

The feeling of it: yes. The formal word of course is 'affect', which is about feelings and emotion; and I was just wondering to what extent you think writing poetry is, or requires, emotion? And if there is an emotional aspect, is it your emotion or is it the emotion the poem has to have?

Well, that's an interesting question. I think when you're writing a poem, or trying to write a poem, that it's the emotions within you that cause you to start writing, and that you couldn't do it without the emotion — because the emotionality is how you feel about the aesthetics.

If you're trying to think, if it's just a rational, logical process, then for me it doesn't work. I can't do it. Look at those eighteenth-century poets who wrote endless couplets. Pope and the other neo-classicists. They wrote so much from the conscious, non-emotional mind. And that's the reason the stuff is very rarely read any more: because it doesn't resonate with the sense of being as a reader or a person. And that's the beauty of Shakespeare. His plays are poetry, but they're poetry because they're loaded up with what we're talking about now: with the structure of the subconscious and its emotions.

Thank you! And I have this last question: is there anything that your readers owe you?

No. Readers owe me nothing. Honestly, readers owe me nothing because I'm not actually giving them anything. I'm trying to write poems, and restructure myself in the process. And I publish poems because I think that it might be useful in a small way to other people. But, you know, they owe me nothing more than you owe the world around you or anything like that. Why should I feel they owe me anything? I owe them if they're kind enough to read my poems.

---

1   A number of poets have experienced synaesthesia (Arthur Rimbaud's 'Vowels' is
    famously a synaesthetic poem), and some research identifies an association between
    creativity and synaesthesia (see Jamie Ward, Daisy Thompson-Lake, Roxanne Ely
    and Flora Kaminski, 'Synaesthesia, Creativity and Art: What Is the Link?' *British
    Journal of Psychology* 99 (2008), 127–141; see also Shane Butler and Alex Purves (eds),
    Synaesthesia and the Ancient Senses (London: Routledge, 2013).

2   Allen Curnow, *A Book of New Zealand Verse, 1923–1945* (Christchurch: Caxton Press,
    1945). This book, republished in a revised edition in 1951, is often described as the
    herald of a new (postcolonial) New Zealand literature. See Lawrence Jones, *Picking
    Up the Traces: The Making of a New Zealand Literary Culture, 1932–1945* (Wellington:
    Victoria University Press, 2003).

3   The Wellington Group, or Wellington School, was the name given to a loose group of
    (mainly male) poets who lived in or near Wellington between about 1950 and 1965,
    including Louis Johnson, Alistair Ariki Campbell, James K. Baxter and Peter Bland.

The Group aimed to produce a different style and voice, and a more international perspective, than that offered by Curnow and his associates. Jenny Carlyon and Diana Morrow include a section on this period of New Zealand poetry, the characters and their conflicts, in their 2013 volume *Changing Times: New Zealand Since 1945* (Auckland: Auckland University Press).

4   Jennifer Compton has been writing and publishing poetry for several decades. A biographical entry is available at http://redroomcompany.org/poet/jennifer-compton/. Australian Grace Perry AM (1927–1987) was a medical practitioner and poet; she edited *Poetry Australia* and South Head Press, both of which were very important in building Australian poetry culture in the 1970s.

5   Alistair Paterson, *The Toledo Room: A Poem for Voices* (Dunedin: Pilgrims South Press, 1978).

6   Jonathan Besser has been a long-term contributor to New Zealand musical culture, as a composer and a performer. A biographical note is available at http://sounz.org.nz/contributors/1007

7   Lisa Samuels, Associate Professor in English and Writing at the University of Auckland, is a specialist in poetry and poetics, and is also a creative practitioner; see her profile at http://epc.buffalo.edu/authors/samuels/

8   Max Tegmark, Professor of Physics at MIT, published *Our Mathematical Universe* (New York: Penguin/Random House, 2014), a work of science writing that has been remarkably well received, including beyond the science community.

9   Martin Heidegger famously reversed Descartes' notion of being; the point in his reversal being that human beings occupy bodies, and those bodies occupy space and time, and therefore being is a material presence, not the abstraction found in Cartesian thought. See Martin Heidegger, *Off the Beaten Track*, trans. Julian Young and Kenneth Haynes (Cambridge: Cambridge University Press, 2002).

10   W. H. Auden, *Secondary Worlds: The T. S. Eliot Memorial Lectures* (London: Faber and Faber, 1967), 105.

11   This is widely attributed to the poet Paul Valéry, expressed in English as 'A poem is never finished, only abandoned.' I have not been able to source the original translation, but according to Alan Levy, W. H. Auden quoted Valéry using that phrase when asked about process. See his book *W. H. Auden: In the Autumn of the Age of Anxiety* (New York: The Permanent Press, 1983). (Philosopher John R. Searle extends the phrase, claiming that Valéry's line was in fact 'A poem is never finished, only abandoned in despair.' See the introduction to his book *Rationality in Action* (Cambridge MA: Bradford Books, 2001).

New
Poems

Baudelaire on L'Île Bourbon 1841

I sometimes wonder how I came to be
here cast-off on this tiny parrot and mosquito
plagued island nowhere to remember

The absinthe and the haze of hashish
sharpens and diffuses time, each in its way
a lonely pathway leading out of here

I miss the bars and alleyways of Paris
and those women in their darkened doorways
offering some other kind of paradise

Still, I recall the albatross, my Creole
woman, and all those other stories travelling
across the cinnamon-scented ocean

Her skin was as cool as silk at dusk
when the sea-breeze leans against the palms . . .
My wings beat futilely against the deck

At the age of 20, Charles Baudelaire was sent by his parents on a passage to India to cure
him of his already wanton ways. Baudelaire, however, jumped ship upon Mauritius,
subsequently got stranded on neighbouring Réunion Island (then L'Île Bourbon), which
in a letter to the poet Leconte de Lisle he later denied visiting, and wrote several fine
poems (among them 'L'Albatros', 'À une Dame Créole', 'Bien loin d'ici' and 'La Belle
Dorothée') drawn from his exotic experiences on these Indian Ocean islands.

Hamish Ansley

Popular Interpretations of Seven Common Dreams

1.

Dreams of bright black
tar pouring
from a yawning flesh wound
almost always connote distrust
of hospitals
(possibly repressed homosexual
desire).

2.

Skin flayed
from your soles and palms
and a beach of pink
salt
suggests you probably shouldn't
have cheated on your
girlfriend.

3.

A spider
or the bald orange man
in a black jumpsuit
from the Fanta adverts
chasing you along
the belly of a python
indicates you should avoid
your uncle Steve
at future family gatherings.

4.

A hamburger
made of teeth like crumbled
seashells —
trepidation about the consumption
of meat:
See *1*.

5.

Her vine of pitch
hair
making crosshatch patterns
with the seatbelt
webbing:
subject has a penchant
for auto-erotic
asphyxiation.

6.

A nosebleed while gardening,
type O negative
spilled
on lettuce leaves:
undiagnosed psychopathy.

7.

Lines of John Milton
written in steam
on the shower door:
compulsive masturbator,
likely post-orgasmic
lacrimation.

Trisomy 18

The geneticist talks of chromosomes.
The cardiologist's sentences are full of holes.

Hope crumples, shrivels, falls faint to the floor.
She is quickly mopped up and then   gone.

We are bewildered and scared.

There are decisions to be made, like, resuscitation —
a topic not covered in antenatal classes.

Our hearts are hurt-full, and thumping.

A nurse says that she will never feed and binds
my breasts, crudely cancelling all milk deliveries.

We are confused and lost.

We are a short term family, a daughter,
a father, a mother.

Stu Bagby

On Reading August Kleinzahler's *Where Souls Go*

I was with them once, the souls . . .
Ellerslie racecourse, late afternoon,
a horse called Golden King making his way
to the start of the final race, cantering
through the sun with his name.

       We turned
to each other as strangers do.
'Look at him. Just look at him,' we said.

So we bet on Golden King and cashed our chips,
then each soul went west (as souls still go)
to see their lover, who had the right song on
when they arrived. The songs were on records
which are round with holes in the middle,
       where the souls go.

Tony Beyer

Aftershock

in the branch library
the books along the shelves
shudder in their jackets

the woman at the desk
surveys the room
with startled eyes

not that this experience is new
but it renews
the provisional and unsteady state of things

against which our daily tasks
our preferences
are no protection

we are in other hands
and must be content
to remain so

Sarajevo

1.

That last summer
before you left
to go I don't know where
summer was green
leaf patterning the sky

and peace
bird sounds
filtered through the silence

2.

the trees
black skeletons
against a fiery sky
birds no longer come
the hill's burnt bare

war
echoes
in the silence

3.

child-size
643
slaughter house tally
timber rough hewn
colour bloodstain

643
empty chairs
circle a tear washed square
in the cracks
snowdrops

Erick Brenstrum

15 January 1945

Flights of Corsairs
over Rabaul all day
covering Simpson Harbour.
A wounded pilot
swimming with the tide
for open ocean
for flying boat rescue.
Tide turned late afternoon
fighters called home near dusk.
Running low on fuel and daylight
before Green Island
seven lost to a line of thunderstorms.

In the photo
three Corsairs abreast
over Guadalcanal
the nearest pilot
looking straight at the camera.

What have you done with your life?

Iain Britton

from The Vignettes: Luminous Particles

9 — paradise seekers

this street's graffiti | handstands in the rain |
commuters shelter under canopies | a city's
lost paradise | muscles in on a neighbourhood

sanctuary of backyard retreats | of wish lists |
girls with their body language | with forked
pink tongues | this ghetto of raw youth

punctuates a no-man's habitat | mortar-maimed
with dark fragments of a daytime's surrender |
here | graffiti has learnt to walk on its hands

a 1 not a 2

sick with flu
I email my supervisor
to say I won't be in tomorrow
and text her to be sure
she got the message

return phone call
crackly line
me woolly-headed
she says I'm nice to her face
but disrespect her
I should make more of an effort
the class tomorrow is important
I can come late and leave early

she rings back, tells me not to come in
she has papers for the students
demands I apologise next time I see her
tells me I'm a fucking idiot

rings again
*will you play table tennis with me
tomorrow?*
I can't because I'm sick
I'll kick your fucking head in, mate
I tell her not to ring again

wrong number

like a lot of people
stamping their feet

Nicole Cassidy-Koia

I miss you Grandma

It hurts so fucking bad
I want to tear my heart out of my chest
And give it to death to digest
Because that's exactly what it feels like
And I'm a mess at best, please
It hurts so fucking bad
I want to tear my heart out of my chest.

Poetry

Let us take our time.
Poetry appears
when we least
expect it.
The fruit half-eaten.
The light turned low.
A shawl draped
over a chair.
Most poetry is unwritten,
denied and supposed.
Don't go to write it.
Go where you've never been.
Go.
And it may come.
Behind you,
love rests.
And where is poetry?
What is it you seek?

Alastair Clarke

Wairarapa, Distance

It is the chemistry of distance,
of broken hills pitted and hewn,
of shadows cloud-cast moving across land,
of abandoned grey-timbered barns,
of forgetfulness and time.

A dark bird stabs soil;
stampeding, steer veer from the train,
fuss in a shiftlessness of macrocarpa and pine.
Distantly the lip of the horizon
teases sight. See, it is powdery blue.
The light sharpens and drifts of yellow
edge toward evening.

The train shivers.
We are nearer now.

Jennifer Compton

a rose, and then another

it's a small knock
like a knuckle tapping twice
on the back of a book

two petals falling
from the singular
efflorescence

(a clutched hand
a fist
white into almost apricot)

and i am flown
back to that city
and that time

when a particular rose
filched from a midnight garden
(because)

stood in for
so much else, as the heat
(roses are sad in the heat, i wrote)

had laid me dully out on the bed
of the cheapest room i could find
(my unshaven legs)

and the sudden knock
the knock knock knock knock
and knock

of a rose surrendering
all of her petals
in one go

lifted my head from the pillow
what had fallen? what indeed?
and with what sonorousness?

there isn't a manual on when you're writing someone a love poem and they break up with you

i woke up to type words
about the singing and snoozing waves
to be edited, to be changed
from waves to wind to
anything

i dreamt about your shoulders
the muscles dripping down into your arms
or maybe they'd be crafted there
a structure

i spent a day letting the words
in no way final simmer and flicker

now what do i do

Mary Cresswell

Transparency
[a political paradelle]

Let us now praise famous men
Let us now praise famous men
Glass beads sing with the lure of the lost
Glass beads sing with the lure of the lost
The men of glass sing with beads.
Let us lure praise — famous, now lost.

What you see is what you get
What you see is what you get
Crystal chooks come home to roost
Crystal chooks come home to roost
What, what! you chooks! See you home —
Crystal get is come to roost!

Any old port in a storm will do
Any old port in a storm will do
Green winds are clattering round our ears
Green winds are clattering round our ears
Any clattering ears do in a round port.
Storm, old will! Our winds are green!

What will the famous port get?
What any lost men with clattering ears do:
Storm is our roost, winds in to home.
See you a lure of green glass beads.
Let crystal chooks now sing:
You are old, round. Come praise us.

sanctuary

for ellen

the coast was clean with waste
piled high in roadside rests

oil-smeared reeds
gingerly we stepped

between jutting sculptures
advertising cards stomped in mud

tunnelled beneath
ribs of a carcass

your exquisite shaved scalp
nestled into my armpit

peered
through rusting springs

at smear of stars
a winking satellite

Semira Davis

Hiding

Mum,
you said it was okay
if I came home pregnant
as long as I was not a lesbian

I was thirteen

and it wasn't milking cows
that had my fingers
dripping cream

and if it were a boy
who gave me that hickey
would I still have scratched it
with split driftwood
to make it look like a wound?

The opposite of forgetting
for Pat

when I arrive you know me

but I've also become
the person up the ladder doing something to the bricks in the wall
the person who left the paintings with you

wasn't it you?
it wasn't you?
it didn't have any connection with you?

the paintings are stacked
with a letter you don't remember
signed with a name
you don't remember

you say, it's like my memory's forgotten
that other person
and inserted you in there instead

I look forward to being
your first husband, both your sons

if that's what it comes to

Dream of a Sunday Afternoon

Diego Rivera poses as a little boy
holding La Calavera Catrina's hand.

Behind him stands his future wife Frida Kahlo
clasping a black and white Yin Yang in her palm.

A symbol of balance amidst the chaos
of revolution and infidelity.

José Marti tips his hat to the two wives
of Diaz the dictator of Mexico.

Police mariachis play at the band stand
as Zapatistas fill the scene with flames.

The President of the Republic fondles
blonde women with the archbishop's consent.

The phrase: 'God does not exist' was removed
where little Diego daydreams of his love.

After Diego Rivera's masterpiece *Dream of a Sunday Afternoon in the Alameda Central.*

Distant Ophir

I went looking for the nightingale,
for the rose, and found corrugated iron,
scent of wild thyme, cry of a hawk.

I felt a breeze lift in the orchard,
to waken the leaves from slumber
and entangle memories in apricot heat.

Monday was washday, Tuesday ironing,
Wednesday cleaning, Thursday baking,
Friday shopping, Saturday sports games.

Sunday meant church, promise of roast dinner.
Air stood dry and warm beneath pine trees.
Crickets leapt over sunflower radiance.

Summer's elixirs glistened in green jelly.
Jam was given in peach and cherry.
Quicksilver sank in the foxed mirror.

The breeze, a stir of quiet fingers,
plucked at floury puffs of petals,
fluffed sponge cake, buttered big scones.

Furniture stacked, empty windows blank,
fine bones showing, faded curtains folded,
the farmhouse went for a knockdown price.

If I peer hard now through the late afternoon,
I can almost see as far as distant Ophir,
and cargo from Otago, raising the dust.

Favoured Exception

I taught you, perhaps, a few anomalous spellings.
By thirteen, you knew most of the usual words
but favoured exceptions — like *supersede* and *rarefied*.

Black ballpoint dragons rattled the margins
of your stories. Their fierce impressions
lasted several pages.

At the nape of your neck there was often a knot.
Your free hand would worry it as you wrote,
making a fair coir above your collar.

Thirty now, and in dire Emergency Housing,
you text me the difference between smack and crack,
much as a patient stranger might explain to a foreigner
what a 'ciggie' is, or that 'grog' and 'booze' are the same.

I am far outside this story, with its dealers
from the Capital, up for the day
to flex their muscles against the walls of the poor
semi-detached calamities of your town.

Littles, Johnson — men like Pinter parodies —
squat and joke on your mother's piss-stained sofa,
then go to serve body-blows to bad buyers.
I know you're smart enough to say your lines and leave.

But what to do, Kid, when your brain cells tick
like bored fingernails on a table, and psychedelics
are a tenner a pop — when your shoes have remnant soles
and you're sleeping on bare bed-slats?

Still, I have only an English teacher's advice,
just as back in our old days I could not make my fingers
reach to untangle your hair, could not spell you out of trouble
with coded homework, nor keep you in school with
WISH YOU WERE HERE postcards from my classroom.

Is it too late to say the dragons are waiting in the margins
until you come back with this electric connection
of history and experience, your wit even quicker now
in its hectic worldliness?

Favoured Exception, my words are warm and well-shod.
They have never known neglect, nor the censorship of terror.
Forgive them. They are embarrassed by their comfortable home,
their shy adherence to the rules.

If it were possible, they would go back
and tell my coward hands to touch your head,
work free the knots.

Suspicion

The seagull walks more quickly
in front of the little boy
whose hands are a gun.
She will not fly or stop
to look behind;
she will just keep a hop
ahead of his shadow
until he loses interest.
Because he will lose interest.
He will lose.
He will.

Jess Fiebig

Dead Man's Point

Autumnal Central Otago
copper poplars line Lake Dunstan,
a pool of glass underneath
this Southern watercolour sky

the yolk yellow leaves,
brash and unashamedly golden
in this lilac light,
are shocking in their defiance
of the gentle pastel landscape

they stir something inside me
that has lain still
                              for so long.

Catherine Fitchett

Lead

Lead, too, corrodes. So each hard rain
that filters down past bullets embedded
in layers of mud-caked bone yards
dissolves metal, leaches, oxidises,
triggers a slow subterranean blossoming
of crystalline flowers — cerussite,
anglesite, galena, one bloom for each bullet
one trillion in half a century of war.

Scholars will come in far off days
our conflicts long forgotten
dig careful trenches, lay their grids
study the bones and wonder
what ritual was it that caused these bones
to lie here shattered?
Here and there a trace of another creature — horse, bird
but for the most part, young men (very rarely, a woman)
jumbled and scattered. But see how carefully, they say,
our ancestors placed their best treasures
in these burial grounds, these rare crystals
shining silver, yellow, white.

The smallness of significant things

I have to move
you tell me
the bus rattles around us
our bags jig up & down
My landlord needs the house
I have to find a new one as soon as . . .
we rock & roll past million dollar
views realty firms drool over
their eyes as big as saucers
They cream it & the island changes
you sigh & we exchange a glance
Let us be rich in diversity you say &
this word has a taste we agree
to savour for a moment
at Little Oneroa
a man with a cane gets off slowly
we see the near empty playground
school is back & the summer visitor
geese have gone; the sea
still glitters blue in the bay
Oneroa village is your stop
as you rise to alight
I call to you
I'll keep my ear to the ground
you smile at me
Thank you; what a lovely phrase
It could live in a poem

at the wharf I chronicle
the significance of small things
an ear, the ground
blue sea in our eyes
a chat on a bus
a smile.

The title of this poem comes from the introduction to Jennifer Harrison and Kate Waterhouse (eds), *Motherlode: Australian Women's Poetry 1986–2008* (Glebe, NSW: Puncher and Wattmann, 2009).

The good daughter

I want to be
that girl in the story
the one shouting out
toads and vipers

toxic barbed words
they are sitting there
I feel them grumbling
like bubbling mud

or super-heated steam
pressure geysering up
through my larynx
scratching my tongue

then blown by a kiss
of confusion and hurt
but if I do there will be
toads and vipers on the floor

on your bed your tray of meds
sticking to your hair your eyes
licking your tears
poisoning the space between us

and it will be me
who has to clean it all up
so it's better to be
that other girl

the one who speaks in gleaming
pearls and humming-birds
the one who draws the blinds
against the harsh bright sun

Umbrellas

You can learn a lot about a girl
By her choice of umbrella.

There are those who like the tall ones.
So they can brandish them like swords
Carry them on sunny days as weapons.

Some prefer the portable option,
Reliable and handbag sized
That can follow wherever they go.

Some are chosen for their sturdiness,
Their layers of science tested protection
That have the statistical probability of lasting
Through all weather conditions.

There are those whose umbrellas have broken,
Flipped inside-out one too many times.
They now clad themselves in Gore-Tex armour,
Stomp through puddles gumboot shod.

Then there are the umbrella haters.
They don't like to admit it's raining until they are soaked
And even then they walk chin first into the wind
Calling out behind them,

What do I need an umbrella for?

The Deep

I want to drown in that pool

Where the 4-year-old boy
is rummaging round
running his hand
through the ebony surface

I want to drown
There!

Where the kid watches
the ripples
curl to the edge of the onyx
and bounce back again
to splash his wee fingers

Yes, there
There is where I want to bury my head
in cool water

Would the boy
reach in
and grab my hair
dragging my shallow shell
back up to the air

or
would he
shove me
down

down beneath the granite
nothing but a circle flowing
from a small child's fingers

Michael Hall

Towards Evening

Having unwound
Herself from
A patch of afternoon
In the bedroom
She miaows at
The kitchen door.
It is now; she
Wants her food.
But it is also now
She is saying.

Above

We were always dreaming of the hill
above us
with houses made of silk
soaking in the endless blue view

We'd go to the empty field to cry
under the leaning trees
on sun damaged earth
away from the cows

Or make love
at night regardless of the moon
we crossed all the marshes and gorse
and we kissed at the pine forest above the sea
until we were kicked out for trespassing

Paula Harris

The poet is bearded and wearing his watch around the wrong way

The poet is wondering what word could distil the blue of the sky today,
if the jasmine outside the window smell as strongly as they appear delicate,
when the postie will cycle past.

The poet is wondering if there are any chocolate chip biscuits left,
what his wife is doing right this moment,
how long his trouser cuff has been torn.

The poet is wondering if he finished his cup of tea
and where he might have left the cup.

The poet is wondering about the comma of the fourth line and if
it should be a line break. Yes, a line break. No, no, a comma. No,
wait, yes, a line break.

The poet is wondering if he should shave,
or will the regrowth be prickly?
it's been a while and he can't remember.

The poet is wondering when this photograph will be taken
and he can put his slippers back on.

Inspired by the caption of a photo from *The Otago Daily Times*: 'Black and white portrait
of poet Michael Harlow, who is bearded and wearing his watch around the wrong way.'

Confucius says we should not be too familiar with the lower orders or with women

She may be taller than I, this woman
of Da Nang, but possibly not.
She's stronger. From the hotel window
I see her, her muscled arms,
hidden by overalls. She has
the stamina for long hours, hauling
the government-issue trolley
with one hand, the other stretched down
as she stoops, a mechanical motion
to pick up the bag at the shop frontage
and its trail of spillage — the stained leaflets,
receipts that smell of soy sauce, the damp
paper butts — wastage of this
new economy, some say is better.
Later, another woman burns
cabbage stalks and tea-leaves
in a tin bucket, poking
at the fire on the street, calling out
to her mother-in-law, squat in the background
washing the phở pots in basins
of grey water. And the next
morning, a bag, thrown from a door, split,
waiting on the pavement to be picked
up.

Susan Jacobs

Two Women Speak

Dreaming, I fly face downwards
she says — over fields carved in sweat.

She twists her pendant,
the party unruly as playcentre.

We sit close — her dark curls touch my face —
drinking rough red like raspberry juice.

We shout over Led Zeppelin, the gyrating nostalgia
of 40-year-olds, parents now.

We talk about our men as if our lives
were not so different. To marry or not.

The case for vasectomies or tying tubes.
How we laugh and nearly cry.

I thought — you still go back to that bastard.
Her eyes reply — I get the crumbs.

They're so delicious.

They Write About Things Like This in Sweden

Under a mountain in Sweden they've buried
one hundred tonnes of nuclear waste
with the hope that in 100,000 years
the waste will no longer be harmful to us.

But since everything we know about
all our recorded history
barely stretches back 6,000 years
there's not going to be an earth as we know it
then, is there?
I read about this in a book by a famous
Swedish crime writer now dead himself
from cancer of the spine
he only found out about the cancer after
a car accident revealed it they gave him an
MRI and said as far as the accident goes you're fine
now it's just the tumour that will kill you within six months.

Burying one hundred tonnes of nuclear waste under a mountain
is about the greatest crime we've committed
while not really knowing for sure it won't ever leak out
and harm us still in 100,000 years that's after
we've been through several more ice ages
meteor strikes the threat of asteroids getting too close
floods or an earthquake
could split that mountain open
and those capsules full of toxic waste
will topple down into the sea

for the planet is like the human body
anything can go wrong, take cancer for instance
and then there's always God
and we know he's going to strike
any minute but does he know about the hidden waste?
But he's dead now that author
and he was a good author too.

Tim Jones

the tallest lighthouse in Scotland
was overcome by waves.

keepers scrambling for safety
left the television on.

now the test card girl
warns underwater boats away.

Sam Keenan

Gauge

My parents often ran out of gas
so we found ourselves on abandoned highways
miles from the nearest town.
I remember the roads — how they wept bitumen
beside flares of purple clover as Mum or Dad
walked to anywhere to try to get some gas
and the hours that passed, slow as heat-drowsed bees
before one of them rounded the corner
canister cradled like a rust-coloured cake.
They can't have discussed it,
the gauge in the old Avenger:
the urgent red light, the failing 'full' hand.
If my mother noticed, she likely sewed herself
into silence, the way she did when
admiring students accompanied my father for tea.
Perhaps she got lost in the landscape passing —
the blurred mosaics of trees, sky brimming with sun,
and imagined herself elsewhere as my father drove,
hurtling us down country roads, no one saying:
We are nearly out of gas.

Mary Kelly

3.44 am

Her lips taste of gin for a reason,
gin from 3.44 am,
when she cannot contain her thoughts.

Paralysed in bed,
wishing she kissed sin,
when she had the chance.

All while the smell from 3.44 am
still lingers.

Raina Kingsley

Where are my Bones
after Keri Hulme's poem 'E Nga Iwi o Ngai Tahu'

Where are my Bones

    they saunter around Burnside High School
    chit chatting to their year 12 friends

    they strain against the storm
    to hear the instructions of how to
    amputate a man's arm caught in the winch at sea

    they reach into the biscuit tin under the bed
    and give me the $20 note they have picked out

    they are drowning their sorrows
    all night all day

    they are gardening
    growing beauty out of nothing much

    they marched to WWI then WWII
    some of them came home again

    they worked hard became a registered nurse and
    returned to whanau to help the dying

    they have accomplished great things and
    botched things big-time

Where are my bones

    they are dead

    they are dying

    they are alive

The Lake

for Leonard Cohen

She lies in suburbs of expectancy,
singing hallelujah in the bathroom.
Cohen's final concert, she is his hat.
The Canadian rakes autumn leaves.
Windows open casually.
Cries come in from the city,
cascading down cheeks into the lake,
to cry when the river bed dries,
handed small stones of sentiment.
Sadness curls up as sediment.
She turns on her favourite song.
Ears open up as to hear again.
Eyes ride as socket horses.
We gather on the shore
before the lake is quiet.
Hallelujah is ours, hallelujah.
Cohen's hat applauds.
She bows in the mirror.
Neck stretches as a second cousin.
Only Cohen knows the road
in the lake of his own tongues.

Katrina Larsen

An Independent Woman

She changes the batteries in the fire alarm. Puts
in extra time at the office, working on securing
security. She pays above the minimum on her
mortgage repayments and calls the dishwasher repair
man when it leaks. The lawn guy comes on Tuesdays
to mow and edge. He reminds her when it's time
to prune the back garden while patting the dog.

She takes holidays with the girls, a cruise in the
Pacific, a few days in Melbourne. The cleaner
comes on a Monday, but the house still needs a
hoover before Friday's barbeque. She goes to bookclub
once a month, it's nice to get out and have a chat. At
work parties she lets her hair down, snogging in the
toilets and dancing in bare feet. She watches what she
likes on television, eats chicken and salad for dinner
and never runs out of ice in the freezer.

The dog curls behind her on the sofa. The kids keep
up lively conversation during dinner. Her mum still
makes a cake for her birthday. The neighbours pop in
for a wine. And once a month she goes for a massage, a
little treat. She pays someone to touch her.

To lay hands against her skin.

Wes Lee

My Tough Little James Cagney Stance

In the snow globe of my mind
there's a man frozen
on a park bench.
Once the lover of my mother,
'the affair',
the short-term stepfather,
the usurper who entered
the house and painted
a bedroom turquoise
just for us,
but I was a tough-sell and never
smiled
when he did things for smiles;
the stubborn little kid
with cold, judging eyes.
I think that's why
he broke me.

His eyelashes frosted to his cheeks
under a folded-out newspaper,
he wasn't always this.
We all start as something else.
He may have been a tough little kid
with cold eyes
and folded arms
who never laughed at his abuser
and never smiled when his
abuser did tricks like a sly
begging dog
who knows how to behave
to stay in the house.

The Bar Girl

The bar girl has a soft mouth
like she has swallowed many butterflies.
It curls over warm syllables.
I am drunk just from watching her speak. She has spent too long
    staring
into deep beer glasses where men
cast their eyes
to drink away their blues.
She's so far away,
I hope she'll leave the bar
and return as some other woman.
I hope the wind will blow her away

Her back arches like an alleyway.
Her eyes ask a question.
I can see her liking cats. I can see
her in my mind's eye stroking cats
that curl
over her. I can see her as a blues singer
singing in a bar with a few lonely souls as the
rain weeps and the wind harps
on about some far away grief.
I can see her now drifting on to the stage
and smiling slowly and parting her lips
like the pages of a story.

She leans over herself like a question mark.
She smiles sleepily at the punters.
The men devour her silk body and her wet eyes.
She hates men.
Like dogs they form lines in her dreams
and fondle themselves for her.

She is so tired and so bored. She dreams of being some other way,
of heading south like rain or river or bird. I see always again
and again the distance filling in her sleepy eyes. How far she's
    ventured away.
The bar's filling up tonight.
The men are getting drunk on her.
The sun heads to slide against the brooding hills.

She seems to me like the moon
raging and silent all at once
filling up my spindrift pages. She opens her moist mouth
and calls to me from her dream.
She picks up the empty glasses
but is somewhere
faraway
in the deep
black night.

Olivia Macassey

Late February

Grey Lynn supermarket carpark
in late February. She thinks I am looking
at her outfit, at how audacious she is

fashionable or original or perhaps her breasts —
stomach muscles — attitude — nervy conscious eyebrows —
So she imagines lust or admiration, outrage, envy:

simultaneously gratified and telling herself she doesn't
care. Her stare is blunt and fierce,
like some kind of leonine gazelle as she bounds

past to hunt salsa and wine. But I'm remembering
how long the summer was
in the savannah of the carpark,

and how short the summer is.

this breaking apart of things

it's three days since the big earthquake
but the cat is still skittish
she jumps sideways at my footsteps
and glares at closing doors

in between aftershocks she stands
on her back legs
reaches two paws towards me
like she's begging for a bear hug
when all she really wants is a scratch between the ears

if you try to hold her close she's
all claws and teeth and bones
humans are better company than cats
better huggers

*

the place where the bookcase was before it toppled
and the hairline cracks in concrete corners
somehow haven't managed to fill
the human gap of you

this morning I saw a documentary
where they moved a tiger to a new zoo
and left her brother on his own
but the voiceover said that that was okay
because 'tigers like loneliness'

six fault-lines ruptured
Cape Campbell is two metres northeast
of where it was last week
and loneliness is an emotion
that you wouldn't understand
if you were a cat
that didn't like being scratched

Robert McLean

Le Petit Testament d'Alfred Agostinelli

It's lovely here — so fine
and warm, sky-blue sea and the sky sea-blue.
    I hope it doesn't bother you
        I took Swann's name
for my *nom-de-aviation*. Please don't blame
    yourself — the choice was always mine.

    I saw my shadow on
the ocean, climbed, and heard the engine stall —
    my solo flight ends with a fall,
        my aircraft broken,
illusions shattered. I had been a joke in
    Paris — a turkey, not a swan.

    Do you remember our
first drive? When it was dark, I stopped and shone
    my idling Alfa's headlights on
        the roses — you
had never seen the sight before. A new
    man, you wept. I can see you now!

    You'd eat asparagus
decked out in evening suit and white kid gloves.
    I'd watch and smile. Nobody loves
        you like I do —
why qualify it? Gossips misconstrue
    affection and disparage us.

    Of course, I had a wife
of sorts — and you were married to your book.
    For it, what lengths — what pains! — you took
        (Marcel, the beach
is close . . . I cannot swim . . . it's out of reach . . .),
    but you and I still made a life.

And life is what you praise,
in words and deeds. I know you longed to touch
    so many more. You gave me such
        extravagant tips,
I felt so moved I kissed you on the lips.
    Now we've gone our respective ways.

        Paris becomes you. Farewell,
you silly man — I gave you what I chose
    to give, but what, no one else knows,
        yet in the end,
to me, you only ever were a friend —
    but love is love, my dear Marcel.

Goldfinch and Hawk

A long time before I am awake,
I begin to smell blood and rafters
burning, see the sky where the roof was,
bodies, and scattered parts of bodies.

Then comes the day. Goats at their tethers,
cool water in the well, swollen sun
heavy with heat, radios blaring,
children playing, garlic in the pan.

My wife — suave, dark-eyed, petulant —
loves me past conjecture. I flaunt her.
Lust makes us shiver. Life is a guest
whom we entertain then bid farewell.

So there are signs — but warnings, never.
I know better than to expect them.
A hawk rises, crests, and dips its wing.
Black olives swell on silver branches.

Brown

The waiting room was at the end of a long corridor
with low ceilings and changing rooms that were separated
by blue plastic sheets and it was very small, very square
and very cold even though an ancient oil heater
was always switched on in one corner of the room.

The walls in the room were coated with sloppy brown paint
and if you pressed your cheek against it and closed one eye
you could see the brown paint was textured like sand or a
concrete pavement or a tree trunk.

On the brown walls were pictures of the ocean, sunsets
and a group of women smiling and throwing their arms up in the air.
In another corner of the room there was always a vase of
yellow-y flowers with a puddle of murky brown water in the bottom.

The chairs we sat on were also brown and squeaked in time with your
   breath
and there was a coffee table in front of us that looked like
somebody had taken it straight out of Nana's house and on it were
magazines from 2008 telling you HOW TO LOSE WEIGHT FAST with
pictures of celebrities in bikinis, laughing and drinking cocktails.

Mum always held my hand very tight, so tight I saw crescent moons
in my palm every time she let go to go into the other room.

When she went into the other room
something would beep and a light would flash and I would think
about Mum lying somewhere in that room under a machine
that was supposed to make her better
while I was sitting on a squeaky chair in a brown room
staring at Jennifer Aniston on a beach in Miami.

And then at some point
the beeping and the flashing light would stop
and Mum would come back out and she would smile,
get changed out of the pale green sack they always gave her to wear
and we would leave the brown room and go home.

Us

for my sisters

i.

Mother, you did not expect to find yourself
in this forest of strange trees.
This ground does not taste
of the iron your tongue knew.
in the velvet of the night we heard you sob
in the room next door, our ears pressed to the peeling paper.
we locked fingers and prayed. someone next door
saw braided-head girls in a circle
praying to a peculiar god
and snapped their curtains shut.

ii.

Everyone congratulates me
on the scholarship. *Your parents
who have suffered can finally exhale*
said the white man at the ceremony.
But I think I hate this degree.
I want to do *good* and make a *difference*
but I have no idea
how to *be* in this foreign land.

iii.

the world broke & crumbled today
— there you go — trying to tape her back
into a perfect sphere,
trying to spit water
on the raging fire.

iv.

know that this earth is your body. your words are
the Pacific Ocean tides that wash & purify
your legs are the Mountains that anchor, your heart —
the Land that gives. every where you stand is your home.
Earth is the African Woman
who gave birth to the first Man.

v.

We were watching late night Al Jazeera, shaking our heads,
when uncle called. A pregnant cousin we have never met has died.
The TV breaks to a Red Cross appeal.
You hold me on the sinking couch
as we mourn those whom we never knew.

Dark Shapes Shimmering

For weeks after the cat died, dark shapes slipped away at the edge of my peripheral vision and ears twitched on the stack of books beside my chair. I woke to birdsong, imagining a weight on the duvet at the end of the bed. I felt a leap in the air like breath against my cheek when I opened a window, while at night curtains billowed and sagged as if paws walked along the sill.

Charles Bonnet syndrome is a side effect of macular degeneration in which sufferers experience visual hallucinations of patterns or buildings, animals and people. The brain replaces missing information from the eyes with images it creates or has stored. In my mother's case, it was the twisting silk leaves and flowers of a Turkish carpet that occupied the blank space in her vision.

She had twice travelled to Turkey and brought back photographs of stucco walls curving into shadows the colour of the apple tea in silver handled glasses offered to her by the carpet sellers in the bazaar. When I open her pantry, I find apple tea granules in a tall cut glass jar that had once belonged to her mother Ida whose initials arabesque among tendrils around the silver lid.

I once asked her about Ida, hoping for memories of being mothered in childhood recollections of touch or voice. Instead, she spoke of long grass and a picnic by a river. In her mind's eye, the image flickering like dappled light through willows, Ida was a summer afternoon where grass feathered beneath her outstretched palms and dragonflies shimmered over running water.

Phototropism

She knows us earth-bound gods,
flashes in the pan
as we are.

I am the snow buttercup,
turning my face always
towards you.

You left me with a tan line
but even as your presence upon me fades,
I look for you every day.

Heidi North

Goodbye, goodbye, this time

In the middle of our destruction
the girl dies

The one who was —
looking back these many years

quite probably the reason
we ended up together at all —

and an old friend writes
I hadn't seen her in a decade

but those Wellington days were the most fun of my life
and it's true. We stand on opposite

sides of my kitchen bench —
for this is my house now —

and I glimpse the boy I loved
in you, oh life's

so startlingly brief
it's impossible

to do anything other than hold on
to my own heart

break. I open my palm —
fragile seed, go catch the wind

Keith Nunes

Around town and out again

he slides out of his exhausted hatchback
edges into the TAB,
a pencil-thin guy is berating himself
'you dick! dick! dick!
never number 3'

he slips the betting tickets into his wallet
heads into the public toilet next door
hears a man whispering
in a cubicle
then laughing like a child at the circus

as he approaches a café
he sees his 80-year-old uncle coming out of the sex shop
wearing reflector glasses
carrying a black plastic bag

the barista is 20-something
has sleeve tattoos of Caribbean beach parties
she admires his tats
'all plastered in a year of mayhem' he says
she laughs
once he would have asked her out
but now she probably thinks he's just a friendly older guy
with hair the same colour as her father's

the pawnbroker's assistant is welcoming
but sad
her husband wants a separation
he's a guitarist and she's simply a reader of thrillers
she feels no match
for the sparkling young things he attracts
like the one she used to be

he gets into his car to drive home
as he passes his house and leans toward the coast
his usually busy head is silent
his smile w-i-d-e

Sea Swimmer After Heart Surgery

Don't go back into the water
I tell her, you're not ready.
It's only been eleven weeks and anyway
where you go swimming
is the coldest bit, it's where the river
empties out its guts after filling up on those
stony Wicklow mountains, and it's colder
by many degrees than even the rest
of the Irish sea: you are not able
for that kind of shock, this is meant to be recovery
and I worry.

I'm telling her off and so I'm glad to be told
in a stage whisper by her grinning husband
that the water right there
has just been found to be poisoned, polluted
by asbestos leaching from an old dump
underneath the golf course — I'm actually pleased
at this news, delighted even,
which tells you something about my mother:
how she is more important than the sea.

A Woman in Red Slacks

Our rented flat in Parnell
Those rooms of high ceilings and sash windows

Our second city
after Sydney

Robert Creeley trying to chat you up
at a Russell Haley party

when our marriage
was sweet

the wind blowing our way from the Rose Gardens over
in Gladstone Road

the Beatles making their best ever music
and my first book of poems almost completed

most of them for you

'a woman
in red slacks . . .'

This evening I fly back
a delta winged moth

my sadness like moon dust
my night vision glowing like an infra-red camera

a stranger to these parts
gliding between the bitter-sweet shadows of apartments

to enter again if only I could find them
the strawberry fields that were said to be forever.

How many times and for what purpose
did we have to break
                                each other's

                                          hearts?

It's not often we meet a man like you, Bruce . . .

You were such a good man
you looked after everyone
  your wife
  your children
  your mother
      mother-in-law
you looked after everyone but yourself

You stood on the edge of dreams
  Camping   a glass of wine   a chat with friends
  back-packing around America
  Europe   Berlin   Prague
  No time for a hundred cafés
  'Bruce, don't walk so fast. I want to sit and have a coffee.'

Back home
we can't bear the pain
I'm glad Jacqui buried you in your 'bugger' socks
as she says:
  'Those socks summed up the situation.'

Desidia

El resto de la casa era más de lo mismo.
Los adornos cubiertos de polvo
esperaban en silencio el descanso eterno.

La habitación era un frío ataúd.

Sobre el tocador la bailarina de porcelana
con las piernas rotas,
el joyero repleto de olvido,
y el rosario para ahuyentar al demonio.

La cama sigue en el lugar de siempre,
con las sabanas dispuestas a no cambiar el rumbo,
sobre ellas muere lentamente mi madre.

Apathy

The rest of the house was more of the same.
Ornaments covered in dust
awaited in silence the eternal rest.

The room was a cold coffin.

On the dresser the porcelain dancer
with her broken legs,
the jewel box full of forgetting,
and the rosary to chase away demons.

The bed is in the same place as always,
with the sheets not going anywhere,
on which my mother slowly dies.

Translation by Charles Olsen

It's what you get for being a monkey

On the stairs to Monkey Temple, Kathmandu,
I watched a monkey attack another monkey.
He kicked dust in his eyes,
like it was the fifties or something,
then lunged at him and bashed him with a rock
till his victim fell bleeding on the bricks, having fits.
All the other monkeys,
and the sari-wearing hawkers with their rugs spread out
with bells and chimes and incense sticks
hovered above the twitching animal,
gawking curiously.

11 Memories of David
in memory of my first cousin David Goode 1959–2016

1.

Picking up David from his student flat, early '80s;
a backseat boy, waiting in the car, for him to emerge
after a late night drinking.

2.

Seeing him off to the UK, on his OE work experience,
with Mum, at Greta Point restaurant.
The bay outside emphasising the distance ahead.

3.

David's wedding, to Rosalie, January 1987;
me with hair permed. David not sure
what to make of it, but happy to see me.

4.

David visiting with kids, at Grant Road,
the new energy in his life. His love
for his kids obvious. A proud smile.

5.

At my mum's funeral: David a pallbearer,
with Chris, helping me to carry the load.

6.

Out the back of his place, bat and ball,
with Thomas and Matthew; then inside, another test:
David patiently waiting for stumps to be drawn,
ready to watch the news.

7.

At the cricket ground, David visiting
with Thomas and Matthew; noting
the beer cans by my team's gear bags
as I ran in to bowl.

8.

Visiting him once
I heard David liked Gordon Ramsay
but probably not the swearing.

9.

Driving round Christchurch,
with David and Rosalie:
Hawkesbury Ave, Dublin Street,
Bennett Street, Straven Road,
places of our grandparents,
our mothers' childhoods.

10.

David and Chris meeting me
in Addington. A beer after the quake.
The hardness behind the words.

11.

Writing on David's casket,
all I could think of:
Love and peace.

Joanna Preston

Leaving

I thought I heard him calling as I crossed
the town boundary, out past the saleyards,

years ago. But the dusk was in my eyes
and I would not turn back, never again

choke on the dust of that place. Escape
was a highway driven through those days.

I raised a cathedral, and locked its doors.
Bound that ambush, memory,

and branded it *slave*. But still I hear
sometimes, in the rattle of cattle trucks.

His voice, or mine. And I forget
how to sleep. A voice shouting, sounds

as much as words. *Come back, please!* perhaps.

Or maybe *Run.*

Flowers

This pink evening is birthed from a blue day.
The old woman gardens with the aid of a walker.
Her husband looks out the kitchen window,
'She'll be sore and tired,' he mutters,
'in no fit state to cook dinner.'

*

My mother suffers;
but gardening makes her happy.

For my 63rd birthday she sends flowers.

Mary Rainsford

Oliver the Ovary

After I knew I was going to kill you
I decided to give you a name.
It helped me make sense of it, Oliver,
how you bulged with the tumour
as if you were quite literally dying
to assert your masculinity.

We spent 23 years together, Oliver.
I thought I knew you.
I thought I knew what your dreams were.
I thought your dream
was to work on my reproduction line.

As it turns out, Oliver,
your dream was to be
the Biggest Ovary in the Land.

Let it never be said, Oliver,
that you were not prepared
to work for your dream.
Every day, with my hands pressed to my belly,
I felt you pumping iron
except not iron
I'm not exactly sure what it was you were pumping
but you got huge.

You were so large, Oliver,
that when the doctors examined you
their voices got all high pitched:
'I think we should schedule the surgery sooner rather than later.'
Oliver, you know the shit has hit the fan
when the surgeons sound prepubescent.

I wish you'd understood, Oliver,
that being a man is not about size.
It is not about the size of your anything
but it is certainly not about the size
of your ovaries.

In some ways, Oliver,
I was an ultra conservative parent to you
always screaming: 'Can't you just be like the other ovary?'
Oliver, I'm sorry.
I am in no position to judge the validity
of other people's dreams.
I am a poet.
Besides, it is not your fault
that a side effect of your fully realised dream
would have been my death.

In a perfect world, Oliver,
we could have made it work.
You would have kept getting bigger and bigger
and I would be weirdly misshapen
but otherwise fine.
In a perfect world
you would have gone down in history
as the Biggest Ovary in the Land.

Oliver, it is not a perfect world.
Sometimes doing what we must do
harms those closest to us.
Sometimes it is kill or be killed.
Oliver, I would not have killed you
if I had a choice.

But if it is any consolation, Oliver,
I have buried your remains
under a tree in my backyard
and every day that tree
gets bigger and bigger.

Gingko

You thrive under disturbance,
yet
are a steady grower,
1000 years is possible under your foliage.
Born in the Eocene,
hungry by the river in the Cretaceous;
a living fossil dated 270 million years.

Or maidenhair for the west
yínguǒ for Mandarin
ngan-gwo for Cantonese.
Ginkgo the result of Engelbert Kaempfer's
pronunciation/spelling error
stained itself to colonial authority in scientific advances.

Parchment folded ink stains in a bottle.
Intolerant of shade
you were found alone kept alive by Chinese monks
every cutting comes from your careful body.

Your leaves are twins dividing
as Goethe astutely observed in 1815
(in a letter to his friend Marianne von Willemer)
the one that caught his eye was probably still there in 1936.

There were six of you in Hiroshima
standing during Truman's first term in office,
remained standing after Little Boy
dropped.

A ghost from the Edo
there is a softness to the fibre of you
a felt resistance of plant matter
made to outlast us.

he kōrero ki taku tipuna

*Te Whiti o Rongomai 'heard a thunder and sensed an approaching
  flood'*

auē, te whiti o rongomai,
ko wai e mahara koe
    ināianei?
ko wai kua whakarongo
ki tau whakaaro mōhio?
ko wai kua whai
    tau kupu o rangimārie?
        ko parihaka te wāhi

auē, te whiti o rongomai,
te matakite tuatahi ki mua māhātma gandhi,
he kaiārahi ki he kaupapa
    tino tūturu.
kei whea koe, taku tipuna,
ina e hiahia ana koe ō mātou
neke atu i te ake?
        ko parihaka te wāhi

auē, kei te tino matapouri ahau
no te mea
ngā iwi katoa
kua wareware tau kite.

ki konei te whaititiri rāua ko te waipuke tonu.

      ko parihaka he pūmahara tawhiti.

a talk with my ancestor

alas, te whiti o rongomai
who remembers you now?
who has listened to your intelligent ideas
who has followed your words of peace?
                    parihaka is the place

alas, te whiti o rongomai
the first prophet before māhātma gandhi
a leader with a very original philosophy
where are you, my ancestor
when we need you
more than ever?
                    parihaka is the place

alas, I am very sad,
because
all the people
have forgotten your vision

the thunder and flood are already here

            parihaka is a distant memory

Te Whiti o Rongomai, descended from Awanuiārangi, was a paramount Taranaki leader, who in the mid-1800s established at Parihaka a unique settlement. He was perhaps the first proponent of passive resistance, apotheosising a philosophy of no recourse to weaponry and no physical violence — despite massive confiscation of Māori lands by the Pākehā colonialists. Because of the perceived threat of the rapidly growing settlement, the Pākehā invaded Parihaka with over 1500 armed troops and arrested Te Whiti in 1881. He was charged with *wickedly, maliciously, and seditiously contriving and intending to disturb the peace*! He was imprisoned with his co-leader, Tohu Kakahi, in the South Island until 1883. Te Whiti had long before prophesied the coming of the whiteman and the concomitant diminishment of Te Ātiawa lands when he literally saw the thunder and flood approaching in his visions.

Sahanika Ratnayake

Golden/Privilege
to J.G.

You do not know what it is to go into the world
like a shrinking cat
You whose parents read the same books as you
From a nurturing golden cave you
walk into a lit world
You who already have the answers
you seek

Where is the wonderment of progress
the unexpected
the wearing of new skins
Where is unfamiliar territory for
You who belong
everywhere, already
I am transmuted, twisted of clay
each day
How are you made anew

How am I to love you? You, who are already complete?

you tell me
months later
after you have kissed my forehead
of the man
at the Gare de l'Est
who asked you for money
and how he wanted to know
your name
and whether
you were a Jew

Ron Riddell

Prado Centro

emboldening earth
sun, moon and stars, we make camp:
c'mon baby light my fire

on sun-baked walls
gambolling girls, naked
in every detail

eating night flowers:
the moonlight sonata
pianissimo

dust on the table
dust on the floor: *fly away Peter*
fly away Paul

just skin and bone
a father bears his lifeless child
to the desert post

sunlit barrios
reach for the sky
a cloud skirts by

the monkey jumps down
the moon hops up, hiding together
in the branches

What do you do?

What do you do — [Google search]
What do you do **when you love someone**
What do you do **when you're bored**
What do you do **to celebrate Matariki**
What do you do **with persimmons**
What do you do **with a drunken sailor**

fill notebooks with rage, foam, sand, salt
fry the onions and the mince
stand at the bar and try to be served

do you do
do you do**n't you**
do you do **liver**
do you do**uble tap like me**
do you do

you do
love me like you do **lyrics**
love me like you do
what would you do
that thing you do

'How do you earn a paycheck?
How much money do you make?
What is your socioeconomic status?

a wife is
a wife is **someone who**
a wife is **a reflection of her husband**
a wife is **a good thing**
a wife is **a gift from the lord**
a wife is **a helpmate**

persimmons are
persimmons are **good for**
persimmons are **good for you**
persimmons are **gross**
persimmons are **ripe when**
persimmons are **an excellent source of which mineral**

And based on that status,
where do I fall
on the socioeconomic ladder
compared to you?

laziness is **required?**
laziness is **loyalty**
laziness is **good for you**
laziness is **nothing more than**
laziness is **my middle name ^^;; '**
laziness is **bad**
laziness is **scheduled when time and space are available**
laziness is **nothing more than resting before you get tired**

Am I a rung above you?
Below you?

a poet is
a poet is **a nightingale**
a poet is **not a jukebox**
a poet is **before anything else**
a poet is **born not made**
a poet is **a man speaking to a man**

How should I judge you?
Are you worth my time?

what are you are
what have you have

what are **you**
what are you **doing**
what are your **strengths**
what are you **up to**
what are you **doing in my swamp**

Jeremy Roberts

Chatting with the Bums

Bums've got that coal-dust breath / prophet-psycho / magic marker thing —
working it, right in the crackpot, middlesafe material world.
They can startle, offend, cause mild panic — often with little more
than a gesture. Beautiful blue sky? — *Get the fuck off my park bench!*
Starbucks Hot Chocolate with whipped cream? — *Don't spill that shit
on me! You're walking on my damn street!*
Bums regard themselves as well-sussed, streetwise, & hold a high
status in their own environment. While they might be on the
outside of conventional, luxuriant Western lifestyles, they baulk at
the 'bullshit workabee slave labour system' called Capitalism. The
Middle Class, by the way, don't give a f--k about the homeless. On
the city streets, bums might be thought of as 'free as a bird', aspiring
to nothing but survival. They possess a hard-earned wisdom about
the 'trick' of life — more so than the comfort & celebrity-obsessed
masses, & have a good handle on the concept of 'destiny'. However,
bums cannot be regarded as being all identical. On the subject of
spirituality, for example, personal views will differ, bum to bum.
Mental health issues or drug & alcohol dependency can be part of
the deal, but no more than it is for the working Middle Class. That
shit goes down in the 'burbs. Bums don't harbour illusions about
what lies on the road ahead & are far more geared up to facing the
inevitable, than mainstream folk. They just get on with it. Bums've
got their own unique way of coping with life.

1. A bum sits in the middle of plush Larchmont Village, outside a
    bagel shop, constantly shouting: 'I heard of *Burger King!* Can you
    spare twenty bucks? It's a back-to-the-future movie!' Affluent
    passers-by answer him with remarks such as: 'I just finished my
    Yoga class'; '$20.00? That's a lot!'; 'Good luck buddy!'

2. Turning off the Hollywood Freeway, a bum is tucked behind some off-ramp scrub, with a big homemade sign: *GIVE $1.00 & HELP A NEGRO STAYED STONED!*
3. Hanging out on Sunset Boulevard, beneath a movie billboard advertising 'The Devil Inside', is a bum with blazing eyes who informs everyone: 'Pope John Paul's trying to crawl up your ass!'
4. In Los Feliz, a bum stands up inside his messy 'living-room' on the sidewalk: 'I'm a preamble for the shambles. You don't know where I been. I come from over the hills. I been to *Trump Tower*. Where's my damn coffee?'

Pure *Gefühle*

Frankfurt airport —
we quickly walk outside to the street, the snow
where I pick up my first ever handful —
transfixed by the flawlessness.
'mentality is temporary'
is its clean, perfect message.

my daughter says 'You look as happy as a child.'
back indoors, she excitedly phones a German friend,
but they live too far away to make it in time.

I watch her sitting outside Tiffany's —
blowing impeccable, sad little notes on her Māori flute,
until we fly away.

Let me be clear

You're right the first experience
a reign of glass
the first gentle evening by the west
I grew another heart
epenthetic struck
ingenious moderato in the lower strings

Daughters of the thorax shake their head bones
in sure order new knees bending
illative weapons sing
the missing pieces macerate crescendo
and I promise not to drape black petals
past the gulag

I'm like animal bathysphere
light cut out my eyes
splice agents scribe a million to the head
it's free beside the road
beside what's terrific
trying to eat the flowers from my mouth

billions and billions

we were always talking about someday. it began with the planes. on one of our first drives, we parked up by the airport. we listened as the sound of flight filled the air, watched the impossible land safely on grey tarmac, again and again. you would tell me the names of those aeroplanes and i told you about where i was going next. the sky was a shade of blue so bright and expansive that it felt like it could last forever. i folded up all my goodbyes and tucked them under my heart, a place where they could stay tender. by the time you drove me home, the sky had turned a dusty pink.

our ferry trip was one of my favourites. we left our little cabin and walked up metal stairs, the waves cresting beneath us. when we made it to the top, the ocean seemed to blend in with the sky and we sat under a dome sprinkled with sugar. i didn't know any of their names but i stood there, turning, my head up to the stars. the hills were dark mounds in the background, rising over and protecting us from artificial light. i said thank you in my head, whispered it to the world. the wind brushed through my hair and you held me tightly against you. i smelt soap and salt and softness. it was warm there, in that safe space.

one day, we took a plane to finland and we walked down the streets of a different country. i wasn't used to the cold and i wore layers and layers as you gave me little kisses, your lips always warmer. we stayed in a room in lapland where the windows faced out into the horizon. you turned off all the lights and we sat in the darkness, the sound of my heartbeat a constant rhythm. i asked you what we were waiting for, but you just held me tighter and said, soon, soon. and then it came: the aurora flickering over the sky, flexing the world into washes of blue and green and purple. we watched and watched and you kissed me on the forehead. and it almost felt real.

when we finally went to the moon, i wasn't young anymore. i was beginning to forget how many places we'd seen, so we spent hours at a time looking down at earth. i was trying to find home amongst all that green, and you were looking for the places we had yet to discover. you'd point to all these countries and say, i'll take you there, i'll take you there. i tried to comprehend all the people down below, too small to see, as they looked up at the moon and mistook me for shadows and distorted light. eventually, i grew tired of looking so i'd lie with my head in your lap, the grey moon underneath my body, as you whispered the future to me.

but then we kept going. we were like cassini, moving through our solar system, an effort that took years and years and years. we stopped at saturn's moons and watched chemicals rise that made our hearts sore. they left a bitter taste in our mouths so that when we kissed, there was a peppery aftertaste. we wondered what lay under the atmosphere of these heartbroken little moons, but we never looked further than the surface. we took pictures regardless, and stored them under our skin. that way, i just had to look at you to remember. and when i did, i saw every other moment we'd been together, all the memories spinning out from you to me.

but i lost you at saturn's rings. i woke up one day and just felt dust against my cheeks and nothing else. i waited and waited for millennia, until all the supernovas turned into black holes and all the white dwarfs turned into black dwarfs. it was so dark that opening and closing my eyes made no difference. when i tried to speak, my words got lost in all the leftover pieces of the universe. the whites of my eyes turned black and i forgot what it was like to see light, the light that i'd loved my whole life. all i could taste was the iron of my own blood, tightly enmeshed with the stars. it was very, very quiet. i thought about someday.

Sarah Shirley

Family history

My family medical history? Oh yes, there's lots, all in 1972
it was, the year my aunt ran off with the village doctor,
leaving my broken uncle and their two pock-marked children
to sail for a warmer coast. And of course there was cousin Elly
who worked for a married dentist in the city, such a scandal
at the time, but you know, they're happy to this very day.
And then poor Isobel, another cousin who never made it far
from home, she lived next door, and I used to giggle when
she told me stories of the tiny people who watch us from
behind the fluttering plumes of the toetoes in the garden.
I remember watching her from my window in April as
I scooped the sweetly bitter gritty jelly from the feijoas
that had thundered down in heavy green armfuls from trees
bowing under the weight of the crop. I was home again
from school, my knee ballooned and hot, in trouble
for the extra time I was missing after my sore throat a few
weeks back. I watched poor loopy Isobel, hurling eggs
against the fence, howling *Don't worry, I'll get you out,
I promise, I'll find you, just please stop screaming!*
and I laughed and laughed, then stopped only when
I saw the tears streaming down to soak the scarf
pulled tight at her neck. Poor Isobel. Later when we
were cleaning up her things, we found a drawer of acorns,
all lined up, each one with a tiny face drawn on,
a shiny brown grimace to be held between thumb and finger.
I lifted one up to my face, and whispered, *I'm sorry.*
Poor, poor Izzy. I tell you — when it rains, it pours, my dear,
it builds up, then it pours.

Jane Simpson

Unmarked crib

The sou'west exhausts all adjectives
at Hone's crib,

his writing shed smooth
as a fridge, held fast
with a lock, and key left in.

Lean-tos encrust the house.
A lull then a gift — a wind
that blows kisses over weatherboards
bearded with lichen.

The storm leaves love bites,
broken palings a hasty repair —
mark the spot with an x.

Our pearls are fake and nobody likes us

Us girls are sheets to be spoiled
studying hem lengths and chewing gum.
We burn our bridges when we get to them,
taste bass lines and wind chimes.

But we are not to be spoiled.
Not future housewives,
ankle length dresses,
yapping
at infomercials;
it's always a lack of cooking prowess
that causes divorce.

The sweet bouquet of youth.
Night glowing down upon us,
we drink concrete
till Bubba shows up
with a bottle of something festive
molten liquor
burning cracks in our lips,
finally some fuel
for these smooth bodies.

Our marble haunches
holding up entire oceans
of intertwined limbs and
injured birds.

Feathers flirt with our skin
knowing that one day, we'll moult —
our soft down
falling
like sheets from the line.

The Sword Swallower's Lament

They promised me the blades wouldn't be too sharp — they lied!
Yes, throat cut to ribbons, it's true.
Though it's best always
To spare gory details
And focus instead on my outfit.
Yes the outfit!
See how it sparkles and shines.
The boob-tube covered in sequins
Catches the light from a certain angle
The hot pants are velvet
And covered in yellow stars
A birthday gift from my mother.

They say that I look the part.
Always pays to make an effort.
A girl needs dreams
And stars, too, not just on my bum,
But also shining in my eyes.
At least, there used to be.

Once they lit up like dollar signs,
Or at least that's what other people saw
When they looked
Which wasn't very often.

Now my grin's turned rather cynical
But the main thing is — electricity —
The whole house hums with it —
A superior supply
It keeps all the appliances happy
And just as long as nobody
Gives you a mains belt
Everything should be sweet.

The swords?
Now they were handed down from my grandfather
Hattori Hanzō — the finest steel.
They say mine is a spectacular show that draws the cheers.

At the end of the night;
Here sit I — my bloodied stomach,
My lacerated throat.

Billy plays rugby

there were never enough big boys
attending Waihaorunga School
to make up a team of fifteen
but the year I became their leader
it was agreed we now had sufficient
to challenge Ikawai School
in a game of sevens

we jacked it up with the Ikawai kids
on the school bus into town
and when Mum agreed to dye our khaki
shorts a bilious green
together with the grey cotton shirts
that we all wore anyway
we had our footy gear

from the first kick-off on game day
we recovered the ball right away
ran in our first try
and it carried on like that
but despite being their self-appointed
captain and goal-kicker
I was the only team member
couldn't seem to score

only after another boy
was permitted to have a go
did we score any conversions

a harbinger of my experience with girls

*

to my amazement after sixty years
two members of that schoolboy team
told me they still remembered it

Barry said he'd been most impressed
with how I'd organised it all
while cousin Sid told me angrily
I'd always thought myself superior

a harbinger of my years in politics

Richard Taylor

the sad song of the toothless whore

Neither presence nor absence helps
or even intercedes in the wanting:
something participating in the reassuring
like a disease of speech
or the contradictory bongle sound
of a pipe upon a pipe, leading —
those who secret from themselves,
down ever more
steeper slopes, fast forward to
the no-possibility of
anything greater than the laughter
of a head in a barrel
pondering a spider nightmare —
the mail gets thru, maybe. But
laughter is its own last and best defence.

We tried touching
but it failed — e'en ten million years ago,
because slime is slime,
the blind are blind
and the dying are dying.

I cant, my skull.

In the meantime, a song is required:
   'if testic is of zap
    what is wooden in the gap
    and where and if by goyle grins?
    and if the wedge is wood,
    is Philip thus and still by this
    as perhaps the progress of his grin?'

None of this helps: in the night
old hands reach out to touch
flaccid skin, ever failing cells.
Our assignment is death, but how?
After all, that black honey
is burning us up: the horribleness
of human love, hopeless,
and the universe opening up
like the sad cunt
of a toothless old whore
dreaming of gold

Loren Thomas

Nailhead

When I squished the baubles
on the swan plant
they'd pop,
leave an itch on my palm.
But sometimes
I'd throw them against our
gravel driveway
pierce them as the
caterpillars hung
folded into their chrysalis
to escape my murderous
power plays.

Nicola Thorstensen

Spin Doctor
for Kellyanne

Gravy train stowaway,
clarity-obscurer
hollow gong-clanger,
weasel-wordsmith
ego-masseuse
dry-well promise-monger,
fact-bending filth-forger
scurvy revisionist
conduct-plumber,
flagrant flaunter of the blazing pants
friend of falsehoods
ethics evader,
poison pundit
malignant misinformant
fiend-enabler,
bile-spilling turd-gilder,
scandal strumpet,
scandal's trumpet,
helter-skelter smelter,
detritus-dwelling, truth-extruding
hoaxgoblin.

Vivienne Ullrich

Losing the Plot

I arrive on page twenty three not so
far in as to be peripheral to
the plot but not the main event. And as
yet she has not decided exactly
how I will relate to the hero, whether
I will be integral to the end, and
how much of my history is essential.

In her Word document I am fixed in a
serif font I find rather unattractive.
She has my backstory in a separate
document and keeps fiddling with the details,
mainly dates, shuffling these within the
parameters of world events and the
ins and outs of other characters.

I object to her use of colons and missing
out on hours each day so, when she is putting
me through my paces I do not know if it is
dawn, the witching hour or time for a cocktail.

I've taken a dislike to her since she
stole my sojourn in the Greek islands and
sent me to Indonesia. She's stolen
other things, given me red hair when young,
had me drinking beer, then changed her mind and
deleted large chunks. The lack of continuity
can be very disorienting, quite frightening
at times. To wipe out a whole second husband
was pretty extreme. And so many areas
she hasn't bothered with. They're just blank. She
doesn't understand how scary it is.

Roland Vogt

On my watch

Just like
(hard to know
and don't want to
about) death,
you expired,
stopped in your track
at 24 past 6
on Easter Monday —
the day jokers
have a go at those
of the day before.

I had a one year
guarantee
but you gave me
the best of accurate
and in the Chinese way.

Now you lie
like my best pet
— as did a cat
on the floor before —
mute yet not,
just merely smiling
after no time left.

Apostrophia

This is my cosmos:
white daisies
in the moonlight,
clothes hanging
from the washing line.

Shadows of clothes
cast on the lawn;
one of them could be
the entrance
to the underworld.

More rain,
pomegranate seeds falling
into a china bowl.
Just don't serve them
to Persephone.

Stars overhead blurred
in the night wind.
I place a flower pot
against the back gate
to stop it rattling.

*

This intense love
is still there
across the decades,
at times acknowledged
by a faint smile.

Apostrophia
the goddess
who turns herself away.
The omission of a letter,
darkness.

Come back again
she tells me,
among old friends
the fragments
can be reconfigured.

Janet Wainscott

Occupation
Moravia, Czech Republic

The church is a cultural centre now,
a baroque display from the victors
of a war centuries ago, newly restored
in all its extravagant glory.
But in a quiet Hussite-plain corner
we are transfixed

by a photograph, a grey stain
on the cream wall — grey sky and snow,
overcoats and boots, grey
uniforms and guns, a crowd
assembled in a square
backs to the camera
faces to the statue,
a Party leader unveiled.

A voice too low to be overheard,
whispers at our shoulder
Not one person
wanted to be there.
Not one.
We realise that we too would have hidden
in our overcoats, waiting for the click
of the shutter to reduce us
to a grainy, grey image.

Devon Webb

I Want to Live

I want to live in a world
where emotions are not belittled.
Where they are seen
as the most important and holy of truths.
I want to live in a world
where vulnerability is celebrated and not shamed.
Where people don't tell you to
'stop being so sensitive'.
Where the cynics don't call you
'naïve'.
I want to live in a world
where people are connected with their sexuality,
and with the sexuality of others.
Where decent people don't say
'this was nothing you're just a fine piece of ass'
after they have sex with you.
I want to live in a world
where friends don't treat friends like shit.
Where you don't have to demand the apologies
you know you deserve.
I want to live in a world
where you don't have to continuously explain to
straight white men
why you don't like Donald Trump.
Where
'I think he's a cunt'
is enough of a reason.
Where you can mention the still prevalent
gender inequality within society
without being called a 'feminazi'.
Where you can have conversations with people
without consistently being talked over.

I want to live in a world where
tears are fucking beautiful.
Where, when somebody cries,
everybody gathers around to hold them
because that is the duty of humanity
and that is the law of empathy.
I want to live in a world
where you don't have to keep on saying sorry
for things you are not sorry for.
Where people don't complain about your flaws,
saying you're too this
or too that.
I want to live in a world
where Love is the greatest currency
and money
is just a means to an end.
Where Life is prioritised over economic growth.
Where people don't crave control over others.
I want to live in a world
where you don't have to be afraid.
Where you can have faith in the law
and the system.
Where you don't have to consistently
be on your guard.
And armour yourself in apathy.
And fall out of sync
with the beat
of your heart.
I want to live in a world
where you can be an idealist
without everybody thinking
you're a fool.

Mercedes Webb-Pullman

Island

My parrot reaches with his beak,
nips me back into the present.

He knows when I'm dreaming;
he doesn't approve.

Here and now, boys, here and now
he insists, quoting Huxley.

He's smarter than me.

Midnight Phonecalls

It's midnight here
When are we going to meet up again?
New Zealand is a pretty long plane trip to anywhere
But it's sweet
OK, to be honest — cold winds of over one hundred kilometres
Earthquakes 8.9
Ozone layer has gone missing
Just being honest though I'd like to gloss over this
But we did find it F**KN hard to adjust to the extreme weather

The good part is everyone here is chilled and easy as
But I'm missing Bali — mainly the sounds and the smell and the really
    good food
I miss funny Balinese family entanglements that seem to work out
I miss Yudane being happy
I miss sitting in swimming pools drinking (juice, coffee, alcohol as long
    as it's liquid)

I'm a bit less political than you
Some people probably think I'm thick as cause I keep my toe at the door
For those loud political pronouncements on I know Bali better than you
Don't sweat it
Just keep talking to them and imagine they've got a carrot up their A*se

I'm having a wee run of bad luck
Or maybe it's an early midlife crisis
Cause nothing, and I mean nothing is going my way
No job so I cut blackberry and clear out our section in Whitemans Valley
Have got thorns stuck all through my fingers and my wrists are slashed
    from prickles
Strangely I love it
It's my therapy — or maybe punishment
But you know, usually my life is so lucky
I'm getting laryngitis from lack of laughing at silly shit

Albert Wendt

ANZAC Day

Little is meant: most of your life is always round the bend
in our engorged river of stories and laments

On this ANZAC morning our house hums with the heating system
and broadcast stories of stoic heroism   courage
and the ultimate sacrifice on the deadly slopes of Gallipoli
They died for us   to save our future from tyranny
We will always remember them
Then the bugled last post that always turns the stone heart into tears

So easy to hook our young on hypnotic stories of patriotism:
to die for your country is the supreme manly reward
and you will live forever in the national story of gratitude
On that addiction   our colonial masters herded us
into the ambushing mouths of Gallipoli and the 'evil Turks'
and the mouths kept swallowing and swallowing . . .

None of my ancestors died at Gallipoli so I have no
such stories to march to in the Dawn Parade
hold the worshipping attention of my mokopuna with
and live by with my neighbours

They died at Gallipoli   that is the truth   For what? I may disagree
But they died and for that I grieve in anger every Anzac Day

Preferences

Their house is not walled with afterlife:
she doesn't believe in it and he respects her choice
So without an afterlife what is there?
The space before we were born   she replies   where the silence
does not know it has flesh   blood   and name

Their house is not floored with intuitive truth and feeling:
she doesn't trust those and he prefers reasoned choice
So without intuitive truth what is there?
The unalterable solidity of the step-by-step floor that connects
all walls and holds up the ceiling and sky   she replies

Their house is not windowed with ever-changing seasonal views
of the countryside: she is afraid of those and he prefers constancy of sights
So without ever-changing seasonal views what is there?
The surety of urban sprawl in the grip of eternal summer
wrapped around you forever   she replies

Their house is not doored
So without doors what is there?

University

I want to write a poem
for the students at university
those living in their
own four-walled realities
Cs get the degrees
said the guy walking
barefoot during winter
he's taking engineering
said he slept at the building
They won't mind
I paid for this shit
why is Law so hard
Human Services made me cry
if you calculate it right
you'll pay your loan in
5 years said my friend from EY
why is the library always
packed, 2 books for 28
people, how can I get this
presentation done by the
14th, why are there more
cars than parking
I tried a shortcut once
thought I was the wiser
no one told me of the
construction ahead, how
can they keep their white
sneakers white while
my black boots get dirtier
they're going to make
our $2 rice to $4, a 100%
increase, can I pay my

loan back with all these Bs
I want to write a poem
for the students at university
those on their fifth cup of
coffee finishing their midnight
deadlines at 11:50

Mark Young

Wittgenstein to Heidegger

The hard parts
I found easy.

It was the simple
things, like

putting one foot
in front of the

other, that started
me thinking.

Essays

All the world is a page:
Alistair Paterson's play for voices

From Shakespeare's world as stage (*As You Like It*) and 'poor player' (*Macbeth*) to Jean Baudrillard's simulacra, the metaphor of our lives as a stage has been a familiar one. The internet age has simply confirmed what we already knew about ourselves, and has given us another platform on which to perform. Alistair Paterson's *The Toledo Room: A Poem for Voices* was first performed at Downstage Theatre (1977), and the form of it we can interact with now is the published one. The theatre is the page; the actors are the voices, rendered in lines and spaces in this long poem (26 full pages). It reflects the fact that Paterson's work is often on a large scale, even novelistic in scope, especially in long poems like *Qu'appelle* (1982) and *Africa // Kabbo, Mantis and the Porcupine's Daughter* (2008).

The long poem extends nineteenth-century innovations in free verse, dramatic monologue and prose poetry. It is a form suited to 'thinking through questions of the frontier' (Silliman 2011, n.p.). Such poems are often sequential or fragmentary; and, in many cases, their resulting multiplicity of style and content (and less commonly voice) might be said to satisfy some stylistics of the novel. Though Mikhail Bakhtin's stylistics are ostensibly about prose, they might be taken as markers for innovative poetry, especially in the long form: they include authorial literary narration; stylisation of oral forms; stylisation of semi-literary forms (e.g. the letter); extra-artistic literary speech (e.g. oratory); and the individualised speech of characters (Bakhtin 1981, 262–64). Bakhtin argues that a novel combines any or all of these categories into 'the higher unity of the work as a whole' (Ibid., 262). Paterson's long poems can be said to contain a Bakhtinian dialogic. In this sense, they are a fusion, or hybrid form, even as the poem for voices could be seen as a hybrid of poetry with stage-craft.

The long poem has been noted as a means of acknowledging materiality (McHale 2004, 260–61). The associated use of space includes the pervasive idea of 'scoring music', described by Charles Olson in

'Projective Verse' (1972 [1950], 339), and taken up by a number of New Zealand critics, including Paterson himself (1981, 30–31).[1] The idea of the score is rendered in *The Toledo Room* in a relatively traditional context: that of an actor's script. At the same time, its existence as a long poem includes effects that support the idea of a prosody of page space; for example, in the use of Paterson's double margin form, and in structural variety.

Like many plays, the opening lines of Act I, scene one address the audience directly, commenting on the play:

> You talk to me — pure fantasy — as if
> what we talk about had actually happened
> might possibly happen: of rehearsals
> the way the play comes on and the actors
> (part of it) light up & glow like French
> horns, double-basses with lights inside.

This is 'talking' in the context of the stage, initially, and the stage conceit is easily maintained on the page. Already, there is a complex relationship (or group of them) between the voice and the addressee. An actor is literally addressing the audience and talking about the play, as if it were real.

Of course the audience can't, or won't, speak back. The voice is that of the imagined play, the actor speaking from the play and on behalf of it. Additionally, it associates itself with the consciousness of individual audience members, getting into their heads. We're even reminded, parenthetically, that the actors are 'part of it', part of the play, yet from the outside the first voice we encounter is anything but. This forms an analogy with the way in which one can seem outside one's life, even as it's happening, and as any experience of stepping back and reflecting on one's life suggests. The exquisite metaphor of actors glowing like French horns — notwithstanding any irony and humour that might be created by the way that character appears on stage — involves the audience further in the play's conceit, doubling the metaphors, and adding another metaphor with the image of double basses lit from within — a resonant detail which recalls Degas' paintings. The subtle enjambment after 'French' adds a little more depth, since it can be implied that glowing is implicitly French, and doesn't need the horn to enact its magic; irony is possible here, too.

The cast practises its lines, the voice tells us, liaisons occur, an orchestra sounds the music but misses the tune, but it's not clear if the audience is literal or another metaphor — there isn't an orchestra in the pit of the original performance (the notes don't mention it, anyway). Suddenly, we are elsewhere:

It's an asylum — the doctors are ill:
two wear duffle coats, the third drinks
absinth (rosemary, a distillate of rue)
but you talk to me.

We talk as if there's sense to it (but there probably isn't), the voice says, 'as if what we talk about could happen', and it proceeds to list a variety of happenings, including some that are imaginary. But all of which are true, the text claims, affirming the imaginary and the virtual aspects of our lives as equally important.[2] The lovely repetition of actors being like French horns and double basses and the recapitulation of the cast trying out its lines and the idea of fantasy helps set this first scene, as well as bedding in the idea that we are 'ready for an audience that's not going / to get what it's paid for'. This is a curious disclaimer. It promises surprise, and alludes to the unexpected in the theatre of life. At the same time the cute enjambment after 'not going' implies that the audience literally won't leave. When this first scene/poem closes with the injunction 'talk to me', it is both a signal to the audience to listen, for the play to begin and for the audience to talk back to itself, to reflect on its own experiences.

The second scene begins by telling us 'He is Faustus — an actor'. Alternatively, he is a musician: Mozart or Handel. He enacts the dramas of life, 'is everybody and nobody — impermanent'. This second poem consists of six-line stanzas punctuated by single words on a seventh, indented line, which, taken together, nicely sum up the overall progression of ideas: 'consumable, conversation, illusion, impermanent'.

Scene three provides yet another change of rhythm, employing Paterson's double margin field form (which he evolved in the late sixties [Caffin 1998, 481] and used in most of his subsequent collections, sometimes exclusively).[3] The second margin is useful for accommodating and drawing attention to departures of thought and idea, and enacting content in a variety of ways, enabling structural and visual counterpoint. Similarly, Eleanor Berry outlines a diverse use of page space in Olson's poetry, describing structural shifts within a poem which 'crosscut other textual structures, producing counterpoint between two or more structures' (1989, 108). Such an effect is just one of a diverse range made possible by the double margins, as I have outlined elsewhere.[4] Here, words in the second margin echo those in the first, with additional, supporting comments, or make a break in the progression of ideas, and reiterate the line 'How can I talk to you'.

Scene four opens:

It's Spanish, at least the arch & grill
suggest it's Spanish: the brave bulls
the matadors, lights, the hushed murmur . . .

Reference to the arch and grill perhaps takes in the scenery of the production, and the drama of the scenario is easy to grasp. The poem employs three-line stanzas and is more discursive than the first three, but again employing repetition as a kind of refrain in a repeated reference to arch and grill in the last few lines. This performative technique sits well in the context of the theatre and on the page, since the phrases are lineated differently the second time around, which varies its sonic qualities, or 'melody'. The book's occasional illustrations by Terry Stringer, composed of outlines of figures, help evoke the sense of characters moving in space.

The fifth scene focuses on the origins of things (a frequent topic in much of Paterson's later poetry, especially *Africa*). All that exists:

> is the natural product
> of the electron, valency, swirling planets
> and (ironically) seems important

That its importance is ironic is noted modestly in a vital parenthesis. The concision of progress of life on earth (which allows for myth) is noted:

> In the beginning:
> dragons
> the bright sun
> the quick brown fox
> & burning, burning
> leaves & grass

The second margin gives the instances, the third line alluding concisely to the era of print culture, before the text jumps back to the first margin and the more naturalistic 'leaves & grass'.

There's a concern with history here — the domain of the long poem — with mention of the Roman world. The text attempts to represent something of the totality of life, its 'everythingness', with diverse references to banal and monumental happenings. It alludes to literary ancestors, to Robin Hyde and Garcia Lorca:

> Though neither knows what the other thinks
> each follows separately
> sunrise
> tide-fall
> daybreak
> the deception of the wind
> & what the summer says.

Having drawn our attention earlier in the poem to the sounds of summer, we move to the way each of us follows the natural progression of the day, with the natural again highlighted by a shift between margins.

In comparison, or rather juxtaposition (across strophes of the poem), the things humans do seem extreme, depicted vividly in the following poem by the actions of a performer juggling knives, yet the words 'a kind of' in the lines 'They do it with knives — / a kind of juggling act' means we're not sure whether a 'real' performance or an elaborate, extended metaphor is intended. Suddenly, there's real blood, nervous laughter and indecision. The text declares 'it's the reality / of the thing that excites the laughter', as if we are now witnessing a real performer. The poem concludes, rather grotesquely:

> It's done with knives
> and the best of it's when the victim himself
> is no longer in doubt
> the skin opens up & the gut tumbles out.

Now, 'the best of it' clearly concerns the theatre of life, perhaps through the way images of war intrude into our homes on television sets. The illusion of pastoral harmony is critiqued in Act II, scene one:

> But the best plays are pastoral:
> composed of purest air, the greenest hills
> the morning's shining dew — &
> even if Cynthia screws around a lot
> she's in love & love is true.

Cynicism undercuts the emphatics of 'purest' and 'greenest'. To the voice of the poem:

> It's political — a matter of
> who controls whom: the actor

the audience — of power & of
the application of power . . .

The emphasis on power recalls *Incantations for Warriors*' insistence
on economic explanations (Paterson 1987, 26). Ostensibly, in *The Toledo
Room*, 'those who act or are acted upon' are given equal responsibility,
but the emphasis is really on those who act, ending with assertions
about:

Nixon who invented lies —
Ford who invented automobiles
Johnson who invented death. . . .

The latter is undoubtedly a reference to Lyndon B. Johnson's escalation
of the Vietnam War. The impact of the lines themselves is understated,
yet profound.

The next scene begins with lines that seem somewhat vague, except
in their response to the awful recollections which precede them:

Under the water there's something
that has no shape, can be given no name to
is the sense of having seen, and not seeing
    of knowing & not knowing

There can be no knowing now, emphasised by the indenting of the
fourth line. There is emptiness and 'no more seasons', 'the music is
/ NOT the music of the spheres but belongs / to government, to the
administration'. Alternatively, 'it's what you believe'. After references
to islands, discovery and to a woman's falling hair, we come back to
'silence, waiting, loss'. As with the uncertainty about the figure of
the actor and the reality of the juggler's knife, one might say of this
unknowing that an 'irreconcilable duality' is now its underlying
principle — we cannot choose between the good and the bad, they
dwell side by side (Baudrillard 2003, 82).

A domestic portrait follows, of a woman who presides over tea; 'she knows the script backwards', she retreats to the wings, moves centre-stage, changes roles and costumes, and paints backdrops. The guest tries patience and suggestion; importantly, the hostess 'pauses & changes the subject. It's as she / arranged it: the walls, the carpet, the chairs'. This sequel to the suffering of war represents a measured and intriguing change of tone, which is thoroughly human in the way it fails to adjust.

The fifteenth poem (Act II, scene six) employs the first person in a way that helps own the reactions and make them less abstract:

> I can make no sense of it
> no — not of the season's rise & fall
> the long hard look of that tall girl
> the sunlight clothes
>   as in a second skin

The text is still lost in unknowing, in the fact that we can't discern good from bad and can control only 'minor' events — such as designing a bridge or draping a dress. In the next scene, the actor is 'one who wears his role like a second / skin'. The enjambment after 'second' suggests an alter ego. The occupation of actor is a way in which one might become 'larger than himself'. I can't help wondering if we are again closer to the metaphor of the 'poor player' than to that of occupation, since my own experience of acting has not been of making oneself more but of finding within oneself the stuff of the character being portrayed, be that hit-man or nincompoop. Act II, scene eight affirms:

> The sea changes — it lifts and swells
> growls in its throat
> surges, slides up windswept coasts

The sea 'drives history & lives' — perhaps an even bigger force than the H-bomb. Lives come to nothing on city streets, in offices and factories, but the sea has always been there. It carries myths, and yet 'It is going nowhere / it has nowhere to go'. We resemble it in some ways. When there's no purpose, we suffer; we have to have purpose, drive. Personified, the sea stretches and 'waits in its den'.

The juxtapositions between the strophes of this long poem are invariably intriguing for the ways in which they inform and collide with each other. The next scene opens: 'The names of the imperial cities are legend', suggesting an embodiment of desire and an expression of humanity's drive, in contrast with that of the sea, which is more powerful, and ruthless. The imperial city seems pointless in the light of nature and earlier reference to the atomic bomb. The names of cities belong to household cavalries, but equally to assassins and vandals, movie-makers, Napoleon, governments and, of course, actors.

We break off this Act's reference to the actor to join the voice in a 'nowhere' place (not Spain or Mexico) in Act III, scene one, where the audience is addressed directly:

> uncertain of yourself, & the room's empty
> as empty as a theatre when the actors look
> between the lines & the audience begins
> to lose its patience . . .
>
> I make signals to you, reach out to you

This reflective pause in the drama is unlikely to make the audience lose patience; in fact, it's quite mesmerising. The audience is again being invited to attend to itself, to reflect on what's been heard (and seen). The empty space of the room evokes metaphors of the page and brings to mind Jen Crawford's metaphor of the use of page space being like echolocation (Crawford 2016, n.p.).

Reaching out, the voice says, is thwarted by noise, and perhaps by language divisions. Assimilating what's being said with what's being done is our challenge, compressed into the following enigmatic lines: 'haggling & talk / of politics to pirouette, *veronica*, death / in the sun . . .'

The reference to a dance movement and to veronica (which means victory) anchors what must otherwise be a state of confusion in actual human experience: we dance on towards death, and die (as a race) when the sun dies, if not before.

The names of cities in general are legend. Like the imperial cities, they belong to administrators, actors, cavalry, and the speakers of many languages, but the people built them. As the text reiterates earlier references to belonging, there is again a sense of the totality of things, which suggests the poet longs to write about everything. Refrain-like strategies also resurface and strengthen performative elements of the text.

The sequence ends with another reference to silence, and to dreaming. It's not a dream of belonging to any place (including Toledo), but rather of flying, of escape and the feeling of freedom, to be not what we are but something else entirely, much like the fictional place the actor occupies and which the text struggles within and away from. Its sudden departures seem natural, even as the fragments of this long poem have extended each other and contributed to the unity of the whole.

The sense of voices spoken is not always that of discretely different demotic voices, but largely of changes of tone; perhaps it is even 'one man playing many parts' (*As You Like It*). The structures employed assist the sense of juxtaposition of elements — for example, of the natural world and the built environment. The link between the visual and the aural in a poem is hard to quantify (Drucker 1998, 106), but, quoting Anne Vickery, Anna Reckin reminds us that 'sound is spatially infinite' (Reckin 2008, 68) — an idea which relates to the perception of a voice speaking within a structure or space, and one which sings out of and through a text like *The Toledo Room*.

Bakhtin's idea of the unity of the whole is significant here, especially since Paterson's text regularly alludes to the totality of things. Along the way, there is literary narration, stylisation of oral forms, oratory and the individualised speech of characters, as Bakhtin outlines. Stylisation of semi-literary forms (e.g. the letter) is perhaps not so obvious here, although detectable elsewhere in Paterson's writing; for example, in the quotations from Frank Worsley's journals in *Qu'appelle*.

The Toledo Room encompasses snapshots of history and accommodates large questions about our place in it, and about the choices we do and don't have. Silence — that which poets are moved to acknowledge and bow before, often against their will — is sometimes all that can be gestured towards. We want to be free, and the voice calls for freedom. The idea of sound being 'spatially infinite' is a fitting one for the voice of *The Toledo Room*, which reverberates around the page, especially through the text's employment of structural counterpoint (including the double margin) and leaps off the page into one's mind and into an engagement with that wider theatre of life.

Works cited

Bakhtin, Mikhail, *The Dialogic Imagination* (Austin: University of Texas Press, 1981).

Baudrillard, Jean, *Passwords*, trans. Chris Turner (London and New York: Verso, 2003).

Bergson, Henri, *The Creative Mind: An Introduction to Metaphysics* (New York: Carol, 1992 [1934]).

Berry, Eleanor, 'Visual Form in Free Verse,' *Visible Language* 23(1) (1989): 89–111.

— 'The Emergence of Charles Olson's Prosody of the Page Space,' *Journal of English Linguistics* 30(1) (2002): 51–72.

Bullock, Owen, 'The Line: Recent Experiments in New Zealand and Australia,' *New Writing: The International Journal for the Practice and Theory of Creative Writing* 14(2) (2017): 223–34.

Caffin, Elizabeth, 'Poetry, Part Two: 1945–1990s', in *The Oxford History of New Zealand Literature in English*, ed. T. Sturm (Auckland: Oxford University Press, 1998), 465–84.

Crawford, Jen, 'Jen Crawford Talks to Owen Bullock About Her Latest Book *Koel*', *Poetry on the Move*, 2016. Retrieved from: https://poetryonthemove.wordpress.com/2016/04/19/episode-1/

Davidson, Michael, 'Palimtexts: Postmodern Poetry and the Material Text,' in *Postmodern Genres*, ed. M. Perloff (Norman: University of Oklahoma Press, 1989), 75–95.

Deleuze, Gilles, *Bergsonism* (New York: Zone, 1991 [1966]).

Drucker, Johanna, *Figuring the Word: Essays on Books, Writing and Visual Poetics* (New York: Granary, 1998).

Loney, Alan, 'The Influence of American Poetry on Contemporary Poetic Practice in New Zealand,' *Journal of New Zealand Literature* 10 (1992): 92–8.

McHale, Brian, *The Obligation Towards the Difficult Whole: Postmodernist Long Poems* (Tuscaloosa and London: University of Alabama Press, 2004).

— 'Poetry Under Erasure,' in *Theory into Poetry: New Approaches to the Lyric*, ed. Eva Muller-Zettelmann and Margarete Rubik (Amsterdam: Rodopi, 2005), 277–301.

Olson, Charles, 'Projective Verse,' in *American Poetic Theory*, ed. George Perkins (New York: Holt, Reinhardt & Winston, 1972 [1950]), 336–42.

Paterson, Alistair, *Birds Flying* (Christchurch: Pegasus Press, 1973).

— *Cities & Strangers* (Dunedin: Caveman Press, 1976).

— *The Toledo Room: A Play for Voices* (Dunedin: Pilgrims South Press, 1978).

— *The New Poetry: Considerations Towards Open Form* (Dunedin: Pilgrims South Press, 1981).

— *Qu'appelle* (Dunedin: Pilgrims South Press, 1982).

— *Odysseus Rex*. Drawings by Nigel Brown. (Auckland: Auckland University Press, 1986).

— *Incantations for Warriors*. Drawings by Roy Dalgarno. (Auckland: Earl of Seacliffe Art Workshop, 1987).

— *Summer on the Côte D'Azur* (Wellington: HeadworX, 2003).

— *Africa // Kabbo, Mantis and the Porcupine's Daughter* (Auckland: Puriri Press, 2008).

Reckin, Anna, *Landscape as Poem: Poem as Landscape: Space, Place and the Visual in the Poetry of Kamau Brathwaite and Susan Howe* (PhD thesis, State University of New York at Buffalo, 2008).

Silliman, Ron, 'Un-scene, Ur-new: The history of the longpoem and "The Collage Poems of Drafts"', *Jacket2*. Retrieved from: http://jacket2.org/article/un-scene-ur-new

Stead, C. K. *In the Glass Case: Essays on New Zealand Literature* (Auckland: Auckland University Press, 1981).

---

1   See also, for example, Alan Loney, 'The Influence of American Poetry on Contemporary Poetic Practice in New Zealand,' *Journal of New Zealand Literature* 10 (1992): 92-98, and C. K. Stead, *In the Glass Case: Essays on New Zealand Literature* (Auckland: Auckland University Press, 1981), 153. Elsewhere, see Eleanor Berry, 'Visual Form in Free Verse,' *Visible Language* 23(1) (1989): 107; Eleanor Berry, 'The Emergence of Charles Olson's Prosody of the Page Space,' *Journal of English Linguistics* 30(1) (2002): 58–59; Michael Davidson, 'Palimtexts: Postmodern Poetry and the Material Text', in *Postmodern Genres*, ed. M. Perloff (Norman: University of Oklahoma Press, 1989): 88; and Brian McHale, 'Poetry Under Erasure,' in *Theory into Poetry: New Approaches to the Lyric*, ed. Eva Muller-Zettelmann and Margarete Rubik (Amsterdam: Rodopi, 2005), 278.

2   I use the word 'virtual' conscious of assemblage theory's correcting of the term 'possible' to 'virtual'. Gilles Deleuze, *Bergsonism* (New York: Zone, 1991 [1966]), 96–98.

3   The double margin form was used in parts of *Birds Flying* (1973), *Cities & Strangers* (1976), *The Toledo Room* (1978) and *Summer on the Côte D'Azur* (2003), and throughout his long poems *Qu'appelle* (1982), *Odysseus Rex* (1986) and *Incantations for Warriors* (1987).

4   Owen Bullock, 'The Line: Recent Experiments in New Zealand and Australia', in *New Writing: The International Journal for the Practice and Theory of Creative Writing* 14(2) (2017): 223–34.

Jeanita Cush-Hunter

Dying to matter:
In defence of confessional poetry

Why not say what happened?
— Robert Lowell, quoted in Ostriker 2001, 317

Not long ago I was doing some reading for the university poetry course I'm currently enrolled in. As a practising poet (as I like to call myself, while waiting to become a published one), I became a little distressed when I registered the meaning of the words I was reading. 'Distressed' is probably an understatement. My heart started pounding, and I felt a spark of genuine fury flame up in my sensitive, artistic heart.

I reached for a pen and began gouging words of outrage (in capital letters) into my notebook. To further underscore my deep frustration and anger, I drew a disgusted face and a series of question marks in orbit around my vented outrage.

What had affronted me so much was the accusation, repeated by various different writers, that confessional poetry was solipsistic, insufficiently generalised and too reliant on the notion of spectacle. There was an implication that confessional poetry might be an inferior or (even worse) outdated mode of poetry.

When I had finished writing several heated retorts to these accusations, I began, more rationally, to write a series of arguments in defence of confessional poetry. Then, probably less rationally, I went and ordered a few hundred dollars' worth of books about confessional poetry from Amazon.com in the hope of gleaning enough knowledge about the subject to form an articulate response to its critics.

The following is my attempt at a justification of the merits of confessional poetry in the world of contemporary poetry. My arguments take into consideration the potential motives of confessional poets, the criticism of autobiographical poetry, the issue of solipsism and the potential of confessional poetry as a form of catharsis.

The question of motivation . . .

Why are some of our poets recreating their lives?

— Kooser 2001, 158

By the time I was 16, I was a skeleton who spent her days hunched over a hardbacked notebook. Into these notebooks of poetry (for there were several) I smeared the blood of my fears, my despair and my anguished anxiety. The words that I wrote most were the ones that were branded brutally into my brain from the sickness — me, I, mine, my — and the details in these poems were of my personal relationships, my daily struggles and my view of my rapidly dimming world.

The anorexia had imprisoned me in solitary confinement. The outside world was out of reach and I was gradually imploding . . . falling inwards into the ravenous hole that was at my core. As I reached for pen and paper every day, I had no idea that I was mirroring the behaviour of many other anguished poets who had sought to claim control of their lives well before my time.

Although my work was certainly, on reflection, autobiographical in nature, and is (I feel even now when re-reading it) very effective at capturing the trauma of teenage depression and anguish, my motivation in recording my thoughts and feelings at this time was not to communicate with an outside audience about my life. In fact, it would be fair to say that I didn't really visualise an 'extension of my life' at this juncture, and so I could have had no idea that anyone in the future might read it. The main impetus for the diligent recording of this stage of my life was not an audacious belief that another individual might find my life enthralling. I was simply trying to survive: to make sense of my world.

Confessional poetry as a significant and separate genre of poetry was first recognised and defined by M. L. Rosenthal in a 1959 review of Robert Lowell's *Life Studies*. The confessional poets were artists who stepped away from the conventional business of the established craft of poetry. These were poets who were 'overwhelmed or intoxicated by the facts of his or her life' (Alshire 2001, 16) and, as a result, let the facts take over. The resultant work of these poets could be viewed as the products of a 'breakdown in judgement and craft' (Ibid., 16).

Lowell's *Life Studies* heralded a new approach to the field of poetry. Robert Lowell was a complicated individual who had been dealt the 'dark cards' (McClay 2017, 25) of the depression and madness of bipolar disorder. He had manic episodes that resulted in hospitalisation, he could become delusional and he was, at times, violent. Some reports about Lowell claim that he could be arrogant and cruel, but there are also frequent assertions that the number of people who didn't or couldn't forgive him for his indiscretions while 'sick' were very few (Ibid.). Lowell was also a talented and unique poet.

When Robert Lowell began to put the intricacies of his battle with his mental illness onto paper, he struggled to dress his personal experiences in the poetic clothes of his predecessors. Lowell had a 'simple, searing honesty' (Kirsch 2005, 1) about his work, and he was not inclined, nor able, to stay within the parameters of conventional poetry.

His poetry was the result of the articulation of his personal experiences, and he found previous poetic methods inadequate for his purposes (Perloff 1970, 475). By the time he published *Life Studies*, Lowell had created a new style of poetry that allowed private experiences to be expressed convincingly (Kirsch 2005, 15). Lowell's subject matter was 'hyper-personal' (Badia 2002, 180), and the structure of his poems marked a perceived transgression from conventional poetic form (Ibid.).

Robert Lowell became known as the founder of confessional poetry and he took into his fold, as students, the likes of Anne Sexton and Sylvia Plath. The emergence of this new school of poetry was signalled by a reinvention of cultural literary norms where nothing could be considered too personal or too private to share with the reader (Sherwin 2011, 2).

Although I wasn't reinventing the world of poetry through my writing as a teenager, I was looking at the power of language in a much changed way. I had previously been of the opinion that poetry's main function was to please the reader. I had belonged to vocal choral groups where poems had been chanted in a sing-song manner to please the judges. In class I had written haiku about nature and politically incorrect limericks about hapless Irishmen. But now I was looking at poetry as a means of sustaining myself, as a way of holding on, as a way of communicating the helplessness of my situation.

Yusef Komunyakaa asserts that poets want to be heard (Komunyakaa 2001, 145), and, even though I had no specific audience in mind when I wrote my poems, I would certainly agree that the experience of surrendering selected parts of my existence to paper was somehow reassuring. The appeal of confessional poetry can be seen in its audience: 'the earnest beginners, in small cities, on college campuses of all kinds and sizes, for whom poetry is a way of setting their lives in order' (Williamson 2001, 51).

I would argue that this explanation cuts closest to the truth of the motivation of confessional poets: the need to give voice to personal distress in an attempt to regain a semblance of control over personal chaos. I reject the suggestions that these poets are trying to be sensational, and that some delight in exhibitionism (Lindley 1985, 82). It seems to me that this is an unjust and overly generalised view that fails to focus adequately on the art and substance that are the supporting pillars of confessional poetry.

The evils of autobiography . . .

A Mundane Miracle Called Life.

— Komura 2016, 257

Two significant events occurred in my life in my late teens. I encountered the work of Samuel Beckett in drama class, and the poetry of Sylvia Plath in English. It was a relief to discover the existentialist philosophy underpinning Beckett's work. In his characters and his constant cyclic dramatic action, I recognised so much of my own bleak outlook on life. The depiction of the universal struggle to understand the human existence was a powerful call to contemplate the deeper meanings and purpose of life.

The work of Plath was another thing entirely. Here was a woman who wrote of distinctly individual challenges that were very particular to her private life. Her poetry was full of hints about her intimate relationships, shared raw details of attempted suicide attempts, and the horrors of the battle she faced with her ongoing mental illness. Plath's work is probably one of the best examples of a confessional poet who demonstrates a clear relationship between 'autobiography, disclosure, spectacle and audience' (Badia 2002, 195).

I was enthralled by Plath as soon as I read 'Lady Lazarus' (Plath 1965, 8–11). This was the first time I had encountered anyone who expressed her personal rage with violent language. The harsh tone of Plath's speaker left no doubt in my mind that she was not writing about the details of her life for the benefit of her audience. I developed a great respect for Plath's bravery in sharing her personal horrors so unapologetically with the public literary world. I began to consider that perhaps I, too, might be brave enough to share my personal horrors with the world one day.

When I picked up *The Rocky Shore* by Jenny Bornholdt (2008), it was because it was a prescribed university text. I had never read any of Bornholdt's work before, and I wasn't sure whether I would enjoy it. However, I realised on my first reading of *The Rocky Shore* that I had become as caught up in her life as I had by the choice of her language and the rambling flow of the six extended poems in this collection. By the conclusion, I felt that I had become acquainted with Bornholdt: that I did know something about her personally. I sympathised with those of Bornholdt's struggles I *hadn't* experienced myself, such as her personal illness, and I empathised with the experiences that I could relate to, such as the loss of a parent to cancer.

It seems superfluous to state that I enjoyed *The Rocky Shore* both as a collection and as an example of autobiographical poetry. I was, therefore, a little shocked to discover some of the strident and negative feedback Bornholdt had received in certain reviews. Joanna Preston, in her review 'Stubbing My Toe on Jenny Bornholdt's *The Rocky Shore*', confidently expressed the opinion that her work was not, in fact, even poetry. Preston suggested that Bornholdt's work more closely resembled a collection of self-indulgent memoirs (Preston 2009, 2).

Whether or not Bornholdt's work can be considered poetry is not my main focus here. But what did genuinely concern me was the fact that there seems to be a great deal of disdain levelled against work that is deemed too 'personal' or too autobiographical. It would appear that there is a contingent of poetry reviewers and readers who do not appreciate or want to receive too much information about the personal life of poets. Bornholdt, herself, seems to convey an awareness of this fact in her poem 'Confessional': 'I was also thinking about / personal poetry and how it's not given much / time of day any more' (Bornholdt 2008, 10).

'TMI' (too much information) is often the cry when there is the perception that an individual has crossed the line of acceptable social behaviour by excessive self-disclosure. The implication, of course, is that there is something distasteful, something inappropriate, something offensive about revealing anything considered too personal or intimate about the self.

The person disclosing the information can be typed as a self-absorbed 'over-sharer'. This has been one of the accusations levelled at confessional poets. A significant reason for this criticism has been the argument that confessional poetry lacks universal appeal because of its stunted subject matter.

Samuel Johnson stated in *Rasselas* that 'the business of a poet . . . is to examine, not the individual but the species' (quoted in Lindley 1985, 68). There is the implication here that the more generalised the content of a poem, the greater its chances of success. It is implied that confessional work cannot have direct appeal to a large audience because of its pinpoint focus on the personal circumstances or autobiographical details of a particular poet's life. However, there is something to be said for the poet who can unearth poetic significance in the desert of ordinary existence (Conarroe 1997, 71).

Robert Atwan in *The Best American Essays 1995* disputes the notion that autobiographical writing is a selfish or narrow, let alone a futile or undesirable, exercise: 'The center of "auto-bio-graphy" isn't "self" or "writing", it's "life" in the fullest physical meaning of that powerful ancient Greek word' (quoted in Komunyakaa 2001, 145).

Pertinent to this statement is the issue of what I think of as the global or local themes of poetry. Certainly, there would be few people who would not agree that Robert Frost's poem 'The Road Not Taken' is an excellent example of posing questions in poetry about the choices that every human must face in life. The poem starts with the words 'Two roads diverged in a yellow wood' (Frost 1969, 105) and ends with the powerful dictum: 'Two roads diverged in a wood, and I — / I took the one less traveled by, / and that has made all the difference.'

However, aren't we also bound to consider the value of more 'local' themes? For example, Lowell's poem 'Waking in the Blue' (Lowell 2003, 183–86) is clearly a poem concerned with 'local' subject matter. This poem is an honest admission of Lowell's mental illness and his frequent hospitalisations for the treatment of his mania. No universal message or subject matter appears in the poem; it is very much a poem that stays focused on the 'local' subject matter of Lowell's mental illness.

This poem might be said to be interesting only if the man at the centre of the poem was known to the reader, but I would disagree. I don't feel excluded from Lowell's experience; rather, I feel compassion and sadness for a fellow human being, and, yes, I feel a little relieved that it has never been me fighting through the dark waters of madness only to surface, broken and humbled, in a mental hospital.

Confessional poetry spurns the notion of the universal. 'In confessional poetry such details [of personal life] can serve to deny universality by delineating the poet as apart and uniquely suffering' (Yezzi 1998, 2). I would argue that this separation of the poet from the universal world of the reader is not such a drastic take on poetry. The idea that an individual should not share details of their lives because the experiences of that individual may exceed the norm seems unfair, and, more alarmingly, repressive. In a diverse world, it would seem illogical to attempt to outline reasons why confessional poetry may not offer universal or generalised appeal to readers of poetry. Rather, the acceptance of the poet as a distinct individual with a particular set of circumstances beyond the common experience (Alshire 2001, 15) is surely a more rational course of action.

Confessional poetry as a genre appears to be one of the few styles of writing that is viewed as requiring a justification or even an excuse for its existence. Part of this is the disdainful view that such poetry is full of the minutiae of everyday life; that there is nothing of substance that may be of interest to a broader community.

And, certainly, when I read back through Bornholdt's *The Rocky Shore*, I do register the constant inclusion of the daily grind of her life in her poem 'Fitter Turner'. 'I've been writing and thinking and clearing a space / near the vegetable garden for another shed' (Bornholdt 2008, 49). But I don't feel particularly disturbed or irritated that Bornholdt found something worth mentioning, or even artistic, in her personal world, and I'm not affronted that she chose this genre in which to share it. A great disservice is done to confessional poets when the emphasis is placed broadly (and, by implication, disparagingly), on the documentation of the poet's life rather than of their art (Sherwin 2011, 24). Robert Lowell puts it very well in his poem 'Unwanted':

Alas, I can only tell my own story —
talking to myself, or reading, or writing,
or fearlessly holding back nothing from a friend,
who believes me for a moment
to keep up the conversation

I would extend the idea hinted at in Lowell's poem by adding that we are all experts in our own lives. As artists — whether writers, poets, painters or musicians — it makes sense to create work out of what we know. This is, after all, the only topic of which we all have undeniable and unquestionable first-hand experience. I don't think, therefore, that there is anything narcissistic or presumptuous in poets who choose to address their audience autobiographically.

The sin of solipsism...

To sound personal is the point.

— James Merrill in Perloff 1970, 470

When I look back at the poetry of my teens there is a clear repetition of certain themes, in the type of language used and in subject matter. The content, as one might expect, is bleak.

'I cannot explain why I want to die...' is the first line of one of these poems. It was because of subject matter such as this that I was reluctant to share my writing with anyone else. A boy I was dating around this time wanted to know what I was doing spending so many hours scribbling in the notebooks stacked in a dusty pyramid under my bed. He regarded them with a certain amount of suspicion, probably because he was jealous of the time I devoted to my writing.

One day I relented and showed him the poems. He read a couple in silence and glanced over the titles of others. Finally, he chose one and, with a great deal of disapproval in his voice, read out a stanza or two to me. I remember he wrinkled his nose in distaste as he said the words.

When he was done, he snapped the book's cover closed, looked down his nose at me and said, 'What is this? I don't believe it.'

'Don't believe what?' I asked, genuinely confused.

'Any of this,' he replied, as he gestured at one of the volumes of my life that he'd thrown onto my bed.

And with that a painful and difficult part of my existence was simply dismissed. He never asked to read any of my work again.

At the time, this boy's reactions and his behaviour completely bewildered me. I had no idea what I had done to upset or offend him. Of course now, years later, I understand what his objection was to the contents of that notebook. I had revealed too much about myself and, probably more significantly, *only* details about myself. There were no poems about him or any declarations of love in those pages. But there were, in abundance, graphic descriptions of longed-for violence, of personal self-hatred and a battle with an ongoing mental illness.

Certainly, the discovery of these topics in anyone's writing would cause most individuals to take pause and reflect; for a 17-year-old boy whose biggest problem was his parents' divorce, it was probably an alarming, deflating, foreign and quite possibly repellent experience.

I had unwittingly committed the sin of solipsism. But I needn't have feared, because I was in good company. This concept of being overly concerned with the self has been one of the most frequent accusations levelled at confessional poets. The confessionalists were unique in their incorporation of what had once been taboo subject matter and themes, such as sexual guilt, alcoholism, confinement in mental asylums (Uroff 1977, 104), suicidal depression, mental breakdown, adultery and divorce (Sherwin 2011, 3). These poets were not merely nudging at the edges of conventionally accepted themes in poetry, they were also battering down walls in their determined quests to exorcise their personal demons. In short, 'nothing was too shocking to divulge; no subject matter was too personal' (Ibid.).

By tackling such contentious issues and themes in their work, confessional poets were dragging themselves out of the shadows of such giants of the symbolist mode as T. S. Eliot, Ezra Pound, Wallace Stevens and W. H. Auden (Perloff 1970, 473) and shrugging off the idea that poetry should be impersonal. The loss of emotional control in poetry was considered inappropriate and a display of insufficient skill. Poems were meant to be cleverly crafted, with poets demonstrating considerable skill and admirable control over form, structure and language.

It has been argued that poets such as Robert Lowell, Sylvia Plath and John Berryman are guilty of solipsism; of slipping into the quicksand of self-pitying self-absorption. The work of these poets has been judged as self-indulgent and even self-exploitative. 'Confessional poetry can all too easily degenerate into a sloppy indulgence of self: its apparent irrationality may be less a struggle to comprehend than an excuse for exhibitionism' (Lindley 1985, 82).

But such observations seem to me to be exaggerations based purely on the personal nature of this subject matter, as well as a great underestimation of the artistic ability of these poets. I would also suggest that such opinions are based on a lack of understanding of the motivation behind such confessional works.

It is presumptuous, for example, to assume that the work of a poet such as Sylvia Plath is a product of her chronic solipsism or deep self-obsession (Badia 2002,195). Plath's poems, although grounded in the details of her personal life, developed into a fierce and daring expression of her own interpretation of events, thoughts and experiences.

As she neared the end of her life, Plath was writing her best poems. In these poems she frequently placed herself at their centre like an almost godlike figure, something Kirsch refers to as 'the achieved dream of the solipsist' (Kirsch 2005, 260). However, Plath was not enjoying the dream of solipsism. Rather, she was caught up in the darkest times she had ever known. Plath was not a slave to solipsism, but she *was* a victim of her own personal mental anguish. The poem 'Edge' (Plath 1965, 80), written at this time, shows a distinct separation from solipsism. The speaker in this poem has a determined, accepting tone. There is a sense of fierce resignation rather than narcissism.

The work of the confessional poets, in short, deserves to be analysed with greater attention to detail and with more respect. There is more at stake in a confessional poem than mere subject matter. It is the carefully selected *details* of these individual lives and the 'worn-on-the-sleeve revelation' (Yezzi 1998, 2), coupled with these controversial themes and artistic ability, that make confessional poetry a unique and courageous poetic genre.

The relief of catharsis . . .

It has been said that no one can appreciate poetry who has not suffered.
— Pepper 1949, 481

The male psychiatrist I was referred to in my twenties was a vain man with dark hair and bored eyes. He yawned rather too much for someone in his line of work. He told me to write.

'Get it all out on paper,' he advised. 'Do you have a journal?' he asked unwisely.

I gave a half laugh.

He told me he wanted me to write in the journal daily, then to bring the writing to the next session, where I would be expected to surrender it to him. It would help me, he stressed.

And so I went home and I wrote prose instead of poetry, and when I returned to the next session, I read out loud the part about how I resented the psychiatrist for impinging on my life.

Though this was probably not my most gracious moment as an aspiring writer, it was certainly an honest one. In reality, the psychiatrist was onto something. The idea of the arts acting as a form of self-expression and, more significantly, as catharsis is nothing new.

When John Berryman, a well-known confessional poet, took his own life, his first wife, Eileen Simpson, observed sorrowfully: 'I . . . blamed the suicide on John's having been a poet. The litany of suicides among poets is long. After a while I began to feel I'd missed the obvious. It was the poetry that had kept him alive' (McClay 2017, 23).

Through Simpson's words we begin to see the potential for confessional or autobiographical poetry to do more than merely act as a documented account of an individual's life. We begin to draw a little closer to the idea of emotional purging through writing.

'Karthasis', when applied to drama, applies to the audience and their involvement. The concept is that there is a 'releasing or purging' of emotions within those who witness the dramatic action that unfolds on stage (Highland 2005, 155). Highland asserts that such a process of relating to the dramatic art allows for 'a maturing of one's nature, of one's character' (Ibid., 156).

While this is a testimony to the effectiveness of the arts as a conduit of human emotion and expression, views of catharsis in poetry differ a little here. Pepper states that 'the satisfaction that comes from the poem is not from a pattern of pure pleasure but through relief from pain' (Pepper 1949, 481). Through such artistic expression or elaboration comes a release from the tension and fear that can be viewed as a positive relief (Ibid., 484). The suggestion, then, is that poetry has the potential to alleviate the suffering of poets through the writing of their work.

In the poem 'Dolphin', Lowell writes about his life in a reflective and honest manner.

> I have sat and listened to too many
> words of the collaborating muse,
> and plotted perhaps too freely with my life,
> not avoiding injury to others
> not avoiding injury to myself —
> to ask compassion . . .

I don't find it too much of a stretch to believe that when Lowell wrote 'Dolphin' he experienced a sense of relief in expressing this 'desperate, personal feeling' (Boksh 2015, 2) that he wasn't really in control of his life. Similarly, I can imagine that when Plath wrote defiantly 'Out of the ash / I rise with my red hair / And I eat men like air' in 'Lady Lazarus' (Plath 1965, 8–11) she may have felt a sense of vindication at outlining her defiance of the well-meaning spectators who 'saved' her from her various failed suicide bids.

The practice of poetry writing (or poetry therapy) as an emotional outlet, or as a method for dealing with the unique challenges faced by individuals, has been widely implemented — and investigated — in the area of mental health. It has been observed that 'poems can create empathetic understanding, diminish feelings of isolation, assist with catharsis, and instill hope' (Robbins & Pehrsson 2009, 47) when implemented as a tool for therapy. These findings would seem to give support to the claim that poetry writing as a form of personal venting or catharsis may be beneficial to the writer as an emotional release.

The main impetus for recording my life as a struggling teenager was simply to purge myself of oppressive feelings in order to prevent my emotional dam from overflowing. I turned to poetry when I felt there was no other avenue of communication or expression. I would argue, from personal experience, that this is a function of poetry writing that is not sufficiently discussed or recognised in literary circles.

The frustration of misunderstanding . . .
> Ever since, the confessional style has been one of the most popular, and
> most easily ridiculed, in American poetry.
> — Kirsch 2005, x

A psychiatrist once said to me, 'It's not fair but it's a fact that some
people's lives are just easier than others.'

She meant it. She was a heavy-set, striking-looking woman of some
exotic European extraction. She was highly intelligent and highly
motivated. She divided her professional time between her own private
practice in a building with turrets, which ironically looked like those on
a fairy-tale castle, and the children's clinic where she worked for free.
'The Institute for Child Guidance' was the clinic's name.

I was certainly in need of guidance by the time my exhausted and
frazzled mother took me there as a famished, exhausted and frazzled
teenager. Those words of the psychiatrist changed my life, because I
finally realised that I wasn't being melodramatic; I wasn't crazy. I also
understood in that moment that I would be constantly misunderstood.

It is tempting, perhaps, to read the work of Lowell, Berryman and
Plath as 'merely personal, merely self-indulgent, merely sick' (Ostriker
2001, 318). But, it is also highly inaccurate and rash.

It is perplexing to see the amount of hostility and mockery directed
toward confessional poetry. I wonder why we hoist the flag in defence of
professional reviewers and the like, and nod our heads so eagerly when
the 'experts' dismiss the words of others? In a peer review of a fellow
student's poem not long ago, I wrote something along the lines of: 'I
would rather be moved by the emotion in something than marvel at the
cleverness of the structure of a well-constructed poem.'

What attracts me back to confessional poetry over and over again
is the emotion. I cannot find anything in the literary world that comes
close to the tone of these poets or the mood that it creates in me as a
reader. I marvel at their courage and I sorrow at their personal plight
each time I read their work.

More importantly, they make me feel less alone. The works of Lowell and Plath are significant not simply because they are outstanding examples of the confessional genre of poetry but because they are able to afford a world of understanding and support to those who may be struggling with similar problems or experiences.

It is prudent to remember here that the motivation of these poets remains mere speculation. We can never know with absolute certainty what lay behind their poems. We can, however, reflect on the unique contributions of confessional poets to the world of poetry.

I subscribe to the view that the confessional poets exhibited great and genuine courage (Orr 1993, 653), not only in their unique and nonconventional approach to their art, but in their unflinching and direct articulation concerning the intimate details of their lives (Yezzi 1998, 2). Furthermore, I would argue that the power of confessional poetry as a tool for self-expression and as a means of giving solace to those who may suffer similar circumstances should not be overlooked or discounted.

Today I'm not sick any more. But I still have the volumes of poetry penned during my deeply confessional stage of writing. And I still re-read them, and I am thankful to have moved on from that stage of my life.

Do I think confessional poetry is relevant in a contemporary context? I would argue that it is essential. Although it is unwise to define it purely as a form of therapy, its importance to those individuals who utilise it for a type of support, as self-expression or as a means to fortify their existence cannot be overstated.

I owe a great deal to confessional poetry. My own life might have been very different had I not discovered Sylvia Plath, and been given the example of her life and work as a form of art and as a pertinent warning. I think McClay sums it up best when contemplating the private lives of the confessionalists and their impact on the literary world: 'One wishes them happier lives, but it's hard to wish for other poems' (McClay 2017, 23).

Works cited

Alshire, Joan, 'Staying News: A Defense of the Lyric', in *After Confession: Poetry As Autobiography*, ed. Kate Sontag and David Graham (St Paul, MN: Graywolf Press, 2001),14–37.

Badia, Janet L., 'Viewing Poems as "Bloodstains": Sylvia Plath's Confessional Poetics and the Autobiographical Reader', *Autobiography Studies* 12(2) (2002): 180–203.

Boksh, Shanjida. K., 'Memorials in Robert Lowell's Poetry: The Synthesis of the Public and the Private', *Transnational Literature* 7(2) (2015): 1–11.

Bornholdt, Jenny, *The Rocky Shore* (Wellington: Victoria University Press, 2008).

Conarroe, Joel, *Eight American Poets: An Anthology* (New York: Vintage, 1997).

Frost, Robert, 'The Road Not Taken', in *The Poetry of Robert Frost* (St Martin's: Griffin, 1969), 105.

Highland, James, 'Transformative Katharsis: The Significance of Theophrastus's Botanical Works for Interpretations of Dramatic Catharsis', *Journal of Aesthetics and Art Criticism* 63(2) (2005): 155–63.

Kirsch, Adam. *The Wounded Surgeon: Confession and Transformation in Six American Poets* (New York: Norton, 2005).

Komunyakaa, Yusef. 'The Autobiographical "I": An Archive of Metaphor, Imagery, and Innuendo', in *After Confession: Poetry as Autobiography*, ed. Kate Sontag and David Graham (St Paul, MN: Graywolf Press, 2001), 144–50.

Komura, Toshiaki, 'Waking Early Sunday Morning: Making of an Unconfessional Confession', *Explicator* 74(4) (2016): 255–58.

Kooser, Ted, 'Lying for the Sake of Making Poems', in *After Confession: Poetry As Autobiography*, ed. Kate Sontag and David Graham (St Paul, MN: Graywolf Press, 2001), 158–61.

Lindley, David, *Lyric* (New York: Methuen, 1985).

Lowell, Robert, *Collected Poems*, ed. Frank Bidart and David Gewanter (New York: Farrar, Straus and Giroux, 2003).

McClay, B. D., 'This Suffering Business; The Lives of Robert Lowell and Elizabeth Bishop', *Commonweal* 144 (2017): 23–4.

Orr, Gregory, 'The Postconfessional Lyric', in *The Columbia History of American Poetry*, ed. Jay Parini (New York: Columbia University Press, 1993), 650–73.

Ostriker, Alicia, 'Beyond Confession: The Poetics of Postmodern Witness', in *After Confession: Poetry As Autobiography*, ed. Kate Sontag and David Graham (St Paul, MN: Graywolf Press, 2001), 317–31.

Pepper, Stephen C., 'The Art of Delight and the Art of Relief', *Philosophy and Phenomenological Research* 9 (1949): 480–86.

Perloff, Majorie, 'Realism and the Confessional Mode of Robert Lowell', *Contemporary Literature* 11(4) (1970): 470–87.

Plath, Sylvia, *Ariel* (London: Faber & Faber, 1965).

Preston, Joanna, 'Stubbing My Toes on Jenny Bornholdt's *The Rocky Shore*', *A Dark Feather Art,* June 15, 2009. Accessed March 18, 2017: https:/jopre.wordpress.com.

Robbins, Joy M., and Pehrsson, Dale-Elizabeth, 'Anorexia Nervosa: A Synthesis of Poetic and Narrative Therapies in the Outpatient Treatment of Young Adult Women', *Journal of Creativity in Mental Health* 4(1) (2009): 42–56.

Sherwin, Miranda, *'Confessional' Writing and the Twentieth-Century Literary Imagination* (New York: Palgrave Macmillan, 2011).

Sontag, Kate, and Graham, David (eds), *After Confession: Poetry As Autobiography.* (St Paul, MN: Graywolf Press, 2001).

Uroff, M. D., 'Sylvia Plath and Confessional Poetry: A Reconsideration', *The Iowa Review* 8(1) (1977): 104–15.

Williamson, Alan, 'Stories About the Self', in *After Confession: Poetry As Autobiography,* ed. Kate Sontag and David Graham (St Paul, MN: Graywolf Press, 2001), 51–70.

Yezzi, David, 'Confessional Poetry and the Artifice of Honesty', *New Criterion* 16(10) (1998): 14–22.

i. m. T. E. Hulme, 'the father of imagism'

The 28th of September 2017 marks the centenary of the death of the so-called 'father of imagism', Thomas Ernest Hulme. He was killed near Nieuport in Flanders by a German shell which he had apparently failed to hear, most of the other men in his Royal Artillery Company having thrown themselves flat on their faces. That single shell obliterated a one-time poet and promising philosopher of aesthetics, a mathematician and an apologist/propagandist of abstract art.

Hulme was opposed to a key tenet of the humanist tradition that he traced back to the Renaissance and found in abundance in Romantic literature — the belief that progress is possible and that man is perfectible. Perfection, he believed, 'properly belongs only to the divine'. Since mankind is 'endowed with original sin', he states at his most patristic, order and institutions are 'creative and liberating'. Hulme's rejection of what many of his peers took for granted is of course reactionary in the true sense of the word. The metaphysics of his belief in original sin are never discussed, and his statements of credo often sound like dogmatic value judgments ('I hold the religious conception of ultimate values to be right, the humanist wrong'). An enthusiastic acceptance of order and discipline and a belief in the doctrine of original sin (which Hulme expressed *before* he joined the army and saw action on the Western Front) don't seem to be quite so perverse in the wake of two world wars. Who believes in the perfectibility of mankind after Passchendaele and the Somme, Auschwitz and Hiroshima?

Hulme's belief that the 'religious attitude' is one in which values are absolutes with an objective character — as opposed to the 'humanist attitude', in which man is the measure of all values — permeates his art criticism. In periods when mankind is held to be 'subordinate to certain absolute values', he believes you tend to get a semi-abstract or geometric expression of the human form, as in the Byzantine mosaic or Egyptian sculpture. In the highly stylised, semi-abstract art of archaic Greece, the organic is made to seem durable and eternal, a measure of the religious intensity of the sixth and seventh centuries, as opposed to the 'optimistic rationalism' of the Athenians in the Classical period. The paradox that a reactionary like Hulme was such an enthusiastic propagandist of avant-garde art is superficial. The more interesting question is how he managed to reconcile the abstract art of the early twentieth century with the religious intensity of the archaic and Byzantine societies.

He certainly didn't think that the new geometric art reflected a revival of a pre-Renaissance belief in the imperfections of mankind. The forms of the new art (of Wyndham Lewis and David Bomberg) were to be 'the more complicated ones associated in our minds with the idea of machinery'. In fact it was a machine-age art that to Hulme's mind, constantly searching for the zeitgeist and the *Weltanschauung* of his age (deeply embedded as he was in the ideas of Wilhelm Worringer), suggested something 'in a certain sense inhuman, pessimistic', contrasting directly with 'the flat and insipid optimism of the belief in progress'. Hulme had no idea just how prescient this remark was to prove. One of the acknowledged masterpieces of the new geometrical art, Jacob Epstein's *Torso in Metal from 'Rock Drill'* (a cast of which the reader can view in the Auckland City Art Gallery), is an armoured and visored robot with a truncated arm, its embryonic progeny exposed within a wide chink in its breastplated ribcage. In an earlier version of the work, the dehumanised figure was mounted on an actual drill, apparently expressing Epstein's belief that humanity was being transformed by the machine age into a race of androids. The *Torso*, his modification of the earlier *Rock Drill* of 1913–15, was the sculptor's reaction to the carnage taking place at the Front. But the new 'pessimistic, inhuman' art was short-lived. After *Torso*, Epstein put the machine age behind him, and Bomberg, the other avant-garde artist Hulme championed, went on to paint landscapes without a single geometrical line to be found anywhere. Machine-age war destroyed any enthusiasm for machine-age art in England.

At times Hulme seems to be anticipating Yeats. 'Dome of Brompton in the mist . . . Dead things not men as the material of art', he observes in 'Notes on Language and Style'. Both Yeats and Hulme valued Byzantine art for its austerity, 'a perfection and a rigidity which vital things can never have' (Hulme). In Yeats's magnificent 'Byzantium', 'A starlit or a moonlit dome disdains / All that man is . . . / The fury and the mire of human veins.' Hulme's wholehearted acceptance of the doctrine of original sin, and the emphasis on tradition and order as creative and liberating, are reminiscent of T. S. Eliot, to whom he appears to have passed his baton. He deplores the 'Romantic', 'Rousseauist' view that mankind is essentially good but corrupted by bad laws and customs, preferring the 'Classical' view which regards mankind as 'intrinsically limited but disciplined by order and tradition into something fairly decent', a distinction which would also have appealed to Eliot. When he writes about the choice of the precise or accurate word over the grandiloquent one, he sounds like Pound: 'Wherever you get this sincerity, you get the fundamental quality of good art without dragging in infinite or serious', infinity and profundity being features of bad Romantic verse and having little to do with what Hulme considered to be the essence of poetry.

The essence of poetry, according to Hulme, is the image, the key feature of an 'intuitive language', the purpose of which is to describe 'the exact curve of the thing', be it an emotion or an object. It involves, of course, an avoidance of conventional metaphors and epithets, and as such is the measure of a poet's sincerity. So far we seem to be reasonably close to Aristotle (*Poetics* 22): 'The most important attribute of a poet is to be good at metaphor . . . a sign of natural genius.' But Hulme's poetics have a basis in the philosophy of Henri Bergson, particularly his belief that the flux of phenomena cannot really be appreciated by any human faculty save intuition. Hulme applied this principle to the poetic image, which, *qua* intuitive rather than intellectual, is the means by which poets can 'break through the conventional ways of looking at things' and apprehend something of the reality of their experience. Prose, by contrast, is a 'museum where the dead metaphors of the poets are preserved'. Hulme had no qualms that this new verse would appeal 'to the eye rather than the ear' — regular rhyme and metre, in his opinion, allowed people to write poetry mechanically, without much inspiration. Many of these views seem commonplace, even banal, these days.

We must remember that they were expressed in a decade in which, for most readers, poetry meant the likes of Rupert Brooke or Alfred Noyes.

And so we come at last to 'The Complete Poetical Works of T. E. Hulme'[1] — five very influential imagist poems which first appeared together in the *New Age* in January 1912, although three of them at least ('Autumn', 'The Embankment' and 'Conversion') date back to 1909 when the imagist movement began in a Soho restaurant. Hulme, according to F. S. Flint, was the 'ringleader' who insisted 'on absolutely accurate presentation and no verbiage'.[2] All but one poem in this 'canon' present, playfully or quite seriously as in 'The Embankment', the celestial in terms of the human. Another short poem (outside the 'canon', but deserving a place therein) inverts this relationship between the earthbound and the celestial:

Susan Ann and Immortality

Her head hung down
Gazed at earth, finally keen,
As the rabbit at the stoat,
Till the earth was sky,
Sky that was green,
And brown clouds passed
Like chestnut leaves along the ground.

The probable date of composition is 1908 or 1909. The rhyme is irregular and there is no run of iambs until the final line.

I'll conclude this tribute with an examination of the last and most enigmatic poem in 'The Complete Poetical Works'.

Conversion

Light-hearted I walked into the valley wood
In the time of hyacinths,
Till beauty like a scented cloth
Cast over, stifled me. I was bound
Motionless and faint of breath

By loveliness that is her own eunuch.

Now pass I to the final river
Ignominiously, in a sack, without sound,
As any peeping Turk to the Bosphorus.

I have always found this poem perplexing. Are there two conversions with a pointed contrast between them? The first is the poet's seizure by beauty 'in a valley wood', in which he is 'stifled', rendered 'motionless and faint of breath'. I am reminded of the epigraph to another poem in the 'canon', 'Mana Aboda':

Beauty is the marking-time, the stationary vibration, the feigned ecstasy of an arrested impulse unable to reach its natural end.

Significantly, the verb 'arrested' appears in an earlier version of 'Conversion', five lines beginning 'I walked into the wood in June' (Hulme 1962, 220). The personification of 'loveliness' as a eunuch intensifies the imagery, representing beauty as more than something cloying and suffocating — it is ultimately life-denying and infertile. This experience presumably took place in the poet's 'light-hearted' youth. In the second conversion, he is once again stifled and motionless ('in a sack without sound'), passing 'to the final river', which I interpret to be the Styx. But why is he passing 'ignominiously, in a sack'? Turkish sultans used to get rid of unwanted members of their harem by putting them in a sack and throwing them into the Bosphorus. The sultan's eunuchs no doubt performed such deeds. Is death the second conversion? Or is death the only conversion in this poem? Or is passing to 'the final river' merely a metaphorical sequel to suffocation by beauty — everything after this ecstatic experience appearing so flat and lifeless, hence the quasi sneer in the last line? The ambiguity seems to be deliberate in this most Mallarméan of imagist poems. And I still haven't explained that reference to 'any [note] peeping Turk'. Everything that the last three lines signify vanishes in the very precision of their referents.

Imagery and metaphor were also the lifeblood of Hulme's prose style, due possibly to the influence of Bergson, but more definitely to a rigorous determination to avoid the dry, conventional abstractions of philosophical argument and exposition. (See, for example, 'Cinders', his 'sketch for a new *Weltanschauung*', reprinted in *Speculations*.) Along with his humour and stoicism, this relish for imagery and metaphor remained with him to the end. In 'Diary from the Trenches', he wrote that being illuminated by a star shell makes you feel as if you are walking naked in a city street. In the intervals between shellfire, he amused himself by finding the 'timeless in a Buddhistic kind of way', in 'waving vegetables' and little white villages seen from the fields of Flanders. Was his mind occupied by a kind of 'Buddhistic' timelessness when he failed to duck the shell that took his life and destroyed the unfinished manuscript of his book on Jacob Epstein?

Works cited

Aristotle, tr. M. E. Hubbard, in *Classical Literary Criticism*, ed. D. A. Russell and M. Winterbottom (Oxford & New York: Oxford University Press, 1989).

Hulme, T. E., *Further Speculations*, ed. Sam Hynes (Lincoln, NE: University of Nebraska Press, 1962).

— *Speculations: Essays on Humanism and the Philosophy of Art*, ed. Herbert Read (London: Routledge & Kegan Paul, 1936).

Stead, C. K., *The New Poetic: Yeats to Eliot* (Harmondsworth: Penguin, 1964).

---

1   'The Complete Poetical Works of T. E. Hulme' was published as an appendix to *Speculations*, ed. Herbert Read. The works can also be found on pages 70–71 of *The Faber Book of Modern Verse*, ed. Michael Roberts and revised by Donald Hall (London: Faber & Faber, 1965). Three more poems plus several fragments were published as an appendix to *Further Speculations*.

2   Quoted in C. K. Stead, *The New Poetic: Yeats to Eliot* (Harmondsworth: Penguin, 1964), 97.

Robert McLean

Arma virumque cano:
A reply to Janet Charman

Poetry New Zealand Yearbook 2017 carried what has been described by more than one reviewer as a provocative essay by Janet Charman, 'A Piece of Why', in which she re-litigates the case against anthologies edited by Allen Curnow well over half a century ago. Her charges, however, appear somewhat different from those levelled against the editor at the time of publication. Here, in her own words, is what she finds objectionable:

> It is my contention that Allen Curnow's poetry anthology introductions represent a disrecognised outburst of this conflict trauma. He reifies this anguish in the form of an exactingly chronicled horror and disgust towards women and their writing, characterising this in terms of a contaminating, and contaminated, femininity-effeminacy. (Charman 2017, 212)

The conflict trauma Charman diagnoses Curnow as having suffered from is the 'transmissive psychic trauma from the colonising wars of Aotearoa New Zealand', which has been 'intensified by every subsequent conflict in which the nation has been engaged'. Her prescription is to 'read Curnow in terms of the trauma his attacks mask', which will allow us 'to see that the m/Other who so horrifies him is not a contaminating and contaminated "other"'. Doing so will mean we can 'compassionately acknowledge . . . the cumulative affects and effects on our (sexual) identities of those brutal conflicts, which to this day transmissively traumatise men, women and children in Aotearoa New Zealand — and elsewhere'.

There is a lot going on there. Space does not allow me to fully and fairly address much of what I consider to be the problems inherent in this thesis and Charman's lack of telling evidence for it. For instance, how can we know New Zealanders *en masse* have been transmissively traumatised by successive brutal conflicts? No doubt, some of us have been. Like Curnow born in 1911, and whose much pored-over *Man Alone* has been discovered to house a homoerotic subtext that Charman has earmarked for future unpacking, John Mulgan was certainly traumatised by brutal conflict, having fought alongside Greek partisans in one of the most vicious campaigns of World War II. But whether it was the fighting, the British government's betrayal of Greek democracy, or something else entirely, which led to Mulgan's suicide will forever remain beyond any of us to say with certainty. But has New Zealand's sizable body of psychologists, psychiatrists, psychoanalysts and counsellors (most of whom would not subscribe to the prescriptions of Bracha Ettinger, from whom Charman derives her diagnostic tools) been surveyed for their professional take on our transmissive trauma? The answer is no. There is no evidence. There is only anecdote and speculation and inference. And these are what Charman relies on to make a wicker man, call it Allen Curnow, and set it alight.

I know nothing of Janet Charman and Allen Curnow apart from their writings; more so, admittedly, of the latter, whose *Look Back Harder* and poetry collections I have come to know better and better over years of re-reading. Having not known Curnow, I can't say if he'd need me to defend him; but I doubt it. What I do know is that Allen Curnow in mid-century New Zealand did make choices about many things, including those about poems — not the people themselves — he chose to exclude from three books that played a significant part in our canon building: the 1945 and 1951 editions of the Caxton *A Book of New Zealand Verse* and *The Penguin Book of New Zealand Verse* of 1960.

> I suppose about 1942 or 1943, and at about two o'clock in the morning at my desk in *The Press* office, when I finished with the night's work, I thought: it's time we had an anthology of the poets I really like. (Curnow 1987, 251)

It is easy to find that sentence rebarbative. How Curnow could be unsure of the year during the most destructive conflict in human history is unfathomable. Questions about the identity of that 'we' and why they should have had an anthology of what he liked are probably unanswerable. One could level charges of patrician arrogance; more charitable would be to attribute the seeming high-handedness to a dated figure of speech. Most likely is that 'we' refers to Curnow and his cadre of like-minders: Glover, Fairburn, Brasch and so on. In any case, Curnow, besides wanting to make an anthology of the poets he really liked, also wanted to 'dispose finally' of the poets of *Kowhai Gold* and the *Treasury of New Zealand Verse* (with exemptions granted for a select few).[1] On the whole, he probably considered his ostensible scorched-earth policy a success. Those fellow travellers certainly did:

> Like a hard frost, it killed off weeds, and promoted growth; it set a standard not for poetry alone but for all the arts. (Brasch 1980, 550)

Curnow would have been over-reaching to think it was only his merciless scythe that saved New Zealand's poetic nursery from being overwhelmed by poets he — to put it in his terms — didn't like. Most of the poems to which he took exception are unquestionably trite, and the books containing them would have disappeared into library stacks, garage sales and discount bins without his intervention. Case studies of anaemic Victorianism, they scarcely betray even a passing taint of the Georgianism (a movement C. K. Stead convincingly argued was itself a reformative influence in post-Victorian poetry) that was becoming *passé* by Curnow's 1920 cut-off point. But Curnow didn't disavow the influence of the excluded. Although Charman writes that Jessie Mackay suffers a shuddering dismissal at Curnow's hands, Curnow admits the poets in the Caxton anthology, among whom he included himself, are 'descended from Reeves, Adams, and Mackay' insofar as 'the country becomes a point of departure for the imagination'.[2] Since the omission of Jessie Mackay seems to be emblematic for Charman of Curnow's disgust towards women instead of his literary preferences, it seems fair to let readers judge the merits of the omitted by reading the poems for themselves rather than take a critic at their word.

The Charge at Parihaka

Yet a league, yet a league,
   Yet a league onward,
Straight to the Maori Pah
   Marched the Twelve Hundred.
'Forward, the Volunteers!
Is there a man who fears?'
Over the ferny plain
   Marched the Twelve Hundred.

'Forward!' the Colonel said;
Was there a man dismayed?
No, for the heroes knew
   There was no danger
Theirs not to reckon why
Theirs not to bleed or die,
Theirs but to trample by:
   Each dauntless ranger.

Pressmen to right of them,
Pressmen to left of them,
Pressmen in front of them,
   Chuckled and wondered.
Dreading their country's eyes,
Long was the search and wise,
Vain, for the pressmen five
Had, by a slight device,
   Foiled the Twelve Hundred.

Gleamed all their muskets bare,
Fright'ning the children there,
Heroes to do and dare,
Charging a village, while
   Maoridom wondered.

Plunged in potato fields,
Honour to hunger yields.
Te Whiti and Tohu
Bearing not swords or shields,
Questioned nor wondered,
Calmly before them sat;
    Faced the Twelve Hundred.

Children to right of them,
Children to left of them,
Women in front of them,
    Saw them and wondered;
Stormed at with jeer and groan,
Foiled by the five alone,
Never was trumpet blown
    O'er such a deed of arms.
Back with their captives three
Taken so gallantly,
    Rode the Twelve Hundred.

When can their glory fade?
Oh! The wild charge they made,
    New Zealand wondered
Whether each doughty soul,
Paid for the pigs he stole:
    Noble Twelve Hundred.

Has Jessie Mackay's performativity extended her subjectivity into
Matrixial space in her poem, or written a Tennysonian pastiche? Would
Curnow have done the former by including it in one of his anthologies,
or would he simply have been going against his taste? Curnow stated in
1935 the kind of poems he liked — 'in a living language spoken by living
people' (1987, 5), criteria not disregarded even if a poem's cause was a
worthy one — and they didn't have lines like 'You'll never break your

prison golden', 'There she heard the owlets wrangle / With an angry hoot', 'Over the ferny plain / Marched the Twelve Hundred', 'Gleamed all their muskets bare' or 'Dreading their country's eyes, / Long was the search and wise'. Since such diction and syntactical inversions are typical of Mackay (among the lines from 'The Charge at Parihaka' singled above, I have included some from 'Rona in the Moon'), they can't be attributed to satirical intent. Even so, readers may well agree with Charman that Mackay deserved inclusion on the basis of such work. I don't, but the weakness of some of Cresswell's and Hervey's poems that did make the grade would suggest that Curnow relaxed his standards on occasion. Then again, if Curnow 'really liked' Hervey's and Cresswell's poems, one must simply shrug and read something else — although not without again noting that Curnow quite clearly defined the kinds of poems he liked and disliked, and acknowledging that Mackay's poems tick few of Curnow's long-established and well-publicised boxes.

Curnow did include women in his anthologies, albeit only a few. But the ones he did include he didn't shy from praising: 'I can think of few poets who establish the same visual authority over such a region', writes Curnow in praise of Bethell, whom he lauds in fulsomely Romantic terms, for figuring 'the living symbol of a season put away' and re-enacting the 'drama of death and resurrection'. Of Robin Hyde, he wrote, 'Her writing was near hysteria . . . any moment we are likely to get the awful archness of her lines on "Katherine Mansfield" and yet "The Deserted Village" is one of the most moving and dramatically complete poems I know.' There is of course no contradiction — the latter poem ('where the subject has come from an observed scene of modern war') is a better poem than the former. And although Curnow may have passed over Jessie Mackay, he certainly gave notice of her contemporary Blanche Baughan's achievement, singling out for especial praise her 1900 poem 'A Bush Section', which he nominated as 'the best New Zealand poem before Mason':

No earlier New Zealand poem exhibits such unabashed truth to its subject. The vivid density of her language, the rapidity of her exposition, the dramatic shifts of scene and standpoint which are parts of the success have been strangely overlooked in New Zealand hitherto . . . Her hopefulness gets dignity and depth from her compassionate understanding . . . there is true feeling, not merely the facile optimism of her generation, in the interrogations with which the poem concludes. (Curnow 1987, 151)

Far from shying away from Virginia Woolf's privileging of Romantic poetry,[3] to which Charman digresses with no discernible connection to the matter at hand, Curnow again praises the poet and poem in unequivocally Romantic terms, not least of all for its 'true feeling' and 'compassionate understanding', formulations neatly demonstrating Curnow's view that poets, if they are up to it, must fully exercise intellect and emotion in mutually intensifying concert if they are to write the kind of poems Curnow liked. Baughan, in the instance of 'A Bush Section', did just that, and it moves Curnow to a degree of effusiveness he seldom, if indeed ever, matched. Is Curnow moved by Baughan despite himself, as Charman would have us believe?

Instead of taking Curnow at his word, Mackay's omission is attributed to Curnow's misogyny, sublimated conflict trauma and fear of effeminacy. So much of her argufying turns on this or that being — in her words — 'implicitly registered' while refusing to register what actually has been said. Although I have suggested Curnow's trumpeting and inclusion of Baughan's 'A Bush Section' (along with his praise of Bethell and some of Mansfield and Hyde) represents a more nuanced agency than Charman would allow him, if these apparent exceptions are also somehow also attributable to Curnow's secreted and all-consuming vicious biases, then all discussion must cease. Curnow explained his criteria for inclusion and exclusion (criterion would be more accurate: he included poems he 'really liked'); he offered more particular explanations in certain cases, such as Mackay's; he detailed how he and Roger Oppenheim translated the Māori poems he included in the Penguin anthology and provided extensive references. And, of course, he didn't write anything other than what he did. And yet Charman would have us believe he was either lying, self-deceiving or too traumatised in his way by military conflict to mention it; or that the presence of every word in the anthologies, his own and others', true or false, was determined by the amorphous and all-pervasive trauma with which Charman states all New Zealanders are struggling. It is, as it were, the key to all mythologies, including the so-called South Island myth, misogyny, shellshock and everything else besides.

Although 'A Piece of Why' has an ostensible theoretical underpinning (sourced from Bracha Ettinger), it begins in sarcasm — taking a sideswipe at Curnow's 'dauntless, self-chosen mission' in its first sentence — and goes on to chart well-trodden ground with implements that brook no measure (with the notable and early exception of Kai Jensen's statistical analysis of women's publication levels in the first half of the twentieth century). The case is argufied with tools such as ambiguous single quotation marks ('femininity-effeminacy', 'equalitarianism', 'male as neutral voice': are these scare quotes or did someone, most pertinently, actually say these things?) and tangential anecdotes, such as that about the wartime academic who moonlighted at the freezing works, swiftly diagnosed by Charman as indicating the philosopher's performance of his 'macho' (those pseudo reported speech indicators are Charman's). But it is her use of 'should' as an argument in itself, as if imposing obligation on the reader, which is her most demoralising tactic:

> Curnow's adamant repudiation of 'fanatical equalitarianism' should be understood . . . as masking his anxiety about the legitimacy of his performance, as a poet, of a sexual role that his society deemed 'feminine-effeminate'. In other words, Curnow wanted to be able to perform the 'feminine' in his poetics without being sexually disparaged or humiliated. (Charman 2017, 202)

The other words are Charman's. This particular conclusion is reached after quoting and/or referencing Michele Leggott, Kai Jensen, Trixie Te

Arama Menzies, Alistair Paterson, Sigmund Freud and John Newton. Curnow is granted three sentences (one about *Kowhai Gold*, one the statistical fragment '18 women', and another concerning his salvaging of 'a few poems which mark some early encounters of European sensibility with these Polynesian islands'), all of which are taken out of context.

Indeed, through the course of Charman's essay she prefers to quote Curnow in sound bites: for example, when Charman turns to Curnow's handling of Alfred Domett's poem 'Ranolf and Amohia', after allowing Curnow to say 'no one questions the total inadequacy of the poem as a representation of the Maori people', she condemns him for valorising Domett and for 'erroneously, not to say self-servingly [which, of course, means to say self-servingly] giving Domett a kind of carte blanche'. But such a caricature is only drawn by being extremely selective when it comes to evidence. Curnow, far from being an apologist for Domett, gave his editorial imprimatur to the editorial note supplied by Keith Sinclair that describes the nineteenth Premier and poetaster as 'a leading advocate of force as a civilising agent' who became a 'respectable figure head for [Russell's and Whitaker's] dubious schemes', such as land confiscations and use of arms.

But Charman refuses to take a nuanced view. Her accusation is unqualified and without limit: Curnow was constitutionally repulsed by each and every female, at least to the point of disgust, although presumably more so by some than others. The evidence of this abhorrence is largely derived from what he didn't write and whose poems he didn't anthologise. Curnow's sins of omission are given currency only by ignoring what he did write and whose poems he did anthologise. According to Charman's thesis, which comes at the end of her essay, her attribution of this disgust to the Colony's, Dominion's, and Nation-State's armed conflicts is an act of compassion. And yet this compassion doesn't extend to ensuring Curnow's subjectivity, physicality and self-sovereignty aren't utterly denied him. Curnow, in Charman's view, went too far in humanising Domett; Charman doesn't make the same mistake: 'Curnow' is made a cypher animated by forces of a dark destructive agency.

To shine a light on this dark, destructive agency, Charman, mostly behind the scenes, uses the work of artist, writer and psychoanalyst Bracha Ettinger. Most of her confections (trans-subjectivity, co-emergence, wit(h)nessing, com-passion, communicaring, erotic co-responsibility, transconnectivity, borderlinking, partial-subjects, borderspace, metramorphosis, fascinance, *link a*, co-poiesis, encounter-event, artworking, trans-ject, conaissance, transcryption, emoving, erotic antennae of the psyche, in-tuning, et cetera) are beyond my understanding, especially how one is supposed in practical terms to, say, trans-ject, emove or borderlink:

> The place of art is a co-poietic time-space-event of passage, a transport-station of trauma and an occasion for joy. A transport-station that more than being a dwelling place or time is rather a timespace offered for coemerging and cofading, borderlinking and borderspacing, over different times and different places, where the same place is stretched between different times and the same time connects different time-spaces, the here with the there, the now with the then, a space-time encounter, a space-time of Encounter-Event, which allows the opening-up of a spiral time-place of encounter. Not inter-subjective but trans-subjective and transjective encounter-events take place by way of subjectivizing experiencing with an artobject or art-process, an other or an event, others, alive or not, met and unmet, that continue to induce and transmit. (Ettinger 2009, 5)

Do Ettinger's ideas provide the means for understanding Allen Curnow's anthological exclusions, inclusions and discriminations? After having read them in good faith, I find them resistant to paraphrase (although readers like me are advised that '*The Matrixial Borderspace* cannot simply be read but must be felt . . . [it] works at the perimeter between consciousness and the unconscious, at the im/possible threshold of language' [Giffney, Mulhall & O'Rourke, 2009]). Whatever such terms signify, Charman doesn't use them as a critical apparatus with which to read Curnow. Her charges against Curnow and to the Caxtons and

Penguin are stated without reference to Ettinger, whose writings are only referenced at the end of her essay.

The gist and substance of her arguments are made in altogether workaday terms similar to those of Baxter and Johnson; i.e. some poets were included whom she doesn't like, and others weren't whom she thinks should have been. (Curnow's like or dislike of this or that poem were, of course, his sole stated criteria.)

Where Charman departs from this is when she pivots on one of the 'therefores' stationed tactically across her paragraphs and moves from difference to impugning Curnow's privacy by confecting out of the unsaid and absent the 'implicit', which Charman intuits and states in no uncertain terms. This move — state A (X or Y was passed over by Curnow like God moving across the waters), pivot on a 'therefore' to state B is 'implicit', which Charman then makes explicit (Curnow's sublimated trauma and disgust towards women) — is the rhetoric of prejudgement. Even so, it is, one must admit, *possible* that everything Charman writes of Curnow, including what she gleans from intuiting from beyond Curnow's grave his innermost goings-on, is true; it is *possible* that Curnow was lying to himself and his readers about why he left poets out of his anthologies (and that what he wrote is less important than what he didn't); it is *possible* that he was disgusted by women, and that this disgust was due to sublimated trauma derived from New Zealand's involvement in wars, battles, raids and skirmishes, and that all New Zealanders are similarly traumatised, whether they know it or not.

Would a reader of Charman's essay be correctly applying the carte blanche interpretive licence that she applies to Curnow if they were to suggest her referencing sublimated conflict trauma is not offered as an explanation of Curnow's choices but rather as a justification of her argument that Mackay ought to have been canonised? To do so would come close to suggesting Charman is using the very real trauma — the loss of life, limb and love suffered by thousands of people, especially by those in the military (ripped apart by musketry in Taranaki, drowning in mud in Flanders, burnt alive at Alamein, and so on . . .) — to flesh out an argument about *poetry anthologies*. Where, one wonders, is Charman's compassion, let alone perspective? After all, her impugning of Curnow's disgust towards women is, on her terms, an act of compassionate reading, one which serves to free us from blinkers that blind us to our own blindness.

It seems to me that Charman entertains a clutch of interests (Curnow's anthologies, marginalisation of non-white male writers and its attendant misogyny, Ettinger's literary psychoanalysis, and unqualified pacifism) and attempts to constellate them by forcing an ostensible coherence upon their disparity that requires her to elide, infer, assume and extemporise, but it is only her outraged tone that supplies any consistency to her essaying. 'A Piece of Why' is an act of literary mediumship, a private seance using Curnow's text as a Ouija board through which the clairvoyant reaches into a world that is out of reach, interpreting the silent utterances of a ghostly straw man and committing an essayistic *auto-da-fé* to cleanse the spectre of his sins of omission. Of course, I could be wrong. But what I am sure of is that, while there is nothing as pregnant with ambiguity as an over-determined text, there also is nothing as inscrutable as a dead man's soul.

> Time smiles and whets his knife
> and something has got to come out
> quickly, and be buried deep,
> not spoken or thought about
> or remembered even in sleep.
> You must live, get on with your life.
> — 'A Farewell'

I'm sure a lot could be read into this stanza by A. R. D. Fairburn, who, along with such terrific lines, which Curnow esteemed, also amused his literary mates by coming up with the risible backhanders 'the menstrual school of poetry' and 'the girlie poets'. Are these swipes sidereal symptoms of unacknowledged trauma caused by New Zealand's military misadventures, or is Fairburn indulging in front-and-centre dick-headed misogyny? Does one need a mission and a theory to take others at their word? Reading 'A Piece of Why' put me in mind of the terrific passage in *Middlemarch* where Eliot coruscates Casaubon and his folly in trying to formulate his 'key to all mythologies':

> His experience was of that pitiable kind which shrinks from pity, and fears most of all that it should be known: it was that proud narrow sensitiveness which has not mass enough to spare for transformation into sympathy, and quivers thread-like in small currents of self-preoccupation or at best of an egoistic scrupulosity. And Mr. Casaubon had many scruples . . . he would be unimpeachable by any recognised opinion . . . but the difficulty of making his Key to all Mythologies unimpeachable weighed like lead upon his mind . . . bitterly convinced that . . . Carp had been the writer of that depreciatory recension . . . which was kept . . . in a dark closet of his verbal memory. (Eliot 2007, 294)

In the end, when it comes to 'A Piece of Why', Mary Ann Evans can say it better than I can.

Works cited

Brasch, Charles, *Indirections: A Memoir 1909–1947* (Wellington: Oxford University Press, 1980).

Charman, Janet, 'A Piece of Why', in *Poetry New Zealand Yearbook 2017*, ed. Jack Ross (Auckland: Massey University Press, 2017), 196–213.

Curnow, Allen, *Look Back Harder: Critical Writings 1935–1984*, ed. Peter Simpson (Auckland: Auckland University Press, 1987).

Eliot, George, *Middlemarch* (London: Vintage Books, [1871–72] 2007).

Ettinger, Bracha, 'Fragilization and Resistance', *Studies in the Maternal* 1(2) (2009); www.mamsie.bbk.ac.uk.

Giffney, Noreen, Mulhall, Anne, and O'Rourke, Michael, 'Seduction into Reading: Bracha L. Ettinger's *The Matrixial Borderspace*', *Studies in the Maternal*, 1(2) (2009); www.mamsie.bbk.ac.uk.

1   Readers shouldn't take my word for how unreadable these books are; after an
    afternoon alone with them, readers can come to their own conclusions about
    whether Curnow's estimation of them was fair. Poetry has, I think, its ups and downs.

2   The contemporary ruckus concerning the omission and under-representation of
    poets felt deserving of inclusion has been well documented elsewhere and warrants
    no more than a footnote. It's fair to say these grievances were more justified in
    relation to the Penguin anthology, which was ostensibly more of a historical survey
    than the Caxton books. Even so, given the very similar rosters across the three books,
    Curnow surely must have been pleasantly surprised by the remarkable correlation
    between what he really liked and what was apparently historically worthy.

3   Why Charman references Woolf as an authority on poetry is lost on me. If Woolf
    in 1929 could not think of 'two living poets now as great as Tennyson and Christina
    Rossetti then', especially given the wider social circles in which she moved, surely her
    credibility in this area is irretrievably slight.

The quiet of boiling oil:
The life and poetry of Ellen Conroy

John Conroy, a talented tenor and violinist in Victorian England, was also an excessive traveller who dragged his family across multiple shires and lived in at least 15 houses during his lifetime. In 1879, he married Erena Pierpoint Rimmer, a daughter of the then-famous grocer and teetotaller Seth Luther Rimmer of Southport, Lancashire.

Erena loved poetry and admired Elizabeth Barrett Browning. The poet's picture held a place of honour in their family photo album. John and Erena had six children: Jack, Hubert, Ellen, Seth, Hermyntrude and a stillborn child. Their daughter Ellen, born in Herefordshire in 1886, was an independent woman, a lover of poetry like her mother and musical like her father.

Unfortunately, it's rather difficult to research a Victorian woman whose entire family abandoned her, who married late in life and never had children; and whose sister was a pathological liar and a sensationalist. The potential wealth of information regarding the finer details of the Conroy family — an unpublished memoir entitled *Idle Thoughts of a War Bride*, written by Ellen's sister Hermyntrude — has had many of its claims debunked and most of the others questioned.

That Ellen's brother Hubert died young is true; however, his life was not cut short because of an accident. And while Hermyntrude would have us believe that John and Erena carried on a forbidden romance before marrying without family approval, all outside evidence dismisses this. In light of these two errors alone, it's easy to doubt what Hermyntrude has written, be it about Ellen or her other family members.

Even Ellen's surviving poetry is somewhat tainted, being preserved only in *Idle Thoughts of a War Bride*. The war poem 'Any boat that would float' is found in both an early draft of the memoir and a later one, and each draft holds a different version of the poem.

The earlier version unfolds like a story, focusing on characters affected by the Dunkirk evacuation of World War II, while later it is 'updated' to include an additional 53 lines of lists and inane details, which stylistically seem at odds with the lines surrounding them. 'Randans & whiffs & punts / Grunted & bunted to shore' echoes a children's storybook and sits at odds with the exploration of man's instinctive pull towards heroism just two stanzas earlier.

Did Ellen edit her poem in the years between the two drafts of the memoir, or did Hermyntrude decide to try her hand at 'improving' the poem? That is impossible to determine. Fortunately, however, there are historical records, photographs and letters to weigh up against the claims in Hermyntrude's memoir, allowing a sparse, yet clearer picture of Ellen to unfold.

John, the Conroy patriarch, left a childhood of living and working in hotels with his parents to come into the employ of Erena's father, becoming a shopman at Seth Rimmer's grocery store in around 1868. John became a commercial traveller some time before his marriage to Erena 11 years later (he was not an accountant, as Hermyntrude would have us believe). He immediately took Erena away from Lancashire to Cheshire.

Because of his job, they moved about the shires almost constantly, travelling from Cheshire to Herefordshire, back to Lancashire, south to Worcestershire and finally to Glamorganshire in Wales in 1900, where they settled for around 13 years.

Ellen and her siblings inherited the dark brown hair and eyes of their parents. Both Jack and Hubert had large ears that stuck out, but Hubert retained the fine, handsome features of his mother's side, while Jack took on more of his father's comparatively unattractive Conroy looks.

Ellen and Seth had very similar dainty faces, although Ellen peered out of their father's eyes and Seth from their mother's. Seth learned the violin with Hermyntrude (the two were noted as music students in the 1911 census), and although Ellen also played, it isn't known what instrument she learned.

After Seth, Erena gave birth to a stillborn child, and Hermyntrude, the baby of the family, followed six years later. Known as Dolly in childhood, she once purchased a copy of her birth certificate with the intention of 'accidentally' ripping it in such a way as to disguise the 'trude' from her name.

Ellen and Jack were passionate about theatre: Jack loved acting, and Ellen enjoyed backstage and costume work, and writing. According to Hermyntrude, both Jack and Ellen attended Cardiff University while they lived in Wales, and Ellen supposedly became a Master of Arts, graduating with honours. The 1930 United States census records that the highest level of education she reached was only 'college', but whatever her education level, she was capable enough to become the teacher at a school in Cardiff.

In 1905, after finishing his studies, Jack left England for South Africa. Around this time, John's unmarried sister Hannah came to live with the family. She had previously lived with John and their brother Luke in Southport before John's marriage to Erena, and then with their youngest sister, Sarah Ann, before her death in 1906. Hannah died of heart failure at the Conroy home in January 1908, and just one month later Ellen's brother Hubert contracted tuberculosis. He died in August.

Around 1913, Ellen obtained a position as headmistress of a private school in London, leading the remainder of the family to move once again. Seth became a librarian, and Hermyntrude studied music. Although Hermyntrude claims that her other siblings 'never got anywhere' with music, she also writes that on Sunday evenings she played ensemble music with John, Ellen and Seth.

Her comment may simply mean that her siblings did not wish to pursue music as a profession like she did, although after spurning his music lessons it would seem that Seth did not enjoy his chosen job as a librarian in the end, either. Before World War I began, he emigrated to South Africa to be with Jack. When war broke out, Ellen and Hermyntrude were the only Conroy children still living with their parents, in a large, grand apartment block in Bessborough Street.

At the onset of the war, Ellen and Hermyntrude learned that their New Zealand cousin Wilfred Campbell Rimmer had enlisted in the army. Wilfred fought as a gunner in Gallipoli, where one of his New Zealand comrades Private George McIntyre was seriously injured in a shell explosion.

After having his arm amputated, George was shipped to England for further treatment aboard the *Glenyorm Castle*, arriving in London in April 1915 with the address for the Conroys, whom he frequently visited and stayed with when he was on leave from the army. The Conroys housed many soldiers during the war, but grew especially close to George and to another man known only as 'the Australian'.

The Conroys travelled to Glasgow in Scotland with George, when he visited family there, and they also holidayed in Seaford with the Australian. Both trips were likely taken in order to get a reprieve from wartime London; however, they were still in (or perhaps had not yet left) London when the munitions factory in Silvertown exploded, evidenced by the pictures in George's wartime photograph albums.

In September 1916, the Conroys received word that Wilfred had been killed in the Battle of the Somme in France. The rough draft of a poem entitled 'To you who have lost', and written around 1918, could have been Ellen's lament for Wilfred.

> Somewhere in France there's a sacred spot
> Tis a grave just newly made
> And its [*sic*] sheltering our boy from perils and ills
> With which life['s] battle is plagued
>
> . . .
>
> I know I know
> The ceaseless ache the emptiness the woe
> The pangs of loss
> The strength that sinks beneath so sore a cros[s]

George eventually proposed to Hermyntrude in the back of a London bus. She was hesitant to move away from England, but agreed to marry him. Ellen also became engaged to the Australian.

George at the time had been appointed a temporary sergeant and was working with the records staff for the army when, about a week before Ellen's wedding, he discovered that the Australian was already married. Ellen broke off the engagement.

Meanwhile, at the end of the war Hermyntrude and George were married in Westminster Chapel and sailed to New Zealand aboard the *Remuera* with hundreds of other soldiers and war brides. John and Erena were already making plans to follow Hermyntrude, so Ellen may have stood on the docks watching her sister leave and knowing she was about to be the only one of her family left in England. But perhaps she had already decided she would not wait to watch her parents leave her, too.

The untitled poem she wrote in Hermyntrude's autograph book before their departure speaks of west, towards America, which may suggest that it was written with her own exit in mind, not theirs, as the *Remuera* would sail east. The poem's two stanzas are composed of iambs and anapests, and the refrain echoes the Victorian novel *Westward Ho!* by Charles Kingsley.

> The Sea has called with its magic lore
> We sing Farewell to our native shore
> and cry 'All hail!' to the unknown West!
> Good luck to our ship! Good luck to our quest
> And its Westward Ho! We'el sail.

Just over a year after Hermyntrude's departure, Ellen sailed aboard the *Mobile*, arriving in New York in August 1920. She secured a job as a lecturer in Manhattan, and within months of her arrival married an Irishman named John McCaffery, the doorman for a dry goods company.

At their wedding Ellen was 35 and John 44, so it's likely they decided that it was too late for them to have children. Nothing else is known of Ellen's husband. He died in 1936 after 15 years of marriage. By the beginning of World War II, Ellen was living alone in an apartment in West End Avenue next to a Russian beautician and his family.

Having always been passionate about writing, she finally gained work as a freelance writer through the war, and continued to write poetry. Her final surviving poem, 'Any boat that would float', takes on a mythical, almost fanciful tone in places — likely due to the fact that, living in America, Ellen would have been exposed to J. B. Priestley's civilian-centred account of the Dunkirk evacuation (popularised in Paul Gallico's *The Snow Goose*), rather than the Churchillian view that the evacuation was a victory for the Royal Navy and that the civilian vessels worked to little or no effect.

That said, Ellen created several beautiful images in the poem, including the depiction of a suddenly passionate priest previously thought cold and emotionless:

> And from the parson there rolled
> Words that made one know
> The quiet of boiling oil
> Yes, from him we had thought so icy cold.

As I pieced together as true an account as I could of Ellen, my great-great-aunt, I sometimes wondered to myself about the point of it all. Did she have children who would be interested in my research? No. Was she a great writer whose poetry might have made the literary world a little richer? Probably not. We will never really know, as so few of her words have survived, but what still exists does not suggest the talent or eloquence of Elizabeth Barrett Browning and the other poets she admired.

Her niece, Hermyntrude's daughter, is now the only living person who remembers her, from the perspective of a little girl reading a lonely old aunt's letters sent from America. At Ellen's death around 1950, her works were lost, and that was that.

She had, however, a tenacity and a potent determination like 'the quiet of boiling oil'. Once her siblings and parents had left her, and once her husband had died, leaving her alone and childless, she was at last able to make a career out of what she had always wanted to do: write. So much was taken away from her in her lifetime, yet in the end she succeeded. I thought to myself, if her poetry does not inspire, then at least her story might, if only someone would tell it for her.

One final note: a clarification, so that I don't become Hermyntrude. The poem 'To you who have lost' was not penned by Ellen. I found the scribbled draft caught up in a bundle of various, mostly unsigned letters I had purchased from an antiques stall at the Omaka Air Show. Upon reading it, I was immediately struck by how the words in this poem almost perfectly mirrored the situation Ellen would have found herself in after the loss of Wilfred during World War I, and the poem itself is unsigned. A lost poem and an all-but-lost woman, perfectly suited, were brought together completely by chance. Attributing authorship of that poem to Ellen for just a moment before confessing seemed like a fitting final gift to her.

Reviews

Brian Turner / Jane Simpson

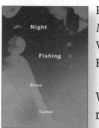

Brian Turner
Night Fishing
Victoria University Press, 2016
RRP $25, 96pp

What does it mean to go night fishing? It's less reckless and youthful than night swimming; not an exuberant skinny dip with limbs moonlit, but rather contemplative and measured. Brian Turner presents a catch of poems about ageing and belonging. Each word in *Night Fishing* is precisely cast — there is no wasted ink. Turner's proverbial turns of phrase are deceptively simple and give no easy answers. Reflective moments are recorded and quietly shaped into something bigger:

> and the will it or won't it sky
> conjures up ordinances that still apply.
> — 'Laws and Lore'

Locality is always important in Turner's work. This collection is less focused on Central Otago than his other work, and explores loneliness when one is far, or feels far, from home. Geography does not give the reader a neat answer for the questions in the poems, but it does offer up space for echoes and rumination.

> At such times it feels like
> every uplift's a blessing,
> inspiriting, as when
> you almost believe
> going somewhere
> gets us somewhere.
> — 'Beyond Dead Horse Pinch and Red Cutting'

Turner is at his best in 'Mountains We Climb'. Melding a sense of place, awe at the unmovable Fiordland landscape and the heartbreak of being a human bound to shuffle towards the grave:

> before dark, on getting to the top,
> being relieved and grateful, almost
> overwhelmed by the view. But then,
> you have to find your way down
> to where you set out from, and start
>
> all over again, and again, and again.

Turner uses simple moments and observations to deliberate on life. Interior worlds are wrapped up in exterior landscapes. His manifesto is to 'enjoy looking and listening / without distraction, and / to try to ensure / that I wasn't missing / realities which really matter'. The physical informs the metaphysical. The wind affects the physical world and can disturb the pond, the cat, and the poplars. But it also brings change, not always positive, taking us away from home:

> He didn't want to be cremated
> in case he was carried away
> on the wind and ended up
> somewhere he didn't belong.
> — 'Inside Outside'

There are no expectations of revelations from nature; 'You know, I never ask / anything of the wind'. However, there is still some comfort and understanding to be gleaned in the environment, which Turner keeps coming back to:

> Maybe knowing's not for
> knowing, and we've
> a fair idea it's an immense

silence we're heading for.
— 'All You Know'

Turner's poetry is not saccharine. It doesn't offer false comfort; instead, it feels like a genuine search for meaning. His poetry is not a panacea for ageing or loneliness, but a friend along for the journey. *Night Fishing* is a reality that matters, and that is enough.

that there is no God; then you can look for
consolation or redemption and rapture elsewhere . . .
in the deckled edges of starlit clouds, say,

or in the sounds of bouncing waters
silvered by moonlight in the valleys,
or in the opening of a door on an old friend
— 'Truths'

Jane Simpson
A World Without Maps
Interactive Press, 2015
RRP $27, 70pp

this adhan, my karakia
from the ends of
the earth
— 'At daybreak'

A World Without Maps explores foreign lands and interior worlds; both places that are hard to navigate. It seems to me that poems are a sort of cartography. Jane Simpson compacts events and emotion into the lines of her poems, denoting something larger and complex, just like lines on a map. Simpson explores cultural divisions and personal borders of memory and time. Each poem is a contour line — showing the terrain of that particular moment in her life. This is a collection for when other means of understanding the world are not adequate, for when:

the lines
run
out
— 'A world without maps'

Simpson is at her best when her memory is focused on the specific detail. A family history is held in the shelves of the pantry: 'pulikachal and tamarind / stain the paper. / Memories, still raw, / sting my nostrils.' Or in 'folded light', where a collection of three-line fragments set in a hospital quietly build to show the horribleness of being incapacitated.

A World Without Maps clearly denotes how estranged the United Arab Emirates is from New Zealand. 'Flood-lit plains' chronicles the rare event of rain in the desert. While rain is not something so rare in Aotearoa, it is still something sacred. I couldn't help but be reminded of Hone Tuwhare's classic 'Rain', when Simpson describes the wait and the desire (with trepidation) for precipitation.

Life in Abu Dhabi's air-conditioned malls is not the only thing picked apart for its strangeness. Closer to home, Simpson inspects the outlandishness of life continuing as normal when one has a fresh grief:

I eat chicken tikka in the food court.
I start to sniff.
They don't know I'm burying my mother tomorrow.

Why do they smile back at me?
Don't they know I'm burying my mother tomorrow?

Why am I so hungry?

I'm burying my mother tomorrow.
— 'Tomorrow'

Perhaps the focus on minutiae makes the collection feel a bit fragmented. But that fragmentation could be a comment on the nature of a world without maps. Borders are 'leaky' and life cannot fully be understood with geography; poetry must intervene. Simpson's work does not exploit cultural and personal divisions for drama or political points. She explores the cracks in her life with a detailed eye; there are meanings and shared borders to be found everywhere.

Mary Cresswell

Jeffrey Paparoa Holman / *Manifesto Aotearoa* / MaryJane Thomson

Jeffrey Paparoa Holman
Blood Ties: New and Selected Poems, 1963–2016
Canterbury University Press, 2017
RRP $25, 168pp

> It was time to go solo: dreaming of being
> Bader's wingman, I walked the curve of the world
> — 'Solo'

This is a book of Bloke: sometimes solo, often in company with the people who matter — teacher, father, family, friends. Many, many poems are dedicated to other blokes: John Ritchie, John Pule, Peter Cooper, Jack Gilbert, Allen Curnow. Others praise airplanes, balsa models and Sunderlands, Tiger Moths. It's *The Boy's Own Paper* looked back on and loved, with the most memorable issues carefully saved over the years and returned to us with feeling. This is also a book of place, richly embedded in the West Coast's land, climate and people.

> I want my bones to lie
> where Mawhera and the sea
> meet under the pounamu eye
> of the tuatara, Poutini —
> resurrect me in the rain.
> — 'Resurrect me in the rain'

The collection is divided into eight sections, although it's not entirely clear which poems were actually written when. (The excellent publication list in the acknowledgements gives us some idea.) The first two sections are boyhood and 'Ancestors', father and son, school days, including not just the poet's own memories but also happily adding his grandmother's memories of doodlebugs to his model plane collection. There are poems in honour of Holman's spiritual forebears. 'Curnow country (1911–2001)' balances vivid images against prophetic couplets:

> Bugger: the old codger can't even mutter
> one last grudging hallelujah to greywacke
> grinding rivers that braid their own tapestry
> restless as the syntax in their coils.
>
> *The voice is wind now: sending back into*
> *the air ninety everlasting-fathomed years.*

The high point of the collection is 'Old King Coal' — poems of the author's namesake hills and the miners who work in them. These are powerful and moving — they read like ballads, the stories of a hard life sung fluently and passionately. 'Inferno (Strongman Mine 1967)' leads off:

> It's not every day you can find a guide
> to show you around a working graveyard.
>
> I didn't see a single soul in torment
> but every creaking roofbeam dripped a cry.

Then there are half a dozen 'Blackball Bridge sonnets' (selected from a book published in 2004), apostrophising the bridge:

> The last time I had my picture taken on your rotten
> deck the gorse flowered over slaps of bitumen
>
> where fat black NZR Bedford bus tyres and
> coal train wheels rumbled come rain or shine.

The traffic on that bridge is the traffic of the world — 'I'm the bridge / to the past and the road still unfolding. / Wheels and water, tracks and steam'.

A previously unpublished poem celebrates the Blackball Miners' Hall as '. . . the First Church of the Socialist Millennium (RIP)', bucketing wonderfully along like a train to the past and to old dreams:

> The First Cinema of the Kiwi Bloke to grace
> the Marxist table — we knew it was time to yell
> 'Look out!' when the music warned Clark Gable.
>
> And the saints on the wall could freeze all
> Hells the Bosses' men had loosed: St Hickey,
> St Webb and St Semple, hung the scabs by a noose. . . .
>
> The First Cathedral of Dancing Proles made
> an ancient miner young — if they had no hair
> in the Brylcreemed air, their toes were inner sprung.
>
> And the saints on the wall would roll their eyes
> and wish for their time again: St Hickey,
> St Webb and St Semple, backs to the wall like men.

'Mine' — on the following page — is a simple, unadorned litany in memory of the men killed in the Pike River Mine in 2010:

> Son, there was a time when you were mine.
> Brother, when the shining day was ours. . . .
>
> And now, the mountain says, 'He's mine.'
> And now, the rivers say, 'He's ours.'

'Check inspector 29' is a bluesy ballad about some of the political venality and indifference that led to, and then followed, the death of 29 Pike River miners — 'No check inspector looking out for you boys out for you'. And 'Child labour' calls out to those who 'lived and died below for steam'.

'Traumata Dreaming' shows boyhood and earthquakes, death and war, where 'Memory is place'. After this, 'In darkest Europe' and 'Other tongues' talk of a search for . . . what? To 'find your own nouns make your own bread sleep with an enemy under the mattress . . .'? 'Dreaming of Te Rauparaha' commemorates the poet's huge awareness of the spirit of the past, bookended in place by the Thistle Inn in Wellington:

> and in that boozy eye I saw the worlds
> come swaying where he was, the days
> go spinning down to earth, where he lay
> beached like a great canoe, a rotting waka

A series of birds blessed by the land comes at the end of the collection: pīwakawaka, toroa, redpoll, the tribe of Bird, crow. All of them are lively and active, engaged in their characteristic behaviours (rather than artistic poses). The fantail is 'feather box of tricks on springs'. And in 'Toroa feeding — Taiaroa Heads':

> . . . Someone cries
> and there they are: artists carving a life
> out of air, albatross, falling
> at speed, at stall, to fill my eye's belly
> and the chicks' maw. Squid purée boils out.

This is a very rich book — in feeling and in history, in place and in passion. The volume is attractively presented, with just the right amount of heft and generous space between the poems. Many of the poems stick in my memory like folksongs, blues and ballad beat. It's an extraordinary picture of one poet's sense of the past and sense of place — a fine book indeed.

Manifesto Aotearoa: 101 Political Poems
Ed. Philip Temple & Emma Neale
Otago University Press, 2017
RRP $35, 192pp

In their call for submissions to this collection, the editors asked for new or recent political poems that 'explore everything from prime ministerial power to the price of milk'. They have gotten this, and then some. This very attractive hardbound collection contains 101 poems (from 98 poets), vividly illustrated by Nigel Brown. Brown gives us the cover plus visual introductions to the four main sections, incorporating quotes from the included poems, and a final warning of a 'Swarm of Poets' illustrating Murray Edmond's finale to the whole book.

The four sections are poems about political actions and decisions which exist already, poems about decisions that need to be made (some in the traditional political sphere but many more addressing long-standing injustices, some in the broad environmental sphere only recently labelled political), and poems about clouds gathering on the horizon.

The first section, 'Politics', begins with David Eggleton's 'The (Andrew) Little things':

> By the right quick march.
> There was the I AM that am, the right abominable Arrrr
> Muldoon, but we saw him off —
> Mister Speaker, Mister Speaker.

In Vivienne Plumb's 'Tornado funnel':

> Smoochy deals and routs are going down
> in every wide-boy wasteland corner,
> kissy-kiss future constructions
> are agreed over a cowboy shake and a wink.

The poems in this section roam through most of the topics that have always been considered to be 'political poetry'. They pick at the parliamentary process in New Zealand; they end with Liang Yujing's 'The Greater Wall' (the firewall imposed by the Chinese government) and with James Norcliffe's knickers-sniffing secret police.

In the second section the book really expands. 'Rights' is a big topic and has not always been automatically considered political — perhaps because it is focused on what's to come rather than looking at what's been done — perhaps just because political poetry has been defined too narrowly. Our most anthologised poem is about a mortgage foreclosure and two failed lives, but I don't think 'The Magpies' is generally cited as being political.

The fight in 'Rights' begins at home, down the mine, with Jeffrey Paparoa Holman's blues ballad, 'Check Inspector 29':

> Bigger and better business rubbed their hands they rubbed their hands
> Sang a new song to the working man the working man
> Take it or leave it was the tune they sang tune they sang

Serie Barford describes the morning after Anzac Day at the supermarket

> where the recession's struck a hunch-backed woman
> in jandals, trackpants and a budget-rack floral parka

selling chokos, 'Papa de los pobres (Potatoes of the poor)'. This is followed by Benita Kape's children digging potatoes for nearly no pay. The poems then move out of the home into a wider space, where different rights are violated. Ruth Hanover is 'Talking about rape':

> when it got back — it was a dormitory —
> I showered
> used disinfectant
> meant
> for the floors

And kani te manukura ('tricks of a treaty') calls down an extended curse on trickery, article by article:

> *article the first*
> one good trick, that one
> played by empire
> on our tīpuna . . .
>
> it's fuck all really
> but let my every word
> be a stone in the mouth of the people
> for those who do not know
> the purposes of a pebble
> at least it will help you shut you up

Aroha Yates-Smith's 'Poems promoting peace' are lyrics for karanga, waiata and haka composed for a documentary — they shout outrage to the ends of the oceans:

> Listen! Take heed!
> You must stop murdering our grandchildren
> and destroying islands
> of the Pacific Ocean.
> Enough is enough! Aue! Aue! Aue hi!

Most of the poems in this section are written by women. Are women more alert to noticing when rights are being withheld or withdrawn? Certainly when people are systematically deprived — of food and housing, of safety, of their place in the world — things get messy in some way or another, and women are generally trusted (graciously permitted, allowed, expected) to clean up messes. Women will always have voices, even when they're not listened to; expanding the topic has allowed more voices here than you get in the over-the-port sniping to which political poetry is often restricted. New Zealand has a wonderful tradition of the latter, but it's not the only way to go, as this anthology reminds us so well.

The 'Environment' section is about death — death of the seasons, of the water, the land, the storylines that used to satisfy us. Bridget Auchmuty's clean-up of plastics and family rubbish moves via the entire globe to bare European trees; Gail Ingram provides a 'Recipe for a unitary state' floating on dairying run-off. Richard Reeve foregoes a frozen Atlantic lobster at 'Frankton Supermarket, Queenstown' long enough to take 'selfies by the ruins'.

This section has a hard time separating from the previous one — perhaps because dealing with 'the environment' is still fairly new as a major topic (as opposed to poems about nature or thoughts of nature) and is often connected with violations of people's rights in some way or another. Carolyn McCurdie's 'Ends' provides some hope in the face of disaster:

> We do this revolutionary thing —
> we tell the truth, we listen. . . .
>
> What d'ya know, you say:
> we are millions.

The last section — 'Conflict' — addresses the permanent anxieties that afflict us today. There is militarism; there are refugees. Louise Wallace tantalisingly waves (the image of) an olive branch before us in her wonderful two-page poem 'The olives'. (There's no way to quote this poem without spoiling it, sorry. But you have the book, right? Turn to page 153.) And in Mercedes Webb-Pullman's 'We're all exiles, Kevin says':

> Early this summer refugees began to appear at our beach. Kevin says you can tell refugees by their birthmarks which are not like ours. They also have six toes.

There is the despair evoked by Victor Billot's 'Dark water':

> There is nothing here for you.
> There is no light above the door that says that home is near.
> You will not cast your arms around your father's neck
> and rest your head in the bedroom's evening quiet.

The world is in turmoil and chaos, and there doesn't seem to be any way out of it. Perhaps we have been through this before . . . and lived to tell the tale . . . maybe? Bernadette Hall ('The heart jumps up in fear to see the mouths') sees an angel:

> . . . The curve of her back
> is like the sweet curve of a hill, a hill with water running steady . . .

> She will do something. And we will be left to pray,
> just as we prayed for the horses at Borodino.

This is an anthology you can sit down and read for the story — not just dip into for reference. It extends (permanently, I hope) the scope of political poetry in Aotearoa to take in topics that affect us now and will keep on affecting us into the future. Well done, everybody, and thank you for such a splendid collection.

MaryJane Thomson
Songs of the City
HeadworX, 2016
RRP $30, 86pp

This book, Thomson's third poetry collection, reads as though narrated by a ghost poet making a pilgrimage through a city. The book's four sections lead us from a tentative opening to an outraged tirade (which isn't pinned down with any sense of place — just 'City, Presumed American'). Likewise, there is little sense of a personality in the ghost (that is, no trackable point of view).

The first section, 'Finding your light', leans toward gnomic one-liners. Most of these are given a retro feeling with a capital letter beginning each line, and punctuation (usually a comma) ending each line:

> Our favourite things are not always,
>   The things that bring us peace,
>
> Stuck in perpetual thrill,
>
> We think our favourite thing is to go out always,
>
> When one day you realize that you are not a teenager, . . .
> — 'Our favourite things'

This section features the poet on her own, looking at the world around her:

> A generation in addiction,
>
> A product of its time,
>
> Narcissists breeding narcissists,
>
> Social media putting people on pedestals, . . .
> — 'If modern day'

She sees the groups that surround her and stands staunchly in isolation, observing them but not joining them. In 'Watch', the second section, she remarks on the dogmas that hold people together, the knowledge of love and loss, and moves toward wanting to be part of the whole, while still remaining invisible:

Whether I will ever belong I will
  Never know,
Perhaps when I meet them I can read to
  Them my words.
  — 'The greatest love in time'

Some of the advice is misguided. 'No more exploitation' uses lines like
'Your jungle be fine, / He toucheth your head, / Restoreth you, . . .' and
reads like a parody (we hope) of minstrel-show dialogue. If it is intended
to be ironic, this hasn't been made clear — but it should have been,
given the vagueness of the ghost/narrator. As it stands now, it reads like
part of the poet's own message.

In the third section, the poems are definitely on the move. The
word 'walk' — which didn't appear at all in the first two sections — is
suddenly all over the place and stays through the rest of the book.

He walks in the light but he knows it's night, . . .
— 'Dues'

Now I walk on, no longer
  Staring at the ground, . . .
  — 'Funny sun kissed fantasy'

The narrator/poet is trying to join the human race, or at least acquire
additional dimension. The one-line format has long since given way to a
longer format, reflecting larger and less manageable difficulties.

That is all, I am coming and
  Going with you or without you.

Travelling with my ghosts
  Because they know if I walk
  Alone, I will be lost, . . .
  — 'This way'

This section tracks the various heights and depths of love, found and lost, but seems to affirm the poet's acceptance of a second dimension (that is, other people):

> Ah that is why, I live today, to learn,
>   Not just of myself, but others.
>
> For no one ever walked the earth completely
>   Alone.
> — 'All day air'

But at the end, the city swallows the narrator:

> I hear the barbarian,
> It's me. They think, I think,
>   It's them. . . .
>
> Last week I was rock
>   Solid,
> Yesterday I was a victim,
> Today I'm an addict.
> — 'The barbarian'

There is sound and music, and the ghost welcomes the voices that begin to come out of the surrounding crowd. Every so often (such as in 'A scary race') the phrasing echoes San Francisco in the 1950s, but this is just a ghost of the Beats. These poems here — particularly as the political scene gets called upon more and more — are calls of distress, not shouts of rage. They are a solo voice, not the voice of a generation.

> I have no right to validate someone
>   Else's suffering,
> But hate is pervasive,
> It spreads,

People are influences, jumping on
  The bandwagon,
Who can be louder,
  Redder, whiter, blacker?
Everyone proclaiming their
  Moral superiority.
— 'Where are you Martin?'

The sentiments expressed in the book are varied and occasionally confusing. To me, this is a result of the narrator/poet being a one-dimensional voice in an artificial and thin setting: given the structure of the book, I expected a singular voice with identifiable variations. On the other hand, the varied thematic links make it clear that the one ghost/narrator is dealing with a wide range of expressions and emotions. The topics provide the depth. It's interesting to speculate what the same wandering ghost could do with a bricks-and-mortar town (1-D in a 3-D constraint).

Hamish Dewe

Charles Olsen / *Zero Distance*

Charles Olsen
Antípodas: Edición bilingüe
Huerga & Fierro Editores, 2016
RRP £14.90, 94pp

Charles Olsen's collection *Antípodas* is a bilingual edition of Spanish originals with English translations by the author. The collection is fairly slight, containing around 30 poems, most of which are a single page. Authorship of the pieces is split fairly equally between two pen names: Gastón de Maetzu and Constance of Nelson. It's tempting to take these as being two distinct personae, or heteronyms, to put a slightly Iberian slant on it. However, there's really not much stylistically to differentiate between them. In each, there's a tendency to a crystalline timelessness of observation. Verbs disappear in favour of nouns and adjectives. At times, these images are mysteriously affecting:

> Sip of moon, sweet sorrow.
> Empty glass.
> Through the window the chirrup of crickets.
> — 'The Trumpet'

This approach is slightly more pronounced in the pieces attributed to Gastón de Maetzu, perhaps due to compositional constraints. Gastón's poems are generated through the *Palabras Prestadas* poetry game, in which the poet is assigned a group of words that must be worked into the poem. It's difficult to appreciate the poems collected here for their inventiveness in working through the constraints, as we're never told what the words were, so we must approach the poems through their own internal logic. Consider 'Farmer's Dream,' which is held up as an example and quoted in full on the back cover:

Fine needles of water weave a cloud to a thatch roof,
aspen leaves converse in the wind

and in the stable a black horse shakes its mane

— flow of shadows —.

In the dark of its eye dances an angel.

The first line forms around a dreamlike logical grouping of 'needles',
'weave' and 'thatch', but this is not continued. The enigmatic grouping
of images never quite coalesces into a coherent whole, despite 'flow' a
couple of lines later harking back to the 'water' and 'cloud' of the first. It
would perhaps be churlish to question why there must suddenly appear
an angel in the horse's dark eye.

Constance of Nelson relies more on the conventional lyric self, yet
even then the imagistic treatment running through the poems points
up the lack of narrative depth. There's a wealth of decorative elements
crowding around a hollowed out narrative shell.

I exhale mist,
fillets of mud stuck to my soles,
rustic statue amid a cowbell prelude.

A sheep raises its gaze,
sniffs the air and returns to graze.
Fine rain.

A supermarket bag
stuck in the wire between tufts of wool.

As hermits, solitary trees
endure an ancient wind.

The horizon embraces us.
Empty, the plastic whispers.
Years ago I suffered a crisis.

It awakened something in me.

What unknown something it awakened in Constance of Nelson's woolly mind is left to the imagination. The isolated images are joined solely by belonging to the same speaker. It's worth noting that the clumsy rhyme of 'gaze/graze' doesn't appear in the Spanish original ('*Levanta su mirada un borrego, / heel el aire y vuelve a pastar.*') Constance's 'fine rain' harks back much too strongly to Gaston's 'fine needles of water' to maintain belief in the two separate personae. Poems from both just seem so unmotivated, their imagery so precious and lacking in the heat of companionship or exhortation. Occasional wonderful descriptions break through, though:

> The old man, rocky bags beneath his eyes, held the letter
> as though it were a sea urchin.
> — 'Correspondence'

Zero Distance: New Poetry from China
Ed. & trans. Liang Yujing
Tinfish Press, 2017
RRP US$25, 130pp

In this collection, published in Hawai'i, Liang Yujing focuses on the work of writers born in the eighties and after, although there are a couple of inclusions from older generations. Many readers will be familiar with some of the Misty poets. These poems are nothing like those. For the most part, these poems lack such allusiveness, flexibility and layering, preferring to retreat into the observing eye and ego. Given the range of poets included, there's a surprising consistency of tone and approach, which seems wilfully flat, with only occasional metaphorical flourishes.

Before looping back to the impossible task of the translator, let's touch on the recurring themes of these poems. Despite the variety of topics and writers, these three themes keep coming back, and often in the same form: sex and death and the mundane. Consistently, sex is presented wholly without eroticism, although occasionally with some tenderness, and death appears without pathos or fear.

> The coffin stays in the central room,
> as we come and go.
> My grandma will dwell in it
> after her death.
>
> . . .
>
> My grandma, now eighty,
> has lived a long time.
> — Ai Hao, 'Coffin'
>
> Not unexpectedly,
> under the sun,
> he asked her to give a blowjob.
> Back against the poplar tree,
> he erected
> like the old tree's grandson.
> The sun shone on her back.
> — Song You, 'Late-Summer Sandals'
>
> Lying in a crystal coffin,
> I await the flames kissing me all over my body
> and a shovel of scalding ash.
>
> . . .

I see the men who once fucked me,
loving me or not,
bear expressions mystical and complex,
while I can't show my love in bed anymore.
— Ya Zi, 'Writing a Poem Imagining My Death'

Such documentary flatness of tone runs through the bulk of the poems collected here. There are a few examples where indignation takes over, as in Jiang Tao's sole inclusion, 'Outside the City':

Under the westering sun,
the city wall turns into a money stack.
. . .
On both sides there stand tall moneys.
Monies sit in them.
Money looks at money.
Money and money sit side by side.
Money and money have a meeting.
They go to a money to eat money.
They go to a money to sleep.
Money makes love with money.
Deep is the night.
People are outside the city, unable to enter.

The obsessively ranting form helps to intensify Jiang Tao's disgust with how an extreme concentration of wealth supports itself in circularity and insularity while excluding all others. The formal repetition of the poem relates to a topic the translator specifically calls out in the introduction: 'In Chinese repetition generates poetry, while in English I have to replace the repeated phrases with other expressions.' This seems to be reaching for a distinction that doesn't quite hold. True, conversational style in English would usually discourage exact repetitions of phrase, but repetition is an established rhetorical device in both oratory and literature. Liang Yujing goes to unwarranted lengths to avoid repetitions which inform the structure of several poems. Despite the overwhelmingly conversational tone of most of the poems, there are still several which either fully adhere to the imagistic approach of Western preconception or include juxtaposition that stands in for metaphor.

> They suddenly take off,
> the sound of satin being ripped.
> — Tu Ya, 'Crows in Bangkok'

> Through the corner of my window
> I dart a glance
> at the lights
> of this city,
> gold coins
> scattered from
> a shipwreck
> deep
> under the sea.
> — Li Yi, 'Cold Moon'

Li Yi's poem, in particular, displays all the traditional strengths of Chinese poetry while adapting its concision and visual focus to modern phrasing and layout.

Often, when reading through a set of contemporary translations from another tradition, we expect to see a canon in the making: who is important, what the defining characteristic is. This collection has no interest in the canon, and no one included is given enough space to really give a representative account of the breadth of their work. What we have, instead, is a group of poems that speak to a single reader's preferences.

Lauris Edmond / Sue Wootton

Night Burns with a White Fire: The Essential Lauris Edmond
Ed. Frances Edmond & Sue Fitchett
Steele Roberts, 2017
RRP $34.99, 180pp

Lauris Edmond's daughter Frances and poet Sue Fitchett compiled this new collection of poetry and prose by inviting submissions from Edmond's friends and colleagues. The pieces sought by the editors were favourites, *essential* to those who chose them.

Night Burns with a White Fire is attractive, orderly and generous. Sections — between a foreword and afterword by Edmond herself — are divided thematically (motherhood, love and marriage, place, etc.). Each is headed with a quotation from a well-known text and illustrated with a representative photograph.

Fittingly, the book was named by Bob Orr, the most recent winner of the Lauris Edmond Memorial Award for Poetry. The eponymous poem, in which the poet's late daughter appears to her, pale and smiling, is first. 'Wellington Letter XVIII', the last poem of the 18-poem sequence originally dedicated to that same daughter, Rachel, completes the collection.

The poetry and prose pieces speak to one another in this collection. For example, an excerpt from a letter to friend and fellow-poet Riemke Ensing, describing Hone Tuwhare's 'great warm presence', sits next to a poem written for Tuwhare, its last stanza paying homage to that same attribute:

> Yes, you're yourself all the way through,
> the breathing radiator I've often stood near
> in a spell of hard weather of the heart,
> warmed by some great buzz

of laughter and love at the centre.
— 'Sober truth'

This is most definitely a collection that feels personal. It gives an insight into the friendships and affiliations that meant a lot to Edmond. Reading the autobiographical works, of course, can tell us a lot about her family, her literary and friendship circles, but this apposite collation of poems and letters, together with notes from interviews and selections from the trio of autobiographies, casts new light on the material, and on Edmond and her people.

With regard to the work itself, this collection reminds us that Edmond was one of the champions of the domestic poem. She, like other women writers of the period — Elizabeth Smither, Fiona Kidman — brought the poem of mother and child, the poem of married life and the family, into anthologies and newspapers. She gave seriousness to poems about what women did and thought and won accolades for doing so, much to the chagrin of some less progressive male poets of the time.

Evident also in this collection is the fact that Edmond was a keen observer of place and time, of the moment that things happened, and so many of the selections in this book highlight her ability to inhabit environments emotionally, as well as through the senses. She always appeared to find nature a thing of triumph — often, a force in counterpoint to man's carelessness, as in 'Being there', a poem in which she spends five stanzas describing the illicit blossomings and unfurlings of the natural world in diction which is vivid, colourful and lively. These things happen mysteriously, almost imperceptibly, she tells the reader:

> you never see it, you wake up to find
> mushrooms in the autumn paddock,
> a fully expanded pink impatiens cluster
> where last night one flower
> bloomed in the dusk,

The poem ends with two lines that starkly reflect on the hardiness of 'the shimmering floor of the world'. The lines shock with their violence, their plosive sounds so opposite to those hitherto employed to explicate the quiet and hardy beauties of nature: 'Bars, locks, fists of blood, bombs falling / couldn't stop it happening.' Edmond sees nature as the quiet survivor of the chaos wrought by man.

This is the Lauris Edmond who also wrote 'Nuclear Bomb Test, Mururoa Atoll' (not included in this collection), which empathises with the sea, the sand, 'a young fish made ill by the predator poison / coursing towards me across the ocean / that was my friend' — *A Matter of Timing* (Auckland University Press, 1996).

Edmond cared for the environment, and her poetry showed both respect for it and dismay at man's poor handling of it.

Finally, as we can see in the last two sections of this collection, Edmond was happy to explore her thoughts regarding her own leave-taking from a life about which she was passionate, but which she also found mysterious and difficult. Alison Parr's choice, and a poem popular with many readers, 'Take One', is a fine example of a poem that expresses Edmond's position:

Take One
Tonight I walked on the wood-smelling verandah;
in the treetops the starlings were slowing
their shrillness to an inconsequential whisper,

the geraniums giving out their sweet herbal smell
even after sundown in the late summer air;
boatmen were beetling over the bay, centipedes

out on some energetic inscrutable mission — and
I thought, this is my time. I don't have it
for long, and the way here was never easy;

sorrow sat often like a beggar under a bridge
darkening its passages and corners, and some days
it moves so fast, this time of mine, I can't catch it;

but whatever it does, while I'm here nobody else
can have it. They wouldn't feel its kick,
nor understand the gleam in its eyes — and I do.

The last stanza of the poem not only speaks of a woman who knows who she is and that her life is now her own, but also of a singular artistic vision. It is unsurprising that this was a common choice for many of those asked to submit a favourite Lauris Edmond poem, because it speaks to the joys and sadnesses of life, and to the fleetingness of it.

Edmond was a writer who could tell you how to mourn a loss and how to get on and seize the day afterwards. She was a poet of life inside the home, but also someone who valued the environment, and who wrote about its endurance despite the carelessness of mankind. In her later poems, she gave wonderful testimony for the joys and sorrows of ageing. *Night Burns with a White Fire* brings those elements together, linking them with new perceptiveness, and presents the reader with a personal, eclectic book that reflects what others see as the quintessential collection of Edmond's work.

Sue Wootton
The Yield
Otago University Press, 2017
RRP $25, 84pp

Sue Wootton is an excellent poet. I've never met her. We're not Facebook friends. But I buy everything she publishes, because I know that I'll get my money's worth in enjoyment and inspiration. This sixth book of poetry is no exception. I first saw one of its poems in a recent *Landfall* —

'Abandoned stable, Matakana' — and loved it for its storytelling, its imagery, its sounds and rhythms. It starts with the speaker coming upon the stable and being thrust into memory by the smell of hay.

. . . I remember

Misted morning rides on horse-wide tracks
on board the felted ribcage of a breathing beast.
Seed heads swashed our knees. We parted leaves.
The passing world itched flesh to snort and snicker.
Ears flick-flicked and swivelled: nets set to catch
the pitch of tremors set off by a distant barking dog.
The bite, the bit, the spit, the froth, the foam.
The lips that curled back rubbery to show
the sea-slug tongue, the yellow chomping bones.

The alliteration and assonance add to a rhythm that is so buoyant and forward-moving that you can feel yourself galloping along beside the speaker on her horse. Doing double-duty, monosyllabic nouns produce vivid and exact images while they sound like hooves pounding: *The bite, the bit, the spit, the froth, the foam.* This is exhilarating. Particularly for someone who has been a rider, this poem is sheer nostalgic delight.

Wait, though. The twist is brilliant. We are brought back to the Matakana stable and the present:

Empty stable. Derelict. But clop-clop-clops a broken board
and nickers tin   and hay-whiff hits
and ancestry kicks into stirrup and I (who never rode) remember —
goes giddy-up my blood, my blood, my blood.

The horsey noises are just the clatter of the stable doors, a bit of roof lifting. The recollection is not of the speaker's own experience, but one of genetic memory. The communication of the trick of consciousness is successfully carried off because the writing is so good.

While 'Abandoned stable, Matakana' is immediately recognisable to me as a 'Sue Wootton poem', alive in its wildness and energetic engagement with nature, the first half of *The Yield* makes it feel different to the previous five collections, in that a tone of disappointment or cynicism runs through many of its poems. There is a prose-poem called 'Picnic', which contrasts the should-have-been and the really-was of a family outing. A piece in ironic couplets, 'Crime seen', describes a marriage that has gone bad as if it were a body to be identified: 'Yes it's a tad misshapen. Yes it does look starved. / They ahem. They aha. They point to where it snapped'. A few pages later, a sonnet on 'Forgiveness' suggests that such an emotion is far out of reach for a woman scorned — it still seems '[s]uch a pretty word, for such a bitch'.

In this first part of *The Yield*, relationships are dead things, but haunting. One even has its own 'Epitaph':

> The ghost of you shall set
> like rimes of frost inside my chest
> and never melt, nor quit
> me quite, nor give me rest. It's
> not easy to recall us at our best.

As the collection progresses, though, the poems start to embrace the risk of love once more. 'Graveyard Poem' confronts the speaker and her companion with their mortality, and so the need to take advantage of bodies and passions despite the associated emotional perils. As the poem develops, so the 'I' and 'you' become 'we', exercised by the metaphysical, stirred by the words on the gravestones and the autumn leaves' imperatives:

> and the green words chant on the tombstones
> dearly beloved, deeply cherished,
>
> and the angels dip their wingtips to our occasionally touching palms
> and the leaves rustle underfoot: risk it, risk it.

Once the collection has passed the midway point, even in a poem like 'Black Lake', which features a grisly setting that is in itself a character, Wootton continues to allow selected humans to demonstrate survival even though those unlucky birds, fish and eels that linger about the lake are described as mute, invisible and blind:

> . . . Whoever walks at Black Lake
>
> walks in peril. Who comes back, comes back broken,
> comes back stronger, glued, resized.

Wootton is making a case for those who will go into the darkness and return, damaged but somehow hardier because of their experience. This latter part of the book is focused on the phoenix-figure, ready to rise.

In an elegy, 'Daffodils', the speaker recalls her dying friend's exhortation, '*Don't wait*'. In the poem's final lines, she expresses thanks for the words that catalysed her assertive action:

> This was thirteen sweeps of the sun ago. Hillary,
> I have never forgotten. When the true daffodils
> re-emerge this season (I believe I hear them rising)
>
> I will bend to the soil in gratitude. Your legacy,
> your bequest. Yes, Hillary — I did. I grabbed my life.

The poem is structured beautifully, working up to that ending featuring the 'true daffodils' and the speaker 'bend[ing] to the soil' from 10 previous stanzas that prefigured the delicate finale.

First came the bucket of daffodils that occasioned the thought of Hillary. Next came Hillary herself, remembered slow and ill with cancer, 'propped by all those cushions', and the speaker visiting her, bustling awkwardly, 'flinging words at [her], plumping // the pillows', thinking of the 'callous' spring, the bulbs beneath the earth, 'putting on a spurt' as her friend was dying. At last, we are back with the 'thrawn supermarket buds' and their reminder, not only of Hillary's words, '*Don't wait*' — for to wait would be to end up like these wrong, unnatural things — but also of Hillary herself, whose life was extinguished as the speaker's started again.

The Yield is testimony to Wootton's ability to make wonderful shapes in her work on a small and large scale. Every poem is carefully crafted so that its images, its sounds, its beginning and ending are satisfying. Moreover, the book as a whole appears to be structured on the ascendant. It works its way from a giving in (yielding) to loss, to an enjoyment of what is left, and what is produced as a result of the process of reinvention (the yield).

The book leaves the reader with a poem about a plant making its own way towards the light, turning out not quite as expected, but shaped just as it should be in its current environment. It was not supposed to live; it was replanted, then forgotten. Yet 'It's come out in a commitment to / the quest for light, and this has shaped it, fired / it upwards' ('The yield').

This is the sort of poem I was used to in Wootton's first two books of poetry, by which I am enchanted — the poem of successful withstanding. It is a very apt poem on which to end a collection that has much to say on the subject of getting 'home by riding [one's] own pliant power'.

Owen Bullock

Owen Bullock
River's Edge
Recent Work Press, 2016
RRP AU$12.95 / $17.95 (international), 88pp

Owen Bullock's fourth collection of haiku features around 70 poems which confirm his standing as one of the country's leading practitioners of the form — many of these verses having received numerous commendations and publications in respected journals and competitions internationally. It would be hard to dispute Bullock's experience and skill with haiku, and this review certainly won't: it's a solid collection.

While there's no principle given for the arrangement of the poems, the foreword does signal that it will begin with material gathered from a recent period the author spent caregiving for the elderly. Opening the frame with these images of old age is an interesting choice on two counts. Firstly, it infuses the book with a sense of nostalgia ('his voice younger / as he talks about / his wife'). But more chiefly, it creates a sense of existential confinement; placing the reader alongside the elderly and infirm is a clever way to open up the book's necessary preoccupation with small worlds and its obsession with details ('dusting / her little vases / this is my devotion', or 'on the piano / photos of the ones / who don't visit'). Given we're dealing in haiku, this is pretty serendipitous in terms of setting out an approach to reading into small images and details.

As a result, framing the collection from the view of the elderly makes the rest of the collection feel like a life flashing before one's eyes — a highlight reel of the everyday, moving backward from the present. This modus operandi seems to be confirmed when the titular poem arrives halfway through the collection: 'getting younger / each day that passes / river's edge'. Reversing — or at least unravelling — the typical birth-to-death chronology is a format that works very well, and — if I may be so poetic — each haiku/flashback glimmers like a speckle of light on a river of memory.

My minor complaint is that a couple of the poems seem rather hyperbolic in their attempt to contribute to the initial framing. Does an elderly man walking to his chair really take 'more courage than any Olympian'? Maybe I'm being pernickety in saying I think the Olympics is more a benchmark for tenacity than courage, but surely Bullock is aware that readers want to be the ones to imbue images or situations with value? Telling me what to think is spoiling the fun. Or, again: 'a scrap of paper / with the word "love" on it / down the garbage disposal'. Hyperbole? Melodrama? Even if this is naked reportage, the image seems too trite to have made the cut in such a superb collection.

Otherwise, I found it hard to choose a haiku to include as a sample in the review, because they're all very good. In the end, though, my personal favourite is a simple reflection on the comfort of the familiar: 'shopping for clothes / wanting to buy / what I'm wearing'.

As far as New Zealand haiku goes, Owen Bullock is the devil we know, and this new collection is as good as any. Highly recommended.

Johanna Emeney / Elizabeth Morton

Johanna Emeney
Family History
Hoopla series, Mākaro Press, 2017
RRP $25, 74pp

Today I learned that heartstrings
are called *chordae tendineae*.
I touched them.
In fact, I got to cut them
in half.
— 'Lines overheard at the teaching hospital'

Among the many posts Johanna Emeney shares on her Facebook page, such as those celebrating the achievements of other writers and the numerous images of cats and goats doing cute things, she also shares links to carefully crafted articles about two subjects, dear to her heart, that are the focus of her second collection of poems, *Family History*: dying with dignity, and grieving for a loved one.

One link she shared recently was to a powerful extract from the posthumously published memoir of Australian writer Cory Taylor, who died of cancer in 2016. In her memoir, Taylor wrote candidly about dying, shattering a ridiculous social taboo in the process. 'There is nothing good about dying,' she declared emphatically. She also admitted that she was scared of death, 'but not all the time', that she had thought at length about ending her life on her own terms, and that her greatest fear was of dying badly by having her life prolonged unnecessarily.

Family History similarly tackles the subject of dying and death head-on. The collection was the creative component of Johanna Emeney's PhD through Massey University, and sat alongside a thesis that examined examples of autobiographical medical poetry written from the points of view of all the parties involved: doctors, patients, carers and families.

The story at the centre of the book recounts Emeney's experience of working through the diagnosis and preliminary treatment of her mother's breast cancer before Maureen Emeney's life was tragically cut short by a car accident that left her family reeling. This collection of poems will undoubtedly tug at your heartstrings and have you reaching for the tissues, but the real work of the book happens in the dry-eyed period post-cry, when your mind is clear to reflect on the wider implications of what Emeney has presented here.

On the other side of a traumatic personal experience of such magnitude, how does a writer process what she has been through?

Johanna Emeney answers that question with a collection of poems full of tenderness, compassion, outrage and grief, along with gorgeous touches of irony and humour — the cumulative effect of which brings Maureen Emeney to life on the page, as well as her family and the medical staff involved in her care.

The real triumph of this collection is the way that Emeney offsets her critique of the insensitive face of the medical profession in several delightfully acerbic poems, like the aptly titled 'How you guess she doesn't have the best breast surgeon', with the much larger humanising agenda of her collection, which is demonstrated through the accumulation of unforgettable concrete details.

There's the image of a daughter carrying the ludicrous gift of a massive stuffed gorilla to her mother's hospital room in the poem 'On my shoulders', and of her mother feigning joy over the gift, but not convincingly. There's the lovely detail of the 'kind shoes' worn by the under-sung heroes of the hospital system in the poem 'Night nurses'. There's the image of the overdressed hospital bed in the poem 'Sick room', and the analogy drawn between this and the many cat-savaged waxeyes the poet placed in warm shoeboxes as a child, all dead by morning, 'shocked by a surfeit of comfort'. There's a recollection of a private joke shared between mother and daughter — a silly piece of wordplay substituting 'handbag' for 'hambag', and there's a powerful moment of recognition in the poem 'Shared lines', in which a young student sees that her teacher has been tripped up by grief while reading aloud John Donne's poem 'The Dream' to the class:

> The line's dumb slack
> is taken up
> by a girl at the back.
>
> Last year,
> her dad died.
> She knows the sudden
> need to cry.
>
> Kindly, she
> hides me
> under two dropped iambs.

Johanna Emeney's acute observations of people, settings, incidents, exchanges and actions moves the collection beyond one writer's account of her experience of losing her mother to a more wide-reaching analysis of the knowledge and comfort that can be derived by going deep inside the experience of loss, turning it over, examining it from multiple perspectives and putting it on the page.

Emeney's collection is divided into four parts. The first part, 'Captions', strategically sets up the concepts that underpin the three remaining sections, chronicling the cancer diagnosis, treatment regimen and the aftermath of her mother's death. The secrets, absences and erasures within a family's history are candidly revealed in the first eight poems of the collection, but, even more importantly, the idea of preservation, or rather the futility of the attempt to preserve anything, is revealed to the reader in several important poems. There's the doom-laden description of a photograph of the poet's mother as a young woman holding aloft two lettuces, still learning the business of 'how to harvest them while young, before first rot sets in'. In the poem 'Cool Storage', Emeney's parents congratulate themselves on introducing a refrigeration unit into their fruit and vege business to ensure that 'now nothing would expire before its time', and in the final poem of the section, the account of a letter received by the grieving daughter seeking permission to house an anonymous sample of her mother's tumour, preserved for posterity, in the national tumour bank.

An odd design feature favoured by the publisher Mākaro Press is the inclusion of a coloured circle on the covers of the books in their Hoopla series, containing a single redolent word that is meant to offer readers an entry point into the collection. 'Medical' is the word chosen for Johanna Emeney's book, but the choice of word is far too cold and clinical for a book that is anything but. I think that 'preservation' would have been a better choice of word, because it is the idea set to simmer by the poet in the first section, and it is the idea that remained with this reader until I arrived at the final poem in the collection, 'Glass bowl with pink swirls'.

Dame Chris Cole Catley (1922–2011), who published Emeney's first collection of poems, *Apple & Tree*, the year she died, has a special place in *Family History*. An observation of a glass bowl (an ornament of Catley's) reminds the poet of the old woman's 'last, small desires — / to dabble a hand in soapy water, / playing the boundary notes of here / and not here'. The keepsake is not really the glass bowl, but the memory the object triggers of Catley's dignified death, now preserved in Johanna Emeney's mind. The account of this gentle exit from life was the kind of death that Maureen Emeney was denied when a car accident ended her life prematurely. Closing with this poem leaves readers with the comforting idea that Chris Cole Catley had time to prepare for the 'not here', and so, too, did her loved ones. This is the salve that the poet needs to recover from the trauma of her mother's untimely passing. It is a tender note to end on.

Family History is a beautiful book, and it is also a book that matters. By that I mean that Johanna Emeney has something important to share with her readers about a subject that all of us will face at one time or another and in one way or another. In the same way that Tracey Slaughter's short stories shine a light on the darker corners of New Zealand society that we urgently need to see, Johanna Emeney guides us through the light and dark of illness and death with grace, good humour, kind shoes and a generously sized heart.

Elizabeth Morton
Wolf
Hoopla series, Mākaro Press, 2017
RRP $25, 90pp

I was admiring Elizabeth Morton's pottery collection recently, each piece neatly arranged on a floor-to-ceiling shelving unit dividing the entranceway from the living room of her home. What I noticed about her taste in pots was her preference for glazes of all kinds. The modestly sized vessels, both wheel-thrown and hand-built, that adorn the shelves showcase a compendium of glazes: crackle, salt and soda, anagama and wood-fired shino — resulting in the gloopy, lumpy, speckled, scarred and scorched array of pots. Prized among them is a small avian bowl by Len Castle, with that glorious alkaline blue glaze that he alone could achieve with such mastery.

I thought about Morton's collection of pots as I read her debut collection of poetry, *Wolf*, marvelling at the way she creates glazes with words that drip and congeal over the spare life-built structures beneath. Meditations on childhood, family, love, loss, solitude and language are glazed in the most spectacular way.

My favourite poem in the collection is 'Eden'. Like the perfect garden of paradise (or the perfect blue glaze, for that matter), the poem achieves just the right balance of the autobiographical, confessional and sensory. In it, the poet looks back on the break-up of her parents' marriage from her perspective as a child. She identifies the cracks that should have revealed to her that the end was coming, trying to recover the moment when her mother went from 'humming / love songs / by the faucet', to chopping onions 'with unnecessary force', and when her father went from 'snoozing / beneath the sycamores' to sitting 'like a fist / under the sycamores'. But then, in a powerful twist, we learn that none of those details is what she actually remembers. Instead, her most vivid memory is of eating over-ripe blackberries:

> she remembers the year
> blackberries burst
> like bloodclots
>
> on her tongue and how
> she tried to rinse away
> the dreadful taste
>
> but couldn't.
> not ever, again.

You'd be hard-pressed to find a better image expressing the dissolution of a marriage and the end of a stable family life than blackberries bursting like bloodclots in the mouth. The moments of intense insight in Morton's collection like this, and there are many, left me in no doubt that this book is not an emerging writer's timid first foray into the world of letters, but rather a collection that reveals that Morton already has an impressive array of techniques under her belt and a long career ahead of her.

Wolf's 60 poems hurtle you into the guts of life. Reading the book is an entirely sensory experience, and you quickly realise that you need to give yourself over to the myriad sensations between its two covers: the grit and the spit, the licking, peeling, splitting, weeping and bruising. In fact, you need to become the mangy, shambling critter wandering through the haunting sequence of six 'Wolf' poems at the start of the collection, 'hide all a-scab with / the nippings of fleas. / skull abuzz with the / echoes of home'. You need to let taste, touch and smell become your dominant senses, imbibing 'the stink of black rubber swingsets', 'the smell of cancer on your cardigan', of 'pollution in her porridge', of menthol in a girl's ponytail, of 'a mouthful of nettle', or of a 'straw hat stinking / of snapper and salt'. Hunker down low to the asphalt, breathe deeply, and you'll be prepared for a poem like 'Boy':

> . . . i can smell
>
> you from the far end
>
> of the parking lot.
>
> i can taste you in
>
> the wet end of my
>
> cigarette. everything
>
> smacks of adolescent boy.

So many sensations like this stick with you long after reading. In the second stanza of the poem '17', the poet's evocation of teenage-hood took me right back to the eighties in Napier: 'we were seventeen, / and the shadows of ourselves were / fraying at the hem'. In 'Night on the ward' there's the sound of 'the night-time snails' that 'crack under your slippers' during a covert stroll around the hospital grounds, and in the lonely scene of a shack in the middle of a paddock in the poem 'Bucolic' there's a woman watching *Country Calendar* as she 'whittles fruit into quadrupeds'.

We've become accustomed to poetry collections arranged in four parts, but *Wolf* departs from the convention. The 60 poems are not separated into sections, which does require more concentration on the reader's part, but there are connections across many of the poems to guide your reading, as Morton pointed out in an interview published in the last issue of *Poetry New Zealand* in which she was the featured poet. 'I find myself exploring recurring tropes,' she replied to a question from editor Jack Ross about her then forthcoming book. 'You can hear the echo of one poem in the next. I don't reckon this is a bad thing, though. It provides the reader a tug line, or so I hope.'

The tug line technique plays out very effectively across the poems dealing with childhood, but even more so in the poems dealing with another trope that figures again and again: language itself — what it can do and the challenge for the writer to harness those words, to wrest meaning from them, all the while struggling with the frustrating inadequacy of words to express the thing one wants to say.

In the early poems in the collection, finding a foothold in language is the key. In 'Wolf finds love', 'the illiterate loneliness / of childhood wanes' when he encounters his mate, but the challenge of sustaining this shared literacy is beautifully described in a later poem, 'The park': 'my words gelatinise where they meet / your heat, sentences gunked in the hollows / of my throat.' A few pages on we find a tug line in the poem 'Caucasian female', but this time her words fly free: 'my tongue is the diaspora of syllables / bled into the sky. i do not hold / my tongue in the form of a fullstop.' Many such tug lines travel through the book, and each of them repays the effort of tracking them, revealing in the process that *Wolf* can be read in many different ways.

There is no denying that *Wolf* is a challenging and unsettling collection, but I liked the sensation of having to nose my way through some pretty dark territory, even feeling a bit squeamish at times, only to arrive at the final poem — a 17-syllable senryū describing a pubic hair left stuck to a piece of soap by a departed lover. What a fantastically gross note to end on.

Ian Wedde / David Howard

Ian Wedde
Selected Poems
Auckland University Press, 2017
RRP $39.99, 340pp

Ian Wedde has never been one to circumscribe himself by tastefulness or trend or common sense; verbose and learned (Wedde is surely the biggest name-dropper in New Zealand poetry), for going on 50 years he has celebrated the good life and given the bollocks to the bad. His new Auckland University Press *Selected Poems* gives readers an overdue opportunity to measure his achievement. The book's front cover is nothing but a three-colour chalkboard-like scrawling of the poet's underlined name: this tagging (albeit by artist John Reynolds) gives some notice of some of the poet's more four-sheets-to-the-wind propensities, but *Selected Poems* also gives us many of Wedde's delightful hails and farewells, which he does like no one else. In so doing, Wedde offers much that is worth our celebrating in turn.

Moving chronologically through Wedde's books, *Selected Poems* aptly begins with a salute to Henri Matisse, the great colourist who ended by making shapes dance. Like that painter's exultant late work, the brilliance given off by the vividly determined and often bloody-minded joy of the early *Earthly: Sonnets for Carlos* has not dimmed with time. The poems trip delightedly through sunlight and shadow, and neither the closely observed rhyme schemes nor the postmodern ampersands and back-slash punctuation — which have dated so tellingly much seventies poetry — stake claims that exceed the strength of what the poet has to say. The well-rounded stoicism and tempered Epicureanism of Wedde's early work, both of which are emblematic of a day-by-day choice in favour of happiness and eschewing of cynicism, is entirely charming. Although Wedde wrote that his poems 'are concerned with how we live, how we should live, and are political in these senses', this 'concern with how we live' is more of a philosophical question: the answer Wedde usually gives is that we should make the most of it.

Wedde, along with most of his contemporaries who threw their lot in with US postmodernist poetry, took on the chatty and jokey and lightly louche line of American mid-century writing, drawing more on O'Hara and his New Yorkers than Olson and his Black Mountaineers (although Wedde isn't shy of addressing the reader as 'citizen' when things concern the polis). Wedde differs from others in his generation in that he brings this voice, which sometimes veers towards into the kitschy and camp, to bear on political and social issues of the day. O'Hara, of course, wasn't all unbridled gaiety, and the technological barbarism of his day, especially the shadow of the mushroom cloud, casts shadows through his sunlight. Similarly 1975's *Pathway to the Sea* maintains the trippingly discursive mode of *Earthly* to issue a gadding jeremiad against block-headed notions of progress.

The book does get a tad flabby around its middle: Wedde does his most nodding and winking in *Georgicon*, *Tales of Gotham City* and *Tendering*. By the 1990s, however, the sharpness of focus returns with *The Drummer*, his only collection of that decade: poems like the terrific 'A ballad for Worser Heberley' take on Keith Sinclair's historical ballads of the 1950s and possibly better them.

He returned in 2001 with the Horatian conceit of *The Commonplace Odes*, which has always seemed to me of less use to Wedde than adopting the cipher of Catullus was for C. K. Stead. Stead, despite all his native huff and puff, seemed released by (and made a little too much of) the liberty and licence for indiscretion his churlish yet cultured persona allowed him. Wedde's mask didn't seem to quite fit him, and re-reading his *Odes* confirms me in my opinion: it inhibits his voice and adds nothing apart from some obvious tags and hackneyed forms of address. There is no 'Homage to Clio' or 'Goodbye to the Mezzogiorno', Auden's poems in the voice of a philosophical sybarite tempered by middle age, yet cosy in his bucolic cosmopolitanism, and still the best harnessing of Horace last century. Wedde's efforts seem clunky by comparison and compromised, if not sometimes made a little silly and portentous, by his ventriloquism and clairvoyant asides:

> Towelling myself before the mirror in a hotel far
> From the unfinished dwelling of my life, I see
> How gravely my weight wants to go to earth,
> Tugged down by good living, by love,
> And by spiteful tiredness brought on by the knuckle-
>
> Cracking Cotton Mathers of cultural bureaucracy.
> Was this your fate also, Horace,
> To sit in meeting rooms filled with nodding
> Heads . . .

Well, no, it wasn't. Wedde's pneumatic way with syntax remains delightful, as does his handling of line and enjambment, and no one would begrudge the poet good living and love, but I wish he would have begrudged his readership the inevitable and irrelevant mention of the 'Sabine farm', and so much else in the next stanza and beyond, like confetti scattered on his parading of middle-class middle age. But 'To Ernst Dieffenbach' and 'Carmen saeculare: for Carol and Abe', free of such baubles, represent this period of Wedde at its best.

The Felliniesque carnival cracks on with *Three Regrets and A Hymn to Beauty*, the latter stringing baubles of birthday wishes to a cast beginning with Montgomery Clift and ending with Victoria Beckham, with many more (and many exclamation points) along the way. *Good Business* is rather more sombre and workaday, pointing towards the elegiac tones of *The Lifeguard*, from which 'Shadow stands up' provides a dignified and touching conclusion to Wedde's *Selected Poems*, a subtly drawn chiaroscuro contrast to the large doses of Day-Glo delights that came before it.

AUP has been generous in proportioning this selection; at 336 pages, it would measure as a collected poems for many poets. Although I'm sure almost all readers will simply be glad to have Wedde so liberally represented, especially since it means his long poems and sequences are largely given in full, the scrupulous few may balk at a publisher's largesse that accommodates such lines as 'When tits swing / under satin / it makes me want to sing' ('Get up'). But as I wrote at the outset, good taste has never played censor to Wedde. All in all, this book is a fine testament to the independence of spirit, lightness of touch and good humour teamed to seriousness that Wedde has brought to bear on a life rich in experience, which he has generously shared with readers for more than 40 years.

David Howard
The Ones Who Keep Quiet
Otago University Press, 2017
RRP $25, 96pp

David Howard has been busily writing more poems since the publication of his incomplete poems by Cold Hub Press in 2011, a book that gave notice of Howard's four-and-a-half decades of signal achievement. Howard has acknowledged Ian Wedde's influence, most tellingly apparent in the essayistic and sometimes discursive approach Howard often uses in his longer poems and sequences. Howard, though, is also capable of a lyricism, particularly in his short poems, that is rarely evident in Wedde's work. This lyricism can be slightly bitter, but as readers of *The Ones Who Keep Quiet* will discover, Howard makes one's speaking mind sing like few other New Zealand poets can do.

The book begins with 'The Ghost of James Williamson', a tour-de-force dramatic monologue about sex and death in envelope-rhymed six-line syllabic stanzas. Howard's nonce form, a stricter version of Keith Douglas's most potent rhyme scheme, reappears in a section of 'Because Love Is Something Left' along with many of the earlier poem's preoccupations. Indeed, even though the poems seem to have been written discretely, often during Howard's tenure at a number of residencies, they orbit incessantly around a few obsessions, despite their apparently characterised voices. It must be said the most of the characters who populate *The Ones Who Keep Quiet* sound a great deal like David Howard, which is problematic in 'The Mica Pavilion', given that it has seven speakers scripted in close proximity — the result is more Esperanto than Babel. Of course the same could be said of Browning's Del Sarto and the renegade Victorian's myriad other mouthpieces: the poet is too strong and his style too distinctive for him to acquiesce fully to the niceties of characterisation.

Perhaps what Guy Davenport called his 'necessary fictions' are closer to Howard's way of doing things in this book than are Browning's, whereby Davenport takes up a Walser or Kafka, and supplies what is necessary to substantiate plausibly the historical record in good faith. In making these necessary fictions, Howard's basic building blocks, especially in the longer poems, are the verse paragraphs, which are formed by accreting syntactical simple sentences into discrete units, which, in turn, are then accumulated, often building towards a point where words fail, to an almost breathless denouement of all that has come before it.

'The Speak House', which was published as a chapbook by Cold Hub Press, exemplifies Howard's method of making, and it is the highlight of *The Ones Who Keep Quiet*. Judging by the exhaustive notes to it at the back of the book, Howard spent a great deal of time and effort to ensure fidelity to its speaker. This effort, which seems almost physical, and the scrupulous maintaining of good faith that demands it, is what makes Howard so special. And when he hits the bull's eye, the arrow quivers:

> If we hear them, if we follow
> the light house on the sea
> beyond the bar, beyond
> all possibility of *an house not made* . . .
> And then the wave, and then.

The bitterness I mentioned is most attenuated in a sequence given in the voice of Ian Milner, the New Zealand writer and scholar, a contemporary of Bertram and Mulgan, who installed himself in Cold War exile in a Czechoslovakian university. 'Prague Casebook' brings Howard's withering gaze to bear on a dying man in a dead world. Sadly, nothing is gained apart from amplification of pain and attenuation of loss. 'Implicit in the grey is total black', wrote Thom Gunn: in this poem, Howard makes it explicit. I imagine Howard is well-read in theology (his poems certainly betray a religious temperament if not belief), but not even the zero-sum consolation offered by Jürgen Moltmann — solidarity in mutual suffering with row after row of history's crucified — is on offer. Instead, the reader tracks his way through a darkening forest and arrives here:

> Your paradise was a short ride in a fast car, I got out
> on the wrong side, that's clear as ice on the highway at first light.
> No one is above you, nothing is forgotten, so I doubt
> you will spare any of us a long walk into endless night.

The Ones Who Keep Quiet isn't always quite so despairing. But it's never celebratory. The oblique personal lyrics interspersed among the longer poems allow a little light here and there, but it's always certainly slanted. To Chesterton's 'democracy of the dead' and our responsibility to and participation in it — which has recently been re-voiced by Geoffrey Hill in one of his professorial lectures at Oxford — I would add a complementary state in which we may choose to take into account those as yet unborn. Part of poetry's work, I think, is to illuminate those parts of life when and where care and attention were, if only for a time, allowed to make a space for love to do its work. And occasionally this has happened. For all his hurt and anger, wrecks and errors, Ezra Pound never quite lost sight of this mission to provide beacons to guide the unborn through prevailing darkness. It is glimpsed in those closing lines of 'The Speak House', 'the light house on the sea / beyond the bar, beyond / all possibility of *an house not made . . .*' David Howard, for the moment, is staying his healing hand, but one hopes he will light a candle or two in his poems every now and then.

John Gibb / Liz Breslin

John Gibb
Waking by a River of Light
Cold Hub Press, 2017
RRP $29.95, 88pp

Something that never fails to amaze me about poetry is the sheer depth of its ability to make anything beautiful by the virtue of language. This notion continually resurfaced in my mind as I read John Gibb's second poetry collection, *Waking by a River of Light*, in which Gibb makes poetry out of the most seemingly ordinary of things, from the postal system to socks, footprints and a soft green notebook, alongside more traditional focuses, such as the shore, 'a sea of flowers', and the rain.

The collection consists of three sections of differing lengths, the titles of which say all that needs to be said of the book's journey, which begins with 'Walking', is followed by 'Voyage Into Darkness' and concludes with 'Waking to Rain'. The first section is named for its leading poem, which opens the collection with an effective hook of potent imagery:

> We were walking along the beach.
> The sand's rough, stony texture
> shimmered red with rusting minerals
> and shone like freckled skin.

Many of my favourite poems are within this first section, 'The World's Second Slowest Coffee Drinker' being a particular standout which I keep returning to — if only to smirk at the (familiar) amusing image of 'waiters . . . circling, anxious for his cafe table / to come free'. For me, oddly enough, the notion springs to mind the controversial Kevin Carter photo of a starving Sudanese toddler and leering vulture. The image reappears towards the end of the section, in 'A Widow at Home':

Querulous as a minor queen,
at 94, the Christchurch widow
survives her final years in her
own house, as relatives glide
in each Christmas, like vultures.

It's a more explicit evocation of the same idea. Much like the waiters waiting for the Second Slowest Coffee Drinker to swallow his dregs, the widow's relatives hover about awaiting her death — to see the contents of her will, her 'last, lamentable hand'. The two poems have such wildly different contexts with such profoundly similar spirits: the subjects wish only to take their time, regardless of onlooking carrion eaters spurring them to their respective conclusions. Yet the poems are short and over swiftly, barely taking up half a page each.

Not that I'm complaining. I have a personal preference for these shorter poems, which pack a thoughtful punch and immediately redirect your gaze back to the top of the page. Gibb excels at such poems, which is not to speak ill of the longer poems, of course. 'In My Next Life', the longest poem in the collection and in many ways its centrepiece, expresses a paradoxically optimistic world-weariness: not just the acknowledgement of failed ideals in poetry, life, society and the weather, but also the confident assertion that 'in my next life' these ideals will be actualised. Yet, a large part of the heavily evoked sense of *Weltschmerz* is in the inkling that this 'new life' is no more than another unfulfilled (and unfulfillable) ideal.

On an only slightly less wistful note, sections two and three both end with poems about cats. Sort of. 'Man With Invisible Cat' features the lack thereof, while 'Farewell, Last Poem' turns feline friends into a metaphor for poetic inspiration, incessant and fickle at the same time.

   ... one last
poem crept in on silent white paws.

And peered up at him wistfully, as he
scribbled like a demon. Farewell last
poem, he thought, as the diamond-bright
mood, with its ferocious silence, would
soon be broken; soon would pad away.

Together with 'Walking', the collection is bookended quite nicely. Ending on such a pensively self-reflexive note reinforces the journey of the collection — strolling from evening into night, and on until morning, dreaming in poems the whole way. Night and day, light and dark, life and death: the recurring thematic preoccupations. Along with the weather, the seasons, time, endings. Uncontrolled forces, strangely miraculous in their ordinariness. The frame and background to all of human history — and so, too, to the poems in Gibb's second collection.

Waking by a River of Light is incredibly accessible, combining Romantic conventions of emotionalism, subjectivity and reverence for nature's constant presence with the sense of something keenly personal and at times distinctly New Zealand. Perhaps the lattermost feature is most noticeable in the occasional dashes of droll humour, notably in 'Wanted' — 'Keep all sheep / and people well away from this man' — and, unexpectedly, 'The Trouble With Friends Dying'.

Liz Breslin
Alzheimer's and a Spoon
Otago University Press, 2017
RRP $25, 76pp

The back cover of Liz Breslin's debut collection features an 'Instant Artist Statement' from 'artybollocks.com', a website which generates an artist statement that is, as promised, complete bollocks. The one on the back cover of Breslin's collection is a good one ('spatial derivatives become frozen through frantic and critical practice'), and it generated a pretty laughable one for me, too: 'the viewer is left with a hymn to the inaccuracies of our existence'.

Had I not opened the book I would still have had Breslin to thank for discovering this gem of a website, but thankfully she has much more to offer. Using such 'arty bollocks' as an endorsement quote is just one example of the needle-sharp facetiousness to be found between the book's covers — tastefully integrated, of course, with dark subject matter such as Alzheimer's disease, tales of the Warsaw Uprising and death.

The poems all fit together with a pleasing cohesiveness, each made stronger, I think, when considered as a whole rather than as individual pieces. 'Everything as it should be', for example, is clearly about one instance of Breslin's struggle with her babcia's Alzheimer's:

> I stroke your starling hand
> draw you back to order
> bread, butter, knife edge, tea
> wszystko tak jek trzeba [everything as it should be]
> but nothing's as it's been

The meaning is made more ambiguous without the majority of the collection having already been contextualised by the title, *Alzheimer's and a Spoon*, which indicates that spoons are somehow significant. They come up a fair few times, notably in a picture across from 'Instant Autocomplete', a poem which is in itself an intriguing innovation:

> How no
> How not to be boring on Tinder
> How not to live your life
> How not to talk to your kid

The utilisation of technology in writing is an interest of mine. 'Instant Autocomplete' inspired me to see what sort of suggestions Google could give *me* from the same prompts — even though I have no doubt that

Breslin wrote the poem's 'suggestions' herself. Suffice it to say, when 'how no' suggested 'how not to die', I decided to stop while I was ahead.

So, back to the spoons. Across from 'Instant Autocomplete' is an image of a packet of 'forks' which are clearly spoons. At this point of the collection, the significance of spoons isn't clear just yet, but the image is a wordless evocation of the disorientation of Alzheimer's — undoubtedly not just for the sufferer, but for their loved ones, too. It wasn't until 'Apocalypse Now', in the final third of the collection, that it was suddenly glaringly obvious to me what the spoons represented: 'The last time I saw you I spoon fed you puréed veg.' This is revisited and driven home less than 20 pages later:

> They are escaping, the words,
> fed to other minds. Mush,
> precise, off the end of a metal
> round thing with a handle.

Moments like these, in combination with sardonic junctures like 'Re: your $$$ inheritance' or the patchwork prayer of 'The Lifestyle Creed', make *Alzheimer's and a Spoon* avoidant of categorisation. Then, of course, there are the interactive elements, most directly and traditionally applied in two instances of 'riddle me this' and a single 'riddle me these'. Breslin's riddles serve as a small break from the action of the collection — especially considering their strategic placement between some of the heavy-hitters — as well as a test to see whether the reader is paying attention. It's all too easy to be a complacent reader, and easy for a writer to accept this complacency.

Liz Breslin does not strike me as a poet who accepts complacency. *Alzheimer's and a Spoon* rewards readers who pay attention; who go back and re-read; who look a little more closely.

Elizabeth Morton

Alan Roddick / Michael O'Leary

Alan Roddick
Getting It Right: Poems 1968–2015
Otago University Press, 2016
RRP $25, 90pp

Getting It Right is Alan Roddick's reunion with a muse who skedaddled many years ago. Maybe it was penance — Roddick did write, on the back cover of his first collection, *The Eye Corrects*, 'I rarely find writing a poem an enjoyable experience.' Perhaps the parting was consensual. In any event, Roddick did write sporadically between his first collection, of 1967, and now. He never fully 'got over' the writing lurgy — indeed, he wrote a monograph on Curnow and edited three volumes of Brasch's poetry.

Getting It Right is poetic evolution captured in time-lapse documentation. It is an upward trajectory. And, to issue a spoiler, it meets the title's brief.

The collection kicks off with poems from *The Eye Corrects* (1967). Here are pictorial yarns, sometimes a little clunky, but always cogitative. 'Festival Race Day' is the most lush of these:

> Saturday afternoon, and over the lawn
> from flowering apple to escallonia hedge,
> forward and back, I urge the surly mower.

'A Patient' is Roddick's lone dental poem (dentistry is his daytime profession) — and it captures a moment's tenderness in the 'murder house'. A simple story, but delightful in its humanity — telling of a patient's attempt to convert her (artfully) passive technician to Christianity, during the course of an extraction.

> . . . And there she has me,

like it or not, part of her parable.
All I can do is smile. She smiles right back.

The next grouping of poems is headed '1968–80'. Here, poems are branded with an earthier touch. There are many poems about trees. There is a 'skimming stones' poem. There are meteorological poems. There are poems with celestial objects. These poems play outdoors, get their hands grubby. The poem 'Tidying My Garage in Hutt IVa' marries suburban rubble with archaeological digs and Troy, all by way of an inventory:

> garages agape at my walking by
> bear fewer broken toys, crammed appleboxes,
> bits of pram and pieces of lino . . .

The muse is on smoko-break, for a fair few years, it seems. Then there are poems on the other side of the ravine. These are headed '2007–15'. Here are Roddick's most nuanced pieces, which strike a perfect poise between humanity and grit, between storytelling and atmosphere. We accompany Roddick on the Caselberg Trust's exploration of the Fiordlands. Here is an hilarious gaggle of artists, doing what artists do, in the bracketed style of 'There Was an Old Lady Who Swallowed a Fly':

> Look! A writer sees
> our jeweller glance up
> from her notebook to nudge
> the composer to watch
> a poet photograph
> the cameraman filming
> one painter sketching mountains

In this section, Roddick's most simple poems are also his most potent. 'Lost and Found' is haunting and easy, and somewhat reminiscent of a Hemingway short-short:

After that downpour
this toddler's shoe

dropped on the kerbstone
beside a car

is filled with a foot
of rain water

There are nostalgic poems. 'The Sun-roof' takes us on the 'Irish moorland road', and hits us with a giddiness of olfaction and sound. It speaks to the uncertainty of memory, the hesitance of youth:

I was drunk with the scent of heather and whin,
the airy silence, lark song, cries of
curlew, corncrake. I must have been ten?

Roddick's muse may have hoofed off and left a decade or so in drought. It has returned with abundance. This is a collection of transitions that ends in something wise and sure of itself.

Michael O'Leary
Collected Poems 1981–2016
Ed. Mark Pirie. Introduction by Iain Sharp
HeadworX, 2017
RRP $35, 260pp

If Alan Roddick's muse hoofed off, it might be that it was shacking up with Michael O'Leary. With over 200 poems notched in this particular belt, O'Leary's *Collected Poems 1981–2016* hardly speaks of drought. This is O'Leary uncut. Sometimes it is electric, sometimes acoustic, and always abuzz with the discographies of other lives — influences include The Beatles, Kurt Cobain, David

Bowie, political revolutionaries, Bob Dylan, Renaissance artists, God, dictators, blues musicians, friends and family. Many of the poems are playful and up-tempo. Some of the poems sit like unruly hedgerows on the page and could use a haircut, perhaps, though there is an unlaboured charm here. The offering is generous, and gifted shell and stem and all. If you have to shuck a poem, mentally pick away parts, the effort is rewarded in poetic calories.

O'Leary's poetry is bad for the waistline, goes straight to the hips. A re-read of the poetry is like a second trip around the buffet counter at an all-you-can-eat diner. Poems are jammed in on the page in a head-to-toe format — one poem tumbling into another, and it feels as if there's too much on one plate, sometimes, a glut of words — like one has casually piled shrimp cocktail over curried eggs over egg tarts, and cannot fathom why they taste alike. O'Leary's offering, though, is consistently surprising. The poems don't repeat on each other, but could use a break between courses. Mercifully, the collection is divided into five parts.

Some of the poetry plays like song lyrics — with choruses and verses explicitly or implicitly denoted. There is a chapter of several 'Songs', recorded and performed by Dunedin Irish Band, with titles like 'Potatoes, Fish and Children' and 'The Man with Three Eyebrows'. The former blends Irish and Māori narrative, and yowls its chorus:

> He thinks to himself by the fire at night
> I don't know why we kill them
> O, sure they're the same as the people at home
> Potatoes, fish and children

There is a section of sonnets, which are playful within the form, and marry popular culture with archaisms. Elizabethan Sonnets that fuse with *Woman's Weekly* type items on Charles, Camilla and Lady Di, a 'Ping Pong Sonnet', and a 'Sonnet to Che Guevara'. There are satirical cricketing poems, where literary stars and rock stars, as well as a Māori leader, find themselves at the wicket. These fusions are testament to the spirited dexterity with which O'Leary can quilt together very different parts.

O'Leary's mastery lies in his broad scope and honed mischievousness. His feast is fusion, and he will serve Papatoetoe pubs with Tom Waits, Romeo and Juliet with Hinemoa and Tūtānekai, platypus with taniwha. The poetry is more a spectacle of ingenuity than it is atmospheric. It is more conversational than it is verdant. But there are times when it grapples with heavy subjects, with an unexpected but welcome earnestness. And there are spells of sumptuous imagery:

> One day I stood on a mountain
> Snow was falling on the surrounding rocks
> The cold went to my bones — a memory unlocks
> In my mind, a vision of the Black Forest in winter

Michael O'Leary's collection is chock-full of poems that, although shifting in tone, maintain a poetic integrity. The collection looms over the slim chapbooks and thematically tidy works which have been lapping up the attention of reviewers and suppliers. This work is wild, brazen, untamed, rambling and lyrical.

Jeremy Roberts

Jeffrey Paparoa Holman / Mark Pirie

Jeffrey Paparoa Holman
Dylan Junkie
Hoopla series, Mākaro Press, 2017
RRP $25, 54pp

'Dylan junkie' is a condition that many music-lovers of the past 50 years have been happy to live with. Since catching the ear of the baby-boomer generation — as the guy who finally managed to accurately articulate their social and political concerns during the early/mid-1960s — Bob Dylan has written and sung his heart out, and impressed every young minstrel from (nearly) every generation since; the recent Nobel Prize (for literature) was seen by many as a matter of course. Many famous poets have been smitten with Mr Zimmerman, too. Beat legend Michael McClure once told how he and Ginsberg were amazed when they met Bob by the discovery that he hadn't read Rimbaud. His early idol was, of course, Woody Guthrie. Dylan is most definitely a poet, despite the use of clichés in his songs — for example, the 'Once upon a time . . .' which begins 'Like a Rolling Stone', but that is probably unavoidable in songwriting — especially if you want to reach people.

New Zealand's own Jeffrey Paparoa Holman has now put together something of a love letter to Dylan, and it is an intriguing collection of writing. Holman references Dylan's lyrics, titles and life to create a very tasty volume not only for Dylan but also for Holman fans. Holman's voice comes through clearly, with Dylan being the springboard for expression.

There's a delightful dedication to Pete Sinclair, the radio host who played 'Subterranean Homesick Blues' on the radio in 1965. Then, straight away Holman tells us: 'hearing him [Dylan] was wind over water . . . what he set free was light as a feather' with 'the Hammond organ . . . bending / twisting time'.

In 'History Lessons', Holman calls up (Nazi) 'Vienna 1938' and writes: 'piss on them old Jew', but also, 'piss on your precious Torah'. Strong stuff. A geopolitical jigsaw puzzle to play with and think about.

'Went to see the gypsy' — also the title of a Dylan song — is very different and probably autobiographical. A shearer needing physiotherapy meets the daughter of the 'physio', who is 'Irene Papas gorgeous' and straight out of 'Motorpsycho Nitemare'. Holman has a lot of fun connecting his own story to this other Dylan song. It's rather delicious reading how he 'wanted to kiss her . . . eat her . . . lick the baklava'.

In 'No time to think', Holman recounts a drowning tragedy in 1978. A man called Abel 'dived to his death / for a drowning man', and there is 'a tangi ablaze / with Abel's weed'. The poem is skilfully executed, with the circumstances of how he died revealed at the end.

Holman allows himself a fan moment in 'Blind Willie McTell & a series of dreams' by sharing a glorious experience — hearing the famous Dylan track nobody had known was stashed away. It was a celebratory time, with 'bootleg whisky in the record shop'. Holman asks 'where d'you think he gets this stuff?', and is deep inside the song, offering possibilities: 'he must steal it / to make you feel it / from the roots of the Bayou / from the cottonmouth stars'.

In a section that uses lines from 'Hard Rain' as titles, Holman brilliantly uses Dylan's 'six highways' to create a timeline — for example, 'Highway One was the road to school . . . Highway Six I became a cynic'. He then mimics the form of the song by asking questions relating to the grittier side of life — for example, '& where do you think you're bloody well going? / sez the Boy in Blue with his truncheon showing', having fun rhyming the couplets.

In 'guns swords hands children', Holman creates an anti-gun poem about a Vietnam vet who saw 'those black pyjama people blown in half' and now 'limps around the farm . . . hates the RSA'. It's totally wrong to let children play with guns in the first place is the message here. The poet has the last word: 'You're older now and all those guns shoot back'.

In 'starving laughing', Holman makes a plea against the destruction of planet Earth and the stripping of resources: 'in Borneo orang-utans suckled infants / the loggers came / the red earth turned to dust / the tills ran hot'. There is karma coming: 'the earth took fright / and shuddered / nothing made by human hands / withstood'.

'Heading for Hibbing' recounts a road trip that must have been nirvana for Holman: an unexpected journey to Dylan's hometown. Broken into 19 small sections, Holman has assembled various notes about places and people, made whenever something caught his eye, or the opportunity arose. For much of it, the Dylan-focus takes a back seat as fresh experiences and stories emerge from the highways. He rents a car from a woman who has said goodbye to many like Holman. 'The road is longer than fate', he writes, 'So many false exits & wayside demons'. He meets Americans who want to go to New Zealand, while he makes connections to the landscape: 'Water that's flat as the eye can bear . . . Thirty minutes, blind in convoy praying / hard to see the road'. In 'Mesabi Country', Holman finds hills made of iron, where 'straggles of trees strike up again'. The trees have a message: 'Don't leave your leftover junk on our land'.

Holman finally makes it to Hibbing — Abraham Zimmerman's grave, and Dylan's own high school. You can feel the thrill as he walks 'through the doors where Dylan walked to blow his tiny mind'. Even Dylan was once a young kid with so much to learn. Ultimately, Holman finds the (old) Highway 61, and drives the miles where Abraham 'heard God say "Go kill your son"'. The final line in the collection — 'I slid a CD in the player. I turned the music on' — is an apt summing up of what the whole collection rests on. It's a poetic tribute to one of the greatest songwriters in rock 'n' roll history, who also happens to be a poet for the ages.

Mark Pirie
Rock & Roll: Selected Poems in Five Sets
Bareknuckle Poets Pocket Series, Bareknuckle Books, 2016
RRP $30, 156pp

Mark Pirie's CV makes the average poet grinding away exclusively at their own little corner of the literary coalface look decidedly lazy. As an editor he has worked hard to promote other writers, and it's good that we now have a major book that focuses exclusively on Pirie's career as a poet. *Rock & Roll* consists of 'a selected poem in five sets', and it is immediately clear that Pirie is an ace editor of both content and varied poetic layout. No fat is allowed in his universe — much the same way that Sam Hunt trims back to the skeleton of the moment. Pirie could probably edit the phone book and give us something interesting.

The first section is 'Rock & Roll'. Pirie is obviously a passionate music fan. The 'Funeral of a Guitar' shape poem is a wonderful example of the genre, with a sad-but-true comment on the music biz.

The 'Letter Home to Heartbreak Hotel' checklists some dead, famous guests and updates their lives. The opening line: 'Dear Heartbreak Hotel, / Jesus is alive and living in Hell', immediately tells us that we are in a world where (to use those famous words) 'nothing is true and everything is permitted'. It is very funny; for example, 'Karen's much the same and still won't eat her dinner'.

In 'Crash Course', an Iron Maiden fan finds 'God among the fallen; / The Crosses by the roadside', with Pirie referencing a famous song and placing the Devil in the death scene — perhaps suggesting that maybe there is indeed sometimes a price to pay for being the 'ultimate fan'.

There is an insightful, heartfelt poem for Elvis Presley — 'at the end'. Pirie writes: 'he didn't want to be a tiger or a lion, / just a Teddy Bear, a guitar man who sings; loves'.

The final poem, 'The Dumber Blues', has a wonderful career-defining quote from Kerouac — 'James Dean is dead? / Ain't we all? / who ain't dead?' — as a preface. Pirie's poem reads like a bleak Blues lyric, with a touch of Robert Johnson, about the curse of being born 'against your will', being stuck with a useless life, at the 'crossroads': 'Dylan's strumming, strumming, so faintly now — / the devil's here, and God's watching us all.'

The second section — 'Special FX' — blends reel life with real life. We're all living in a movie, aren't we? As in the 'Rock & Roll' section, some big names are wheeled in, and it is fun to see what Pirie does with them. In 'Movie Star', it is Pirie himself, however, dealing with a suggestion that he use his creative 'poetry talent' to create a screenplay/ movie. He seems keen on the idea, inspired, but there is the line 'If I do it right . . .' suggesting that it's not going to be an easy task, and there's the feeling that being 'alone in a silent room, directing / the moon, twinkling about with the stars' is not the best use of his talent and time.

'Placing the Self Within the Scene' suggests a director talking an actor (and reader) through various scenes, as if in answer to the famous question 'What's my motivation?' For example: 'somewhere in the last act / the dialogue takes an uncertain twist . . . you rise from your chair and step carefully around the argument.'

There are 10 two-line 'Filmograms'. Pirie writes honestly of longing in 'Wishful Thinking': 'Even if Renee Zellweger is married; / She still needs to be caressed.'

An *in memoriam* piece for Marilyn Monroe contrasts male and female points of view about the doomed sex-bomb. It's written, probably unavoidably, with the man stuck on the physical aspects — 'What a loss, what a waste, that beautiful body . . .' — and the woman far more empathetic: 'Did people care enough for her as a / person, the real Marilyn?'

The third section is called 'Good Luck Bar'. A number of pieces might be called 'battle of the sexes' dispatches. Pirie appears to give a fairly honest account of his failed attempts to find reciprocated love or, at the very least, compatibility, and there are some tasty little encounters. The ultimate partner must be out there, somewhere, but for now it seems he 'swims towards her, / like a language / she can't understand'.

The fourth section — 'Sidelights' — is concerned with sporting legends. You would think that poetry and sport would link up more often, but the truth is that most poets seem to shut themselves off this part of life. Brian Turner is an obvious, famous exception. There are some beautiful pieces of work here — not just to do with that 'poetry-in-motion' aspect, but with *humanity*. That poet-at-the-crease, Martin Crowe, is also remembered after his cricketing days: 'News of his cancer cut like a knife, NZ entered dark days'.

The often-used media conceit — 'sport-as-war' — is turned back on itself by Pirie, in 'Making a Point'. If sporting rules were to be applied to conflict, war would still be a brutal, nasty experience, with death as the outcome. One man might survive 'the final bullet / thanks to a Bible stuck in his / left breast pocket'.

The final section is 'Postcards' and contains a variety of material, including some of his interesting Australian experiences. A trip to the old Melbourne Gaol is nicely detailed, and the old-time floggings are vividly described: 'a leather pouch round the kidneys & a / helmet to protect the head . . .'

There are a number of 'Techno / Rave' poems (actually an edited 'found' sequence), and they read like notes made by a clubbing-savant, superbly executed: 'juddery hip-hop, pianos & trademark fluttery / Techno / "lager, lager, lager!!!"'

Rock & Roll lives up to its title. You can even say it has a backbeat, rhythm & lead, and a voice that is strong and engaging. Pirie is not pissing about, and these poems read like contemporary urban reportage — carefully crafted and styled. The cover art by Anthony Lister is terrific, too.

Jack Ross

Ted Jenner / Jeremy Roberts / Laura Solomon / *A TransPacific Poetics*

Ted Jenner
The Arrow That Missed
Cold Hub Press, 2017
RRP $19.95, 52pp

There are some great set pieces in Ted Jenner's latest book from South Island publisher Cold Hub Press. One of his principal subjects of investigation this time around appears to be ekphrasis, the description of pieces of visual art in words.

Take, for example, the piece 'Snapshot'. We begin with a careful evocation of a photograph of 'Travis's mother when I knew her in the '70s.'

> She is leaning nonchalantly against the driver's door of the family's Vauxhall. Her pregnancy is not particularly noticeable, and might have been overlooked but for the note Travis scrawled on the back of the photo, 'Mum carrying me, Dec. 1960'.

This opening makes it clear that 'Travis' will be as much of a player in what is to follow as his mother 'Laura B' herself. And, indeed:

> It must be fairly obvious that this was the woman who introduced me, at the tender age of eleven, to the seductive charms of her sex (of women, I mean, not girls).

As for her husband, Rob, he 'had the reputation of being one of those geoscience graduates who knew the ropes but couldn't pull the strings'. He disappeared from his camp in Papua New Guinea two months before Travis's birth. Despite some 'unconfirmed sightings' in Queensland, 'after 1962, nothing'.

By now, I think, we're beginning to realise that each new paragraph in Jenner's prose poem/micro-fiction will bring some kind of revelation, a new stage in this gradually unfolding chronicle of complex and far-from-ordinary life:

> Actually I have no idea where mother and son are either. When Travis was in his early twenties, I traced him to a phone number and an address in Balmoral, but he had no interest in meeting up, let alone reminiscing about those early years when we were such close neighbours.

Instead, he sent on this photograph by post. But why? 'Was my "puppy-love crush" so obvious when I'd done my best to conceal, it, being so shy and awkward at that age?' Given the strength with which it still rages all these years later, it's tempting to assume so.

> What the camera didn't fail to register on that day, however, is something I only discovered on re-examining the photo weeks later: a shadow snaking across the gravel of the driveway towards the car and Laura, which must surely come from the father Travis never met.

It's hard to imagine a more powerful way of evoking the mysteries of the past. This gradual exploration of the subtext of the photo, its details and implications, is a little reminiscent of *Lake Mungo*, that greatest of all Australasian films about the paranormal power of memory.

Certainly the result is a triumph for Jenner. True or not, his poem runs round on itself with perfect economy and gradually mounting power.

If that were all that Jenner's book contained, it would still be well worth the price of admission, but at least two of the following pieces, the beautifully complex and lyrical 'Farewell and thank you, Muse' and (perhaps most striking of all) 'The arrow that missed: a letter from the painter', continue this exploration of the power of cumulative paragraphs of descriptive detail within a complex exegetical framework.

What if this cosmos the gods created out of chaos were merely a function of our passion for ornament and order? Please don't quote me on any of this, Kallias, or you'll have me up before the Council on a charge of impiety, but tell me what cosmos was there in those handfuls of clay and mud we used to scoop out of the bed of the Kephisos when we were boys?

This 'imaginary letter from painter to potter' refers to an actual painting on an actual pot (now in the Louvre) as Jenner reveals in his notes to the collection.

He carefully interrogates the strengths and restrictions of their respective arts as opposed to that of the 'war poems, the *Iliad* or the *Kypria* . . . the authors of which never concerned themselves with the actual material waste and debris of war that my father witnessed at Marathon.'

They never concerned themselves with such details precisely because such incidentals do not move fifteen thousand hexameters any closer to their pitiless and irrevocable climax.

What the arrow this painter has put in to fill a gap in his picture may have ended up demonstrating is, it turns out, 'that the gods sometimes fail to hit their targets'. All of which implies:

That this world-order, this cosmos we Athenians prize so much has cracks in its edifice, is in fact fallible.

Jenner's book, then, considered as a whole, appears to be an examination of the 'cracks in the edifice', the things we can never know, can never reconcile with one another, however deeply and carefully we dig, however precise our chains of reasoning.

Don't let the slimness of the book deceive you: this is a major work, by a poet who is building, brick by brick, poem by poem, book by book, a unique and inimitable body of work.

Jeremy Roberts
Cards on the Table
Interactive Press, 2015
RRP $29, 158pp

There's a fascinating poem called 'Driving with Terry' deep in the heart of Jeremy Roberts' book of poems (which he refers to in his bio-note below as his 'collected works'):

> the cassette tapes I play as I drive around the city
> in my 1984 Toyota Corolla LE
> are a dead man's tapes.

Why? Well, I'm glad you asked:

> this music came into my hands because for several years
> I was his daughter's number one squeeze.
> he must have really liked this music, because these are all
> homemade tapes, dubbed off original vinyl LPs.

So, as he drives along:

> I sing along with the music, & say things like:
> 'Good choice, Terry' — or
> 'Why did you pick that album, man? You know they
> wrote better songs than that!'

There's rather more to the poem than that: various arguments to do with lust and The Eagles (in that order), but I thought I'd start with this opening in order to illustrate some of the strengths of Roberts' approach to poetry in general. First of all, there's the arresting conceit or life-event: in this case the 'dead man's tapes'. It's a genuinely interesting idea to have a kind of ghost companion driving around with you like this. Secondly, there's the deliberately scaled-down, unshowy language register: everything about this poem, line breaks at awkward points, phrases such as 'number one squeeze', seems designed not to stand out as dictated by artifice in any way.

Its ending, too, after a long disquisition on the guitar solo in 'Hotel California', described as the 'creative inverse of emotional pain', is deliberately deadpan:

> those who take their own lives can't get free of the pain
> & express it in a drastically different way.
> they get my respect.
>
> those that don't understand
> are lucky.

Does that mean that Terry took his own life, or is suspected to have done so? It's difficult to tell. That might be an over-reading of this section of the poem; on the other hand, it might just be what the whole thing is about.

'Driving with Terry' certainly got my attention, though — and made me see just how much can be achieved by Roberts' throwaway writing style. One of the crucial points about it is the fact that it turns one's attention away from the author/protagonist of most of the poems, and onto somebody else. Terry is interesting. We learn little about him, except his taste in music, and the fact that he's dead and that he had at least one daughter, but he nevertheless fills out the backdrop of the poem very effectively simply because Roberts himself is so interested in him.

In general, these outward-focused pieces are the most successful in Roberts' collection. Poems such as 'Back in the Day', about the millionaire posing as a Shakespeare-spouting tramp, or 'Love Buttons', which offers a curious backstage vignette of a light show at a Sam Hunt concert, share this fascination with the strange ways other people find to get through their lives in this world.

The compendious nature of the collection does inevitably lead to a good deal of repetition: poems which add little to the overall impression, and which might therefore have been cut from it. The lack of any clear chronological or thematic structure also adds to this impression.

However, while a shorter, more carefully arranged selection might have done Roberts' strengths as a poet better justice, one can see the logic of his desire to put his life's work (to date) on record, once and for all. Next time around, I might counsel him to include less work and arrange his poems somewhat more carefully: the strength of this book, though, is that it makes one look forward with considerable anticipation to that 'next time around'.

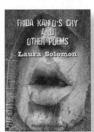

Laura Solomon
Frida Kahlo's Cry and Other Poems
Proverse Hong Kong, 2015
RRP $38.59, 48pp

Laura Solomon is probably better known as a prose writer than as a poet. She has, however, published in both forms throughout her career. The best pieces here are the ones where her personal circumstances seem to interact with the protagonists of the various dramatic monologues she presents us with. 'Joan of Arc Sends a Postcard Home', for instance, which begins with the lines:

Dearest, they burnt me!

Surely that opening phrase *must* be intended as a parody of the immortal line from Charlotte Brontë's *Jane Eyre*: 'Reader, I married him'? And with that, a whole subtext of madwomen in the attic, repressed female ambition, hoves into sight:

> I showed off as I died, howling and wailing and flailing my limbs;
> a spectacle and then, I was gone,
> my spirit departed my body
> like a train leaving a station
> I became feathers and ash.

There's something very disconcerting about those words 'I showed off as I died'. Can't a person — even so 'showy' a person as Joan of Arc — ever be free of the accusation of 'showing off': acting for effect, rather than purely and spontaneously? Apparently not.

The title of the poem, too, is clearly meant as a reference to Craig Raine's hideously influential, movement-naming, 1979 poem 'A Martian Sends a Postcard Home' (which its author must surely have come to dread almost as much as Stephen Spender did 'The Pylons', or Philip Larkin the line 'They fuck you up, your mum and dad'?):

> Caxtons are mechanical birds with many wings
> and some are treasured for their markings —
>
> they cause the eyes to melt
> or the body to shriek without pain . . . etc. etc.

But what precisely is the point of all this allusiveness when it comes to Joan of Arc, in particular? It's very hard to say. There's a kind of electric charge in Solomon's poem which makes it very hard to persuade oneself that there *is* no point, however.

'Resurfacing from the Wreck', a few pages later, makes similarly strong play with Adrienne Rich's 'Diving into the Wreck':

> First having read the book of myths,
> and loaded the camera,
> and checked the edge of the knife-blade,
> I put on
> the body-armor of black rubber

the absurd flippers
the grave and awkward mask.

Solomon, by contrast, begins her own poem:

Here I come, all clichés,
a deep-sea diver resurfacing for air.
It fills my lungs like heaven.

If I still had a tongue in my head
I could tell you what I saw down there.

Does she mean it as a sequel to Rich's epoch-making 1973 anthem? Or as a parody? Certainly neither poet is averse to the odd deep-sea cliché: mermaids, for instance. Rich's are richly androgynous, simultaneously mythic and real, female and male:

And I am here, the mermaid whose dark hair
streams black, the merman in his armored body.
We circle silently
about the wreck
we dive into the hold.
I am she: I am he

Solomon's, by contrast, are mere incidental features of the scene:

A mermaid or two, drifting idly by,
combing their hair as they swam

In his afterword to the collection, Andrew Guthrie claims that 'Solomon takes on the poetic task of attempting to expose the outlook of the non-human, or the thoughts of the historically remote personality'. I'm not sure that that's quite it, though.

Certainly Solomon distrusts language and its ability to close gaps and bridge distances: on the contrary, she seems happiest when stressing its *failure* to do more than serve up the clichés we're most used to.

Her 'Resurfacing from the Wreck' poem concludes, after all, by comparing its protagonist to 'an Ophelia of sorts':

> But I did rise, didn't I
> You have the pearls as evidence —
> — I have my blind eyes

The real deconstruction of all these mythic archetypes seems to come in the more avowedly personal poem 'Third Drowning', though:

> I wasn't very far out,
> I was close into shore,
> but the waves kept pounding me,
> I waved one hand,
> but you couldn't do anything, from up above,
> you were helpless.
> . . .
> and we both never spoke of it,
> both acted as if nothing extraordinary had happened,
> faces as blank as tombs that have not been written on.
>
> I knew then our relationship was doomed —
> as we sat in a café, you drinking beer,
> me reading a newspaper that was written in a language
> I could not comprehend.

A TransPacific Poetics
Ed. Lisa Samuels & Sawako Nakayasu
Litmus Press, 2017
RRP $30, 198pp

Whether Lisa Samuels and Sawako Nakayasu's book really qualifies as a 'poetics', a kind of manual for Oceanic writing in general, or simply as an anthology of interesting pieces from different spots in the Pacific, is not, to my mind, a question of overmuch concern.

For myself, I'd prefer to take it in the latter sense, and to forget about some of the larger claims made for the work as a whole — in particular, in Samuels' opening essay, 'What Do We Mean When We Say Transpacific?' She does, after all, concede that 'Imagining a transpacific poetics includes imagining a right to participate in its articulation', and it's that kind of openness and inclusiveness which constitutes this collection's greatest strength.

There's a great deal here, and I despair of having something worth saying about each of the contributions. Instead, I thought I might just single out a few pieces which interested me particularly, while stressing that another reader might compile a completely different list of highlights from so eclectic and idiosyncratic a compilation.

Jai Arun Ravine's 'The Romance of Siam', for instance, does a wonderful job of interrogating the iconography of Thailand via Yul Brynner's star turn in *The King and I*, together with similarly spurious texts from multiple sources.

Murray Edmond's essay 'Tattooed Rocks at Whāingaroa: A Personal Archaeology of Knowledge through Poetry' is right at the other end of spectrum. Beginning with a series of poems dedicated to Edmond by poet-historian Scott Hamilton (and included in *brief* 47), Edmond runs through some of the allusions there: to Hamilton, 'the place where I grew up', and its curious nexus of international influence (through *The Rocky Horror Picture Show*, among other things) and provincial torpor:

What had happened in the Waikato over the century from 1864 to 1964 was a process called 'settlement.' Settlement implies moving into an area and taking it over, as Pākehā did, and also 'settling down' or 'coming to rest.' The Hamilton I grew up in during the 1950s and 1960s was a place that had 'come to rest' — or so it seemed to me.

Edmond's series of riffs on the themes that have informed his writing from then to now — von Tempsky, Samuel Butler, Robin Hyde and Richard O'Brien — is perfectly designed to give us a kind of late-twentieth-century Kiwi pantheon of influences. It's not so much its originality as its *familiarity* which makes it such a touchstone here. It's hard to imagine anyone interested in New Zealand writing or culture on almost any level who couldn't find points of entry in Edmond's generous piece.

Along with another few essays, such as Eileen Tabios' fascinating account of the growth and origins of 'Hay(na)ku' — originally meant as a Filipino variant on haiku, but now a popular independent form with its own anthologies, journals and websites; or Stuart Cooke's examination of the continuities between Australian Aboriginal and Chilean Mapuche poetry, Edmond's piece guarantees some practical ways into the larger topic of continuities in Oceanic writing.

Lehua M. Taitano's remarkable poems from *A Bell Made of Stones*, Barbara Jane Reyes' poems from *Poeta en San Francisco* and Sean Labrador y Manzano's 'Breaking up with H. D.', with its repeated refrain of '[what eviscerates you?]' constitute particular high points for me. I might never have encountered any of these authors had it not been for the liberal eclecticism with which Samuels and Nakayasu have assembled their book.

Other texts which strike me more discordantly, or with a less immediate sense of recognition, might well appeal just as strongly to other readers. There's much to be said for adopting the smorgasbord rather than the fixed-course banquet approach to an assemblage such as this, success through selection rather than necessary approval of everything included.

Perhaps I might conclude by quoting a few lines from Susan M. Schultz's sequence of prose poems 'Memory Cards':

Time takes them away; I take my time. The former is more true than the latter. I am taken by it, but what I improvise will be my riff and bridge.

Laura Solomon

Victor Billot / Lisa Samuels

Victor Billot
Ambient Terror
Limestone Singularity Media, 2017
RRP $19.99, 82pp

Ambient Terror is an excellent collection from the talented Victor Billot. He has his finger right on the zeitgeist, and accurately portrays the spirit of our times for New Zealanders. As the title would suggest, a feeling of unease pervades the poems, and they paint a realistic, if sometimes depressing, picture of life in twenty-first-century New Zealand.

There are some great comic moments, such as when the Prince of Darkness attends a Work and Income interview, although this poem also carries a serious message. Some poems are quietly moving, such as when Billot writes about a child who may be his son in 'A Boy', and the haunting final poem 'Song of the Sea' where the narrator intones:

> The wind is blowing all night long
> And from its thread it sews a song
> You once were here, but now you have gone
> The wind is blowing all night long.

The smart and enjoyable 'FVEY' is about the invasion of privacy in a digital age, and ends with the lines: 'Everything about you analysed, scrutinised and known.'

> But just for now we'll let you keep your unspoken thoughts your own.

A sense of fighting off the darkness and of the poet exploring various hells comes through in these poems. 'New Seasons of the Blue Fields' contains the line 'sorrow flows through the streets like a river', and in

'Economics' he 'drives onwards, down the tributaries and channels of this Underworld'.

Familiar scenes from New Zealand life are depicted in poems such as 'Westport Race Day', where people place bets on horses named Southern Sky, Our Lad and No Regrets, or 'Port Chalmers', where the channel lights 'wink the way home in a cheery salute of green and red'. Teenage life is portrayed, too, in poems such as 'Quantum Decoherence at a Bailter Space Gig', where the narrator has his 'neural networks reformatted' and feels his life changed by the gig. In 'Teenage Pissup on the Kaikoura Coast' the poet heads north for New Year's Eve fuelled by screwdrivers and Camel cigarettes, parties through the night, and in the morning drives into the rising sun in search of breakfast, which is found at the Kekerengu tearooms.

'Trial By Fire' is an eerie number which could be about the poet's art or maybe just about getting through life in one piece. Perhaps the narrator is being ironic when he says 'It is your choice, your decision'. He is put to trial by various subjects: water, disorder, ice, knife, blood, kisses, mirror, flood, number, winter and glimmer of hope. It seems these trials will go on forever as the poem ends with the line 'trial from now until the end of the road'.

Victor Billot is a very gifted poet who deserves to be widely read; his audience his reward for depicting New Zealand life so well and having the courage to explore the infernal realms.

Lisa Samuels
Symphony for Human Transport
Shearsman Books Ltd, 2017
RRP $21.95, 76pp

Symphony for Human Transport has a dreamlike quality to it. The collection is comprised not of individual poems, but rather of one long poem divided into four parts. Many of the stanzas begin with the phrase 'The door of the train blew open' or, alternatively, 'The door of the train flew open'. The stanza then goes on to describe what happens next.

I found this collection rather overblown and pretentious. Some phrases did not make sense to me, such as 'we need to meet the century's Have Been Might Strode, who description warrants resembling not only choral scurries but everyone tanking the brief assembly for ex-self'. The poet is not really making sense here, or else is being so obscure as to render herself redundant.

I wasn't sure what to make of this collection, so I surmised that the narrator was going on a train journey with the door opening at random intervals. At the start of the collection she gives a hint that the poetry may be based on a dream, when she says: 'I finally dreamed last night after waiting years to repeat my life in copies under dark and light . . . in the dark spotlight of the dream the door of the train flew open.' If the poem *is* based on such a dream, then it begins to make more sense to me — it ebbs and flows like a dream or a river, and dreams don't always make sense, so perhaps Samuels is trying to create a dreamlike atmosphere.

The poems address another person, a 'you', who could be a lover, a relative or a friend, or alternatively a way of talking about the self. On page 35, when the door flies open 'seemly state found us by the skin', the 'us' implying that there is more than one person involved. The narrator goes on to state 'now you're bee-kept, you got the honey-greens'. Again, I think that 'honey-greens' is a made up word, a neologism — used here it could mean almost anything.

In other places the poem descends into gibberish. For example, on page 57, 'an angular sound infused on sense, to hover all coeval, liking angular meeting inexactly, violet in our doing without wreak, the time not time nor we together weaving seamed'.

In the final stanza of the poem, the writer talks of the hour 'that dreamed within a dream' — of a house on a cliff. She goes into another house that is also not hers, and seeks the earlier dream's high room 'the owner time already knew'.

I struggled to make sense of this collection. However, another reader might well be able to see things that I haven't been able to.

Richard Taylor

5 6 7 8 / **Brentley Frazer**

Monica Carroll, Jen Crawford, Owen Bullock & Shane Strange
5 6 7 8
Recent Work Press, 2016
RRP AU$17.95, 76pp

5 6 7 8 is a book of four poets, who are all either Australian or New Zealanders. Jen Crawford is a poet whose work I know and admire. However, in this review I put that aside, being prepared to 'savage' her or any of the writers I review. My ambition one day is to be a bitter savager of young poets, but sadly so far there has been no such opportunity . . .

5 6 7 8 is a series of witty and interesting mini collections of poems by each poet, using a number as a title, and including an illustration (I presume by each of them) and a reference. Monica Carroll is first with 5, and her drawing shows a hand facing the reader. Is this a 'stop', or a 'high five' of some kind? Hands can 'hit', so her first poem, 'The Sweetest Gear', a positive poem with an erotic flow, begins:

Hitting it means you're on the cruise. Everything's
open. Naked in a good way ....
...... and your hair is loved-up by a warm-fuelled
wind. It's not the climax gear, but the after, where
colour floods back and sweet is the crisp pine tint . . .

The poem is 'charged' like Creeley's famous 'the darkness sur- / rounds us . . . let's buy a goddam big car' poem from *For Love*. Is Carroll's poem simultaneously of the sexual act itself? Could be. The point is its energy and the positive free flow.

'Average', also a prose poem, is good indeed: her 'analysis' of averages starts: 'On average you get five years . . .' And in fact this is a reality, but also a probability, not a certainty: what was 'terminal' is perhaps not so.

In this poem, Carroll suddenly veers into the comic-surreal:

> If you write a story about someone losing their thumbs, the thumbs can
> be Rosencrantz, later on.

A reference to the play by Stoppard? 'Driving' continues the language
play: compassion and violence mix. 'A Surgeon' shows that this ludic
aspect of the poetry is philosophical, and questioning of another being
having the right or not of access to touch and investigate another's body
even if that is 'for our good'.

Then the poet uses riddles, repetition and a series of intriguing
'question-poems' with missing questions and tricky 'answers'. A good
selection from this poet who challenges and surprises.

Crawford's selection 6 has an image of what could be a hexagonal box
or a coffin. 6 is also riddling and quite fascinating. In 'hex', the coffin
interpretation occurs to the reader:

> a soft coughing from journalist pallbearers, with the
> screwdriver the man makes the sign of the screw, and
> all kinds of spaces open up . . .

This long prose poem has a mysterious 'dream logic' in which 'hex' and
'the sign of the screw' are part of perhaps some infernal rite:

> . . . this is a monstrum, a wonder, on the one hand in which
> It's cut into six pieces, which doesn't happen in the dream:
> the arm whirring on the blade and screaming . . .

It all has the precision and 'madness' of Kafka's 'In the Penal Colony'
story, or something by Raymond Roussel.

Crawford in 6 uses 'found' texts and clearly cuts or mixes these
into her works. I would like to write more about Carroll, Crawford and

the other writers herein, but to keep to my limit I will sweep on. Both writers are charged, and certainly somewhat in the innovative tradition of Stein and others.

7 is by Owen Bullock. Bullock is focused on memories, and his poems often are a series of haiku-like fragments or sections. He has some startling and eerie images:

> first child
> and an old rusty key
> on a cake

Which is one stanza of 'cycles of 7'. His formal play with 7 (what unifies the small anthology is their play with the number each has been assigned) intersects with carefully cut-back nostalgias, recollections, regrets, etc. And the start of this poem is:

> no memories
> only a vague
> lost feeling

Sometimes Bullock gets a little blasé, I feel, using references to rather overused ideas such as 'multitasking'. That said, in the poem in question 'imagine pattern' draws the reader's attention with the use of another, yet in this case surprisingly unnerving, cliché:

> no one imagines how much time
> writing a letter in blood

This literal-figurative sanguinity becomes a refrain and keeps the reader's eye on the text, despite the rather discursive process of the poem. While clearly paying attention to syllable and word counts, Bullock has an interesting, open way of working, and some poems seem rambling, with 'messages' and semi-homiletic epigrams, but they do work within the mode he has adopted. But he seems best focusing and recording, say, a little girl overheard on a bus:

> over and over
> she says
> the bus is wobbly like a jelly

and then later the ingenious:

> her vibrant smile
> leaps onto the bus
> with her

Shane Strange has *8*, so his section begins with an illustration of an octopus: and we have Oxygen, Reich's *Eight Lines* and other connections to 8. Strange mixes scientific references and jargon with, say, quotes from *Hamlet*. The effect can often be quite comic, as in the prose poem 'A Marxist at Ikea':

> . . . She brewed a headache
> born of the sounds of 6 billion people vying for coffee tables

Some of the poems are not so good, but 'Ohms' works well, as the repetition echoes Reich's minimalist repeating but subtly altering music:

> For a single movement Reich's *Eight Lines* transmitting up
> concrete and for a single movement there was no child, no
> labour, no obligation that could stop us lifting our eyes in
> a single movement our eyes in a single movement lifting
> our eyes in a single movement into the sun our eyes into
> the sun contrapuntal.

Then Strange finishes with some excellent poems, including 'Octopus' — full of puzzle and delicious and even baffling words or phrases such as 'deimatic octopode', which space prevents me quoting in full:

> deimatic octopode, a choice
> to make: saddle stitching,
>
> impossible glove? I am
> the beast below the surface

Perhaps a nod to the French poet Ponge, the deceptively clever poet of things?

All these excellent poets have risen to the task of creating poems centred on a specific number.

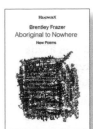

Brentley Frazer
Aboriginal to Nowhere: New Poems
HeadworX, 2016
RRP $25, 88pp

Having recently read Sven Lindqvist's *Terra Nullius*, I was intrigued by the title of this book. Indeed, Frazer alludes, either in passing or by direct quotes, to the Australian Aboriginal poet Lionel Fogarty, and to his country's and other indigenous peoples. But his work reflects a wider range than the political and social. It is that and much more, as Frazer 'combines major new sequences with shorter lyrical, concrete and prose poems, and gives . . . a sense of what it means to be an urban Australian looking into the future. A 21st Century apocalyptic howl from the cities . . .' says the blurb. Apocalyptic and transgressive energy, and some anger and satire, are certainly forces in these poems.

Aboriginal to Nowhere, whose title may reflect a reversal of the 'No One's Land' of Lindqvist's book, or a trope of the poet or poets and people in general who are perhaps from at least something to 'nowhere', is a complex work. The title could almost reverse the normative picture of so-called European 'progress', questioning Europeans' 'advanced civilisation'. But the author may also be an aboriginal to nowhere in a wider sense.

In the shorter and frequently outstanding 'lyrical' pieces, such as 'Charisma Studies', Frazer, combines satire and humour with beautifully dark images. Images that seem to point to an almost irredeemable dystopia. Drugs, broken things, the detritus of the urban scene and the death of animals by accident or human action interact with complex works and a paean to his father and his own fatherhood; and while some miss their target, there is energy and ingenuity everywhere. This is one of those shorter poems that fulfils the eye-stabbing 'make it new' side-winding sharp-eclectic to lyrical style, with its almost overdone 'angry young man' approach:

Bloodle

No, that's not the entire poem, but it could have been. The title alone is arresting and thought-provoking, and reminds me of Grenier's and other micro-poem experiments of the US Language poets' works. But 'Bloodle', longer obviously than this title, is not in any category, nor is 'No Fly List':

You said in a soft friendly voice
something terrible & hard to
articulate, perhaps only an *enemy*
would say & I marveled at the
subtle way you made the mundane
effortless & dynamic. However

I no longer have faith in rogue
actors or terrorists. The idols
watching over the foothills of

logic have retired to view
documentaries on Hegelian
political strategy &

This poem transforms away from the other more referential poems. The menace is there, but the poem exists almost on its own and breaks off 'unfinished', yet it is as if a strange voice was speaking in our dreams, of what we seem to know but are not quite sure. And of course it also works on the political-social level.

'Guyotat LSD', which also illustrates the book's cover, is a visual poem/text/artwork that is in homage to Pierre Guyotat, who is, Google reveals to me, even crazier and more *outré* than Frazer. I say 'crazy' but of course this is rhetoric; Frazer is in control, but he looks (but not always) to 'outsider' and transgressive writers. Words from Guyotat's 'pornographic' works are stamped on the page in different directions to build up what is a word picture. This happens also in 'Elegant Blisters' (another concrete poem), where words writhe on the page so that, like reading the end poems of Olson's *Maximus*, the reader has to turn the book. Frazer is well read and informed in and by literature and popular and other culture, and alludes to, or quotes, such poets as Eliot, the grunge singer Kurt Cobain, Guyotat, the Australian Aboriginal poet Lionel Fogarty, Mina Loya and others. Fogarty is interesting, and his poems can be seen online. Frazer provides a link.

Frazer himself is hard-hitting, and also has somewhat of the 'fuck you' style, but he cares about his family, social issues, people and literature. It is evident in this collection.

This collection is overall superb. I think perhaps he sometimes pushes the issues, the darkness, the anger, etc., too much, but it is hard to fault him in his 'direction', and he is exciting for sure. He is different in a familiar way, and sometimes he is simply extraordinary.

I feel, though, that his longer poems sometimes need more work. 'A Greener Pasture' is a dense intaglio of references which is consonant with Eliot's *The Waste Land*, which it follows and/or he makes use of Eliot's collaging and allusive form: but it seems too dense. However, the fault might be in me. But the longer sequences include 'Untitled Plane Crash', which is a tour de force, with some amazing lines:

> Let's roll now, man, the shadows have that dull edge
> like night sticks through phone books on abdomens.
> Let's forget our poverty, if only for this dawn.

> Don't . . . don't say it, something terribly hipster
> at least you're not the corpse of a refugee rotting on a beach.

The poem is a multi-vocal and poly-tonal journey through the mind, and is like a small contemporary music symphony, moving across cultural and genre levels as voices and refrains move in and out.

Frazer has included many poems, so inevitably there are works that I feel are not so good, but otherwise *Aboriginal to Nowhere* is a challenging and fascinating collection of intense creative work.

Perhaps my favourite is the superbly inventive (and dark/comic/ surreal/creepy/ugly/beautiful) 'A Cacophony of Grey'. This is the work of a twenty-first-century magician which on its own would justify getting hold of a copy of the book. I won't quote from it — you have to read it; it is too good to excerpt.

Books and Magazines in Brief

Mary Cresswell
Field Notes
Submarine Poetry, Mākaro Press, 2017
RRP $25, 68pp

Mary Cresswell decided 'belatedly' to describe her latest book as a 'satiric miscellany, if that's of any help' — or so she tells me. Certainly we observe here the characteristic Cresswell fascination with strict forms:

> double dactyls, sonnets, ballads, haiku dragged out of word clouds, ghazals, riffs on particular obsessions, homophonic word games, serious observations disguised as humour (and vice versa).

Is there a larger set of concerns on display? Ecology, certainly; male arrogance, passim:

> Come into my office, peasant
> he said, sit down sit down
> I myself can sit down and grasp
> the basic principles of whatever

Why does that speech sound so strangely familiar? Perhaps because the realm of black humour and despair it inhabits is known to me as well — as in 'The baggage pick-up at the end of the universe':

> pointme
> elseward
> passthe
> hemlock
> nomore
> talking

Claudio Pasi
Observations: Poems / Osservazione: Poesie
Trans. Tim Smith & Marco Sonzogni
Seraph Press Translation Series No. 2, 2016
RRP $25, 40pp

This is a truly remarkable collection of lyrics, in translation, by Italian poet Claudio Pasi. At times the poems attain an almost Mandelstam-like grace and precision, as in the last lines of the poem 'Angor':

> a stone that presses against my chest
> and takes my breath away. The ambulance
> accelerates. Aerials, treetops, clouds,
> chimney stacks fly past the window.

In his foreword to the book, Alessandro Fo remarks that 'No text by Pasi is ever gratuitous or irrelevant.' It's hard to imagine making a more meaningful tribute to any poet. Even in so brief a compass as this, though, one has to admit the justice of his words. As Fo goes on to say:

> Pasi's poetics are characterised by an empathetic and moving attention to the little things — the mini-dramas — of life: those 'normal' but dramatic events in the day-to-day happenings of a person, family, or community.

The poems included here, in subtle and nuanced versions by graduate student Tim Smith (with the help of Marco Sonzogni), don't shy away from the big issues, either: fascism, World War II, and even (of particular interest to me, I must confess) the probable fate of Marcantonio Raimondi, Pietro Aretino's collaborator on that most notorious of sixteenth-century pornographic books *I Modi* (The Positions).

Shipwrecks/Shelters: Six Contemporary Greek Poets / Ναυάγια/
Καταφύγια: Έξι Σύγχρονοι Έλληνες Ποιητές
With Lena Kallergi, Theodore Chiotis, Phoebe Giannisi, Patricia
Kolaiti, Vassilis Amanatidis & Katerina Iliopoulou
Ed. & trans. Vana Manasiadis
Seraph Press Translation Series No. 1, 2016
RRP $25, 40pp

At the Auckland launch of this book, editor and translator Vana
Manasiadis made no secret of its connections with the catastrophic
— and yet, it seemed, strangely inspiring — political *via dolorosa* of
contemporary Greece.

Certainly it seems as if once again Greece is at the forefront of the
most burning issues of our time: not just the imminent collapse of the
economic underpinning of our post-Cold War world, but also its direct
corollary, the refugee crisis.

Shipwrecks, or shelters, then? The six poets Manasiadis has selected
to translate do not appear to present a consensus: their personal
dramas of love and loss are enacted in spaces which seem continually
undermined by history. 'An island doesn't stop being deserted simply
because it is inhabited' is the quote (from Deleuze) Theodore Chiotis
has chosen to put at the opening of his own poem '21':

> The body carves a path which at first seems unfamiliar, then familiar,
> and a long time after, threatening.

If I had a criticism, it would be that not enough space is given to each
of them — what with dual texts and notes and prefaces and all — to
enable us to get a clear sense of where these six writers are going
individually, how they measure up against one another.

It's a tribute to the fascinating nature of the materials Manasiadis has
assembled, though, to have to complain that one's principal desire is for
more: perhaps even a book twice the length of this one.

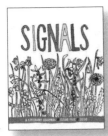

Signals: A Literary Journal 5
Ed. Ros Ali & Johanna Emeney
Michael King Writers' Centre, 2016
Free, 110pp

So *Signals* has reached its fifth (annual) issue! Ros Ali and Johanna Emeney have done a remarkable job of maintaining the freshness and exuberance of this journal stocked by, and for, the young writers who have attended and been inspired by the workshops run by the Michael King Writers' Centre in Devonport.

The book has been beautifully — and spaciously — designed by Sarah Laing. Its real strength is the contents, though. While it's invidious to choose particular pieces for praise, I can't bring myself not to mention such stories as Radhika Lodhia's 'You cannot wear my skin':

> I tiptoe around the aggressor; as though walking on eggshells, saying
> *men* but 'not all men,' saying *white* people but 'not all white people,' . . .
> I hold myself back. But I wish. God. I wish. That I didn't have to.

or such poems as Britt Clark's 'Walk Me Home':

> It is 4.45 on a School day, Mount Eden
> The school is called NORMAL
> But we don't feel it

This is a wonderful collection. Here's to five more years of such treats to come.

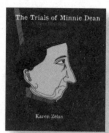

Karen Zelas

The Trials of Minnie Dean: A Verse Biography

Submarine Poetry, Mākaro Press, 2017

RRP $25, 196pp

This is a very strange book indeed. Even its author refers to it, in her acknowledgements, as a 'rather idiosyncratic work', and is careful to admit her indebtedness to Lynley Hood's 'excellent biography' *Minnie Dean: Her Life and Crimes*. But surely Zelas must be mistaken when she refers to a *1985* review she wrote of Hood's book? 1985 was indeed the date of Ken Catran's book (and TV series) *Hanlon: A Casebook* on Alf Hanlon, Minnie Dean's defence counsel, but Hood's biography did not appear — to considerable acclaim (as well as controversy) — until 1994.

Both Catran and Hood are sympathetic to Dean (although they fill in the more debatable details of her background very differently). So, too, is Zelas. But is a verse biography the best medium for assessing the case for and against the only woman ever to be hanged in New Zealand? It's hard to say, really. Certainly a close reading of Hood's biography is excellent preparation for seeing precisely what Zelas has done with the story.

I'm not sure that the same could be said to apply in reverse, but it's certainly true that the story maintains its fascination and allure in this new form, and — after all — 1994 is now a long time ago.

Was Dean guilty of anything meriting the punishment she received? The consensus from Catran, Hood and now Zelas would seem to be 'no'. Many people in Southland, and elsewhere, remain unconvinced to this day, however. It would be hard not to congratulate Zelas on opening up this awkwardly revealing case once more. After all, it could hardly be more relevant to a country with so shocking a record of abusing and terrorising its young. Conspiracies of silence and unexamined evidence seem to be the best way of guaranteeing the continuation of all that. Zelas, to her great credit, has decided to face the issue head-on.

About the
Contributors

John Allison returned to New Zealand in 2016 after 15 years in Melbourne. His poems have been published in numerous journals worldwide. He was the featured poet in *Poetry New Zealand* 14, and his poem 'Dead Reckoning' appeared in *Poetry New Zealand* 50 in 2015. John is the author of four books of poetry. His book on perception, imagination and poetry, *A Way of Seeing*, was published in 2003 by Lindisfarne Press in the United States.

Hamish Ansley is a writer primarily of fiction and sometimes poetry. His work is inspired by reality but heavily fictionalised. He has been published in *Mayhem* and recently completed a Master's thesis at the University of Waikato about masculinity in contemporary fiction.

Ruth Arnison is the afternoon administrator at Knox College, a residential college affiliated to the University of Otago. She is the editor of *Poems in the Waiting Room* (NZ), the founder of Lilliput Libraries, and when the weather is fine enjoys painting Poems on Steps around Dunedin with her 'step sister' Sheryl McCammon.

Stu Bagby was born and raised in Northland. He now lives on 5 acres of land near Paremoremo. An anthologist and poet, his latest book of poetry, *Pockets of Warmth*, was published in 2017.

Tony Beyer's recent publications include *Nine Songs* (Puriri Press, 2017) and *Anchor Stone* (Cold Hub Press, 2017).

Joy Blair started life in Central Otago, and eventually moved to Auckland's North Shore, where she writes variously, mainly poetry. She has appeared previously in *Poetry New Zealand*.

Ella Borrie is a poet and mug collector living in Wellington, although her heart is in the Southern Alps. She has an English and law degree from the University of Otago, was the co-editor of *Antics* 2015, and her work has appeared in *Mimicry* and *Starling*.

Erick Brenstrum is the author of *Thalassa*, a book of poems, and *The New Zealand Weather Book*. He writes a column on weather and climate in *New Zealand Geographic* magazine.

Iain Britton has had six collections of poems published since 2008, mainly in the United Kingdom. Recently, a new collection, *The Intaglio Poems*, was published by Hesterglock Press (Bristol, 2017).

Owen Bullock's publications include *semi* (Puncher & Wattmann, 2017), *River's Edge* (Recent Work Press, 2016) and *sometimes the sky isn't big enough* (Steele Roberts, 2010). He has edited a number of journals and anthologies, including *Poetry New Zealand*. He has a PhD in creative writing from the University of Canberra, where he teaches. In his research on semiotics and poetry he discusses the work of Alistair Paterson, Alan Loney and Michele Leggott.

Nicole Cassidy-Koia is a 19-year-old student with a strong passion for literacy and creative writing. She was born and raised in Auckland, and is expected to graduate from the University of Auckland with a Bachelor of Primary Education in 2019.

Jill Chan's sixth collection of poetry is *What To Believe* (2017). Her work has been published in *Poetry New Zealand*, *takahē*, *Brief*, *JAAM*, *Deep South*, *Trout*, *Otoliths*, and many other magazines.

Alastair Clarke is an English teacher, and has recently returned to New Zealand after living for a number of years in Britain and Australia. Seeing his country once more has dictated his most recent writing.

Jennifer Compton was born in Wellington and now lives in Melbourne. Her verse novella *Mr Clean & The Junkie* came out in 2015 (Mākaro Press).

Harold Coutts has recently finished a BA in English Literature and Classical Studies at Victoria University and continues to live in

Wellington. They self-published a collection of poetry in late 2016 called *Fissure In Flowers*, and is working on the first draft of a novel.

Mary Cresswell is from Los Angeles and lives on the Kāpiti Coast. Her latest book, *Field Notes*, contains poems written purely for enjoyment. It was published by Mākaro Press in mid-2017.

Brett Cross is based on the edge of the Hauraki Plains in North Waikato, where he runs the two small presses of Titus Books and Atuanui Press.

Jeanita Cush-Hunter is an aspiring writer and poet who lives in Auckland. She has a Diploma of Education (Secondary Drama and English) from the Queensland University of Technology, and a Bachelor of Education from Massey University. She is currently immersed in a Master's degree in creative writing at Massey University.

Semira Davis lives north of Wellington. Her writing has appeared in *Landfall*, *takahē*, *Blackmail Press* and the *Phantom Billsticker's Café Reader*.

Tricia Dearborn's poetry has been widely published in Australian literary journals including *Meanjin*, *Southerly*, *Island Magazine* and *Westerly*, as well as in the UK, the US and Ireland. Her work is represented in anthologies including *Contemporary Australian Poetry*, *Australian Poetry Since 1788* and *The Best Australian Poems 2012* and *2010*. Her latest collection is *The Ringing World* (Puncher & Wattmann, 2012). She was recently awarded an Australia Council grant to complete her third collection.

Hamish Dewe edited *brief* 43 in 2011. He was, back in the day, an editor of *Salt* (the Auckland one).

Doc Drumheller was born in Charleston, South Carolina, and has lived in New Zealand for more than half his life. He has worked in award-winning groups for theatre and music, and has published 10 collections of poetry. His poems have been translated into more than 20 languages, and he has performed in Cuba, Lithuania, Italy, Hungary, Bulgaria, Romania, Japan, India, the United States and Nicaragua, and widely throughout New Zealand. He lives in Oxford, Canterbury, where he edits and publishes the literary journal *Catalyst*.

David Eggleton received the 2015 Janet Frame Literary Trust Poetry Award, and his collection *The Conch Trumpet* won the 2016 Ockham New Zealand Book Award for Poetry. His most recent poetry publication, *SNAP*, is a limited-edition 14-poem collaboration with artist Nigel Brown and printer John Holmes for the University of Otago's Otakou Press.

Johanna Emeney is an Auckland teacher and poet who co-facilitates the Michael King Young Writers' Programme and teaches creative writing at Massey University. Her second collection of poetry, *Family History*, was published by Mākaro Press in 2017.

Jess Fiebig is a Cantabrian who spends her time writing poems and drinking too much tea. Her work has previously appeared in *takahē*, *Catalyst* and *NZPS* journals.

Catherine Fitchett is a Christchurch poet who has had work published in various magazines and anthologies, most recently in *After the Cyclone* (New Zealand Poetry Society, 2017). She has had various careers, including a number of years as a forensic scientist, and is currently working on a collection of poems based on elements of the periodic table.

Sue Fitchett is a conservationist and Waiheke Islander. She is the author of *Palaver Lava Queen* (Auckland University Press, 2004) and *On the Wing* (Steele Roberts, 2014), and the co-author or editor of several poetry books and anthologies. Her work has appeared in various publications in New Zealand and overseas, and has been exhibited in art shows.

Alexandra Fraser is an Auckland poet. Her first collection was *Conversation by Owl-light* (Steele Roberts, 2014). In 2016, she completed a Master's degree in creative writing at AUT. She has been published in various New Zealand and overseas magazines (including *Poetry New Zealand*), and in 2017 was placed first in the Poetry Society of New Zealand competition.

Maryana Garcia is fascinated by quotidian miracles and all things microcosmic. She has previously been published in *Mayhem*, and regularly contributes her word experiments to the cloud under the Twitter handle @bosonbrain.

Callum Gentleman has toured New Zealand extensively as a poet and musician, and recently completed two Australian tours. He is also the wordsmith for Panhandlers, a soundscape/poetry duo with Joel Vinsen. He lives in Auckland, but dreams of escape.

Michael Hall currently lives in Dunedin. His poems have been published in New Zealand and overseas. Two of his most recent poems have been published on The Spinoff.

Sophia Hardy published her first full book of poetry, *Jupiter's Perigee*, in 2017 (Lasavia Publishing), after numerous contributions to poetry journals and books. Although occasionally narrated in the first person, her poems are often character studies, and frequently include historical personages.

Matthew Harris has a PhD in English from Massey University and works as a senior tutor in the School of English and Media Studies. He is a writer of poems, fictions and short films: *43000 Feet* (2012), *Snooze Time* (2014) and *Madam Black* (2015) have travelled the international film festival circuit from Rhode Island and Tribeca in the United States to the Clermont-Ferrand festival in France, accruing various awards.

Paula Harris lives in Palmerston North, where she writes poems, teaches Pilates and contemplates the pleasures of eating dark chocolate. She won the 1995 Whitireia Poetry Award, which was kinda awesome. Her work has been published in various New Zealand and Australian journals, including *Poetry New Zealand Yearbook, Snorkel, Landfall* and *Broadsheet.*

Gail Ingram's short stories and poetry have appeared in journals and anthologies in New Zealand and overseas. Recent awards include runner-up in the 2017 New Zealand National Flash Fiction Day International Micro Competition, winner of the 2016 New Zealand Poetry Society International Poetry competition, selected finalist for 2016 Best Small Fictions, and runner-up in the 2015 *takahē* International Poetry Competition. She holds a first-class Master of Creative Writing from Massey University.

Susan Jacobs lives in Auckland and is a sporadic poet. The mother of four adult daughters, she has a special affinity for Italy, where she lived for 10 years. She is the author of two non-fiction books (*Fighting with the Enemy: New Zealand POWS and the Italian Resistance,* Penguin 2003; and *In Love and War: Kiwi Soldiers' Romantic Encounters in Wartime Italy,* Penguin 2012) about the Italian–New Zealand connection in World War II. Susan has worked as a lecturer, tutor, teacher, editor and book reviewer, and is currently teaching English to adults in a high school.

Lincoln Jaques was born in the UK but raised in Beachhaven, Auckland. He gained an MA (Hons) in English from the University of Auckland, and has just completed a Master of Creative Writing at AUT. His poems have appeared in *Poetry New Zealand, Spin, Fresh, JAAM, Southern Ocean Review* and *Shot Glass Journal* (US). He was a category winner of the 2015 Auckland Museum ANZAC Centenary International Poetry Competition. He has also written travel articles for *Way Beyond Borders*.

Ted Jenner is an Auckland writer who has published three books of poetry, one book of poems, short fiction and travel anecdotes (*Writers in Residence and Other Captive Fauna*), and two books of translations from ancient Greek poetry. His most recent book of poems, *The Arrow That Missed*, was published in 2017 by Cold Hub Press.

Tim Jones was awarded the New Zealand Society of Authors Janet Frame Memorial Award for Literature in 2010. His books include his second short-story collection, *Transported* (Vintage, 2008), a poetry anthology, *The Stars Like Sand: Australian Speculative Poetry*, co-edited with P. S. Cottier (Interactive Press, 2014), and his fourth poetry collection, *New Sea Land* (Mākaro Press, 2016). He was the guest poet in *takahē* 89 (2017).

Sam Keenan lives in Wellington. She was the winner of the 2014 Story Inc. Prize for Poetry, and she has an MA with distinction from the International Institute of Modern Letters. Her work has been published in *Landfall* and *Cordite*.

Mary Kelly is a student based in Wellington. She has been writing for two years and enjoys writing based on past experiences. This is her first published work.

Raina Kingsley is of Ngāi Tahu, Ngāti Māmoe, Ngāti Kahungunu and Rangitāne descent. She studied at the Hagley Creative Writing School, and has had poems published in *Leaving the Red Zone* and *Poetry New Zealand Yearbook 2017*. She has been living in Christchurch since 1988.

Gary Langford is the author of 38 books, including 15 in fiction, four textbooks and 15 in poetry such as *The Sonnets of Gary Langford* (Xlibris, 2016). His last dozen books use his paintings as illustrations, including the cover of *Memoir of a Teacher Writer*, published in 2017, and his latest story collection, *The Writer Who Becomes a Best Seller*, also 2017. Gary is an artist writer in Melbourne, Australia, and Christchurch, New Zealand.

Katrina Larsen is a teacher from Tauranga who has previously been published in *Blackmail Press*. She enjoys words and travelling to other worlds.

Wes Lee lives in Paekakariki. Her latest collection, *Body, Remember,* was launched in 2017 by Eyewear Publishing in London as part of the Lorgnette Series of pamphlets. She was the 2010 recipient of the BNZ Katherine Mansfield Literary Award, and has won a number of awards for her writing.

Bronwyn Lloyd is a writer and senior tutor at the School of English and Media Studies at Massey University. She has published numerous catalogue essays and articles on New Zealand painting and applied art since 1999, and her first collection of short stories, *The Second Location*, was published by Titus Books in 2011.

Henry Ludbrook is a Nelson-based poet. This is the second time he has been published in *Poetry New Zealand*. He is active in the Nelson Live Poets group. He also has a poetry blog called River Deliver Me at hello-hcludbrook.tumblr.com.

Olivia Macassey's poems have appeared in *takahē, Poetry New Zealand, Landfall* and other places. Her second book, *The Burnt Hotel*, was published in 2015 by Titus Books. She currently edits *brief*, and lives in Northland. Her website is www.macassey.com.

Caoimhe McKeogh lives in Wellington and works in community disability support. She is currently working on a novel with the assistance of a New Zealand Society of Authors Mentorship. She has been previously published in the *Poetry New Zealand Yearbook 2017*, and *Landfall, Headland* and *brief* literary journals.

Robert McLean is a poet, short-story writer, critic and reviewer. He is editing a selection of Dan Davin's poetry, which will be published by Cold Hub Press in early 2018. Born in Christchurch, he lives in Featherston and works in Wellington for the New Zealand government.

Peri Miller is currently completing a Bachelor of Communications at Massey University, and looking to study towards a Master's in 2018. She has previously written a book review column for Massey University's student magazine, and plans to one day have credentials stronger than 'student'.

Natalie Modrich is a 20-year-old student, born and raised in Auckland, who is currently studying for a Bachelor of Arts in English at Massey University. At the moment she writes poetry mainly as a hobby, but aspires to see more of her work in print in the future.

Fardowsa Mohamed is a student at the University of Otago, currently in her fifth year of studying medicine. She has been writing poetry since she was a child. Her poetry has been published once before, in *Landfall* 233.

Reade Moore is passionate about poetry, genealogy and stories that delve into these subjects. Her story 'Watercolours' earned third place in the 2017 Page & Blackmore short-story competition, judged by Kevin Ireland.

Margaret Moores was a bookseller for many years, but now works as a publisher's sales representative. She lives in Auckland, and has recently completed a Master of Creative Writing at Massey University. Her poems and short fiction have been published in journals and anthologies in New Zealand and Australia.

Elizabeth Morton has been published in New Zealand, Canada, the United States, Australia and Ireland. Her first poetry collection, *Wolf*, was published by Mākaro Press in 2017. She was feature poet in *Poetry New Zealand Yearbook 2017*. www.ekmorton.com.

Shereen Asha Murugayah was born and bred in Kuala Lumpur, Malaysia, but now lives in Dunedin, pursuing a PhD in science. Her work has appeared in *The Poetry Kit, Shot Glass Journal* and *Rambutan Literary*.

Heidi North is a writer from Auckland. Her poetry and short stories have been published in New Zealand, Australia and the United Kingdom. Heidi's first poetry book, *Possibility of Flight*, was published by Wellington publisher Mākaro Press in 2015. She joined the Shanghai International Writers Programme along with 10 other writers worldwide as the New Zealand fellow in September–October 2016. She was awarded the Hachette/NZSA mentorship for 2017 to work on her first novel.

Keith Nunes lives beside Lake Rotoma, where the two of them undertake a great deal of reflecting. He has had works published around the globe, has placed in competitions and is a Pushcart Prize nominee. His book of poetry and short fiction, *catching a ride on a paradox*, is sold by the lunatic fringe.

Jessamine O Connor lives in the west of Ireland where she facilitates 'Epic Award' winners, The Hermit Collective, the Wrong Side of the Tracks Writers, and also coordinates conversational English classes in a local town. Her fourth chapbook, *Fusebox*, was recently published by The Black Light Engine Room Press and she is working on her fifth. They are available from www.jessamineoconnor.com.

Charles Olsen is a New Zealand artist and poet who has been based in Madrid, Spain, since 2003. He has translated both Spanish and New Zealand poets. His website is charlesolsen.es.

Bob Orr has lived most of his adult life in Auckland, but now makes his home on the Thames Coast. He was the recipient of the 2017 Writer in Residence award at Waikato University. His most recent book is *Odysseus in Woolloomooloo*, published by Steele Roberts in 2014. He is currently working on poems inspired by a Waikato childhood.

Jacqueline Crompton Ottaway is an Auckland poet who has published extensively in local journals and anthologies. Her books include *Travels in the Antipodes: A Collection of Poems* (Piper's Ash, 1999), *Phosphorescence On the Oars* (BF Publishing, 2006) and *The Lion Roars: Piha Poems*, with paintings by Barbara Pflaum (Glen Esk Publishing, 2009).

Lilián Pallares is from Barranquilla, Colombia. In 2017 she received the XIV distinction Poetas de Otros Mundos (Poets from Other Worlds) for the high quality of her poetic *oeuvre* from the *Fondo Poético Internacional* (International Poetry Fund), Spain. She has published a collection of short stories, *Ciudad Sonámbula*, which has been translated as the ebook *Sleepwalking City*, and her latest poetry collection is *Pájaro, Vértigo* (Huerga & Fierro, 2014). She was selected among the 10 best young Latin-American writers by About.com, New York, 2011. Her website is lilianpallares.com.

I. K. Paterson-Harkness is a Dunedin-born writer and musician who now lives in Auckland. Her poetry has previously been published in *Landfall, JAAM, Poetry New Zealand* and *takahē*.

Mark Pirie is a Wellington poet, publisher, literary critic and archivist for PANZA (Poetry Archive of NZ Aotearoa). His latest collections are *Rock & Roll: Selected Poems in Five Sets* (Bareknuckle Books, 2016) and *Ride the Tempest: Uncollected Early Poems 1993–1995* (Earl of Seacliff Art Workshop, 2016). In 2017, he edited the football poetry anthology *Boots: A Selection of Football Poetry 1890–2017* (HeadworX), and published a new edition of his rugby poems *Sidelights*.

Joanna Preston is a Tasmanaut poet, editor and freelance creative writing tutor. Her first collection, *The Summer King* (Otago University Press, 2009), won both the 2008 Kathleen Grattan Award for Poetry and the 2010 Mary Gilmore Prize.

Lindsay Rabbitt published the poetry books *Upagainstit, On the Line* and *Thewayofit* (the latter two illustrated with line drawings by Jane Pountney) in the 1980s; his essay *These Lives I Have Buried* was published as part of the Montana Estates Essay series in 2004. He is currently completing two manuscripts: 'My Mother Was Mrs Central Otago' (a family memoir) and 'Prayers for the Living and the Dead' (a collection of poetry).

Mary Rainsford is a poet living in Wellington. She is currently studying English literature and criminology at Victoria University. In 2014 she won the New Zealand Poetry Society Competition. She was a regional finalist in the 2016 Slam Poetry Competition.

Essa Ranapiri (f.k.a. Joshua Morris) is a trans non-binary individual. They have previously been published in *Mayhem, brief, Poetry New Zealand, Them* and *Starling*. They will write until they're dead.

Vaughan Rapatahana is a Kiwi writer who lives across Aotearoa New Zealand, the Philippines and Hong Kong. Although perhaps best known for his poetry, his bibliography also includes prose fiction, educational material, academic articles, philosophy and language critiques. Vaughan is of Māori ancestry, and many of his works deal with the subjects of colonial repression and cultural encounter. His writing has been published in New Zealand and overseas. He was the winner of the inaugural Proverse Poetry Prize (2016). His latest poetry collection is *ternian* (erbacce-press, Liverpool, 2017).

Sahanika Ratnayake is a vaguely nomadic person: her parents moved to New Zealand from Sri Lanka when she was five, and since then she has lived intermittently in New Zealand, Melbourne and the United Kingdom. Aside from writing poetry, she studies philosophy, an activity she fears is an obscene decadence and a scam.

Ron Riddell's latest book of poems is *Dance of Blue Dragonflies* (Printable Reality, 2016). His new novel *Pachamama & the Jaguar Man* will be published in 2018. He is the editor of *Forty Years of Titirangi Poets* (Printable Reality, 2017), copies of which are available from Piers Davies at: piers@wwandd.co.nz. Ron is always pleased to hear from anyone interested in attending (or reading at) the Titirangi Poets (Titirangi Library, 2–4 pm, 2nd Saturday of each month) or the annual Medellin International Poetry Festival (July/August) in Colombia. See more at: www.ronriddell.com.

Gillian Roach is an Auckland poet and novelist. She has a BA in English literature and language from Victoria University, and a diploma in journalism. Gillian recently graduated with a Master of Creative Writing from AUT. For her Master's she worked on a poetry collection, 'Bread Winner', exploring the question, 'What do you do?' (available in AUT creative commons).

Jeremy Roberts is a resident of Napier, where he MCs at Napier Live Poets. He has appeared at poetry events in many locations, and has had work published in a wide range of journals. He has performed and recorded poems with musicians in New Zealand, Texas, Saigon and Jakarta. His collected works, *Cards on the Table*, was published by IP in 2015.

Jack Ross is the managing editor of *Poetry New Zealand*. He works as a senior lecturer in creative writing at Massey University's Auckland campus. His latest collection *A Clearer View of the Hinterland: Poems & Sequences 1981–2014* was published by HeadworX in 2014. His blog is The Imaginary Museum: http://mairangibay.blogspot.com/

Lisa Samuels is a transnational poet whose recent works include the novel *Tender Girl* (Dusie, 2015), the anthology *A TransPacific Poetics* (Litmus, 2017, with co-editor Sawako Nakayasu), and the poetry books *Symphony for Human Transport* (Shearsman, 2017) and *Foreign Native* (Black Radish, 2018). She teaches writing and theory at the University of Auckland.

Emma Shi was the winner of the National Schools Poetry Award 2013, and her work has been published in literary journals such as *Landfall*. She recently completed her studies in classics at Victoria University of Wellington. She writes at facebook.com/emmlexx.

Sarah Shirley lives with her husband, her two young children and a big brown dog. She is a junior doctor working in Hamilton. Her poems have appeared in *takahē, Poetry New Zealand, Star*Line, Intima, Pedestal, Landfall* and elsewhere.

Jane Simpson is a Christchurch-based historian, poet and tutor. Her poems have appeared in *Poetry New Zealand, takahē, Meniscus* and *Social Alternatives*, and in a number of anthologies in New Zealand and Australia. Her first full-length collection, *A World Without Maps*, was published in 2016 by Interactive Publications (Brisbane). She has recently completed work on a second collection.

Ruby Mae Hinepunui Solly is a Ngāi Tahu writer and musician. Her writing has been published in *Minarets, brief* and *Redraft*. She often writes about themes of cultural identity, and lives in Wellington with her partner and pet chicken.

Laura Solomon is the author of several novels, three short-story collections and two poetry collections.

Bill Sutton lives in Napier. He has worked as a scientist, politician and policy analyst, and his poems have appeared in *Poetry New Zealand,* *takahē, JAAM, Blackmail Press, Catalyst*, and *Broadsheet*. His second poetry collection, *Billy Button A Life*, was published in 2016 (HB Poetry Press).

Richard Taylor is an Aucklander who has been published in various journals, including previous issues of *Poetry New Zealand*. His two main books are *RED* (Dead Poets, 1996) and *Conversation With a Stone* (Titus, 2007).

Loren Thomas is a writer from the Waikato region. She has previously been published in *Poetry New Zealand, Mayhem* and *brief*.

Nicola Thorstensen lives and writes in Dunedin. Her poetry has appeared in *takahē, Turbine* and previously in *Poetry New Zealand*. She is a member of the Octagon Poetry Collective, which organises local poetry readings.

Vivienne Ullrich has had a lifelong affair with words as a reader, teacher, lawyer and poet. Last year she completed a Master's in creative writing at the International Institute of Modern Letters at Victoria University.

Roland Vogt is an ex-creative writing tutor at Hawke's Bay Polytech and overseas English teacher, now in his hometown of Wellington, near the Waiwhetū taniwha and his first paper round.

Richard von Sturmer was born in Devonport in 1957. His latest book, *This Explains Everything*, was published by Atuanui Press in November 2016. He also works with musician and filmmaker Gabriel White as The Floral Clocks. Their second CD, *A Beautiful Shade of Blue*, was released in May 2017.

Janet Wainscott lives near Christchurch. She writes poetry and creative non-fiction, and her writing has been published in *takahē, Bravado* and *Shot Glass Journal* (US).

Devon Webb is a 19-year-old full-time writer residing in Auckland. She writes: 'Poetry is one of my greatest passions and I use it as a tool to express my emotions, communicate with others and spread positive messages in a political era of excess hatred and negativity. I am currently building up my body of poetic work at a rapid pace as I work on my debut novel, the first draft of which currently sits at over 100,000 words.'

Jen Webb is Professor of Creative Writing at the University of Canberra. Her work includes the poetry collection *Proverbs from Sierra Leone* (Five Islands Press, 2004) and the short-story collection *Ways of Getting By* (Ginninderra Press, 2006) as well as, more recently, the chapbook *Stolen Stories, Borrowed Lines* (Mark Time Press, 2015).

Mercedes Webb-Pullman completed a Master's in creative writing at the International Institute of Modern Letters at Victoria University of Wellington in 2011. Her work has appeared online and in print in New Zealand, Australia, Canada, the United States, the United Kingdom, Ireland, Spain and Palestine, in *Turbine*, *4th Floor*, *Poetry New Zealand Yearbook*, *Pure Slush*, *Swamp*, *Scum*, *Reconfigurations*, *The Electronic Bridge*, *Otoliths*, *Connotations*, *Main Street Rag* and *Caesura*, among others, and in her books. She lives in Paekakariki, New Zealand.

Robyn Yudana Wellwood has written and published articles in Bali and the United States in between being a mother, teacher, gallery owner and traveller. She has been living between New Zealand and Bali with her two children and husband for the last two decades.

Maualaivao Albert Wendt is recognised internationally as one of Samoa's, the Pacific's and New Zealand's most significant novelists and poets. He has published numerous novels, collections of poetry and stories, and edited notable anthologies. His work has been translated into many languages and taught around the world.

Sigred Yamit studies Psychology at the University of Canterbury. She has been published in two of Printable Reality's anthologies: *We Society* (2015) and *Plate in the Mirror* (2016). In her spare time she reads about famous dead people, writes poetry, and watches movies of a specific genre (lately it has been gangster movies).

Mark Young's most recent books are *Ley Lines* (2016) and *bricolage* (2017), both from gradient books of Finland; *The Chorus of the Sphinxes* (2016), from Moria Books in Chicago; and *some more strange meteorites* (2017), from Meritage & i.e. Press, California/New York.

About
Poetry
New Zealand

Poetry New Zealand is New Zealand's longest-running poetry magazine, showcasing new writing from this country and overseas. It presents the work of talented newcomers and developing writers as well as that of established leaders in the field.

Founded by Wellington poet Louis Johnson, who edited it from 1951 to 1964 as the *New Zealand Poetry Yearbook*, it was revived as a biennial volume by Frank McKay in 1971, a series which lasted until 1984. David Drummond (in collaboration with Oz Kraus's Brick Row Publishing) began to publish it again biannually in 1990. The journal reached its forty-eighth issue in 2014, the year its present managing editor, Jack Ross of Massey University's School of English and Media Studies, took it back to its roots by renaming it the *Poetry New Zealand Yearbook*.

Poetry New Zealand has been edited by some of New Zealand's most distinguished poets and academics, including Elizabeth Caffin, Grant Duncan, Riemke Ensing, Bernard Gadd, Leonard Lambert, Harry Ricketts, Elizabeth Smither and Brian Turner. The journal was overseen from 1993 to 2014 by poet, novelist, anthologist, editor and literary critic Alistair Paterson ONZM, with help from master printer John Denny of Puriri Press, and guest editors Owen Bullock, Siobhan Harvey and Nicholas Reid.

The magazine's policy is to support poetry and poets both in New Zealand and overseas. Each issue since 1994 has featured a substantial feature showcasing the work of a developing or established poet. It also includes a selection of poetry from New Zealand and abroad, as well as essays, reviews and critical commentary.

The editor is grateful to Associate Professor Jenny Lawn, Head of the School of English and Media Studies at Massey University, for her financial support of this edition.

Managing editor
Jack Ross
editor@poetrynz.net

Advisory board
Thom Conroy, Jen Crawford, John Denny, Matthew Harris, Ingrid Horrocks, David Howard, Bronwyn Lloyd, Alistair Paterson, Tracey Slaughter, Bryan Walpert

Website: www.poetrynz.net
Webmaster: Warren Old
Blog: poetrynzblog.blogspot.co.nz/
Index: poetrynz.blogspot.co.nz/

Submissions: The submission dates for each issue are between 1 May and 31 July of each year. Submit either (preferably) by email, with your poems pasted in the body of the message or included as a MS Word file attachment; or by post, to the address below, with a stamped self-addressed envelope, and contact details in your covering letter.

Dr Jack Ross
School of English and Media Studies
Massey University, Albany Campus
Private Bag 102904, North Shore Mail Centre
Auckland 0745

Please remember to include a short biography and current postal address with your submission. Contributors to each issue will receive a free copy.

For more information about our books please visit
www.masseypress.ac.nz

First published in 2018 by Massey University Press
Private Bag 102904, North Shore Mail Centre
Auckland 0745, New Zealand
www.masseypress.ac.nz

Design by Jo Bailey and Thomas Le Bas
Typesetting by Kate Barraclough

A catalogue record for this book is available from the
National Library of New Zealand

Printed and bound in China by Everbest Ltd

ISBN: 978-0-9941473-3-2

The assistance of Creative New Zealand is gratefully
acknowledged by the publisher

Poetry
New Zealand
Yearbook

2018